THE MINING CAMPS SPEAK

The
MINING
CAMPS
SPEAK

A New Way to Explore the Ghost Towns of the American West

BETH AND BILL SAGSTETTER

BENCHMARK PUBLISHING OF COLORADO

BenchMark Publishing of Colorado

2217 Grove Street

Denver, Colorado 80211

(303) 455-0789

FAX: (303) 455-1093

Email: benchmarkcolo@worldnet.att.net

Printed in the United States

ISBN 0-9645824-1-4

9 8 7 6 5 4 3 2

To: Janette Lorayn Miller Trudeau

1950 –1989

A monarch dances
Through a columbined meadow
And I think of you.
A painted lady flutters by
On stained-glass window wings
And I feel you are here,
Your lepidoptery guiding me.
My spirits lift.
And there's a black swallowtail —
Or is it a mourning cloak?
I am confused.
Suddenly the illusion of your presence
Shatters.
I am alone after all.
For you would have known
The difference.

    With love,

    EMS

WARNING:

This is a sight-seeing book to visiting ghost towns. Visiting ghost towns is usually an enjoyable and educational experience, but under some circumstances it can also be dangerous. You should not visit a ghost town by yourself. One or more adults should always travel together. Children must always be under constant supervision by one or more adults. You should not depend exclusively on the information obtained from this book for your personal safety. You should never enter an abandoned mine tunnel or shaft under any conditions. Your safety in abandoned buildings depends on your personal judgment based upon your experience and a realistic assessment of the conditions.

There is no substitute for an experienced guide to help you safely enjoy your visit to a ghost town. Therefore, the information provided in this book should only be used with caution. If you misinterpret the information contained in this book, you may be seriously injured or even killed as a result of the misunderstanding.

There are no express or implied warranties that this sight-seeing book contains accurate and reliable information. There are no warranties as to fitness for a particular purpose. Your use of this book expressly indicates your assumption of the risk of serious injury or death as a result of risks inherently dangerous in visiting a ghost town and is an acknowledgment of your own responsibility for your safety.

CONTENTS

Foreword		xi
Preface		xiii
Acknowledgments		xvii
1	The Language of the Mining Camps	1
2	The Men	13
3	Placer Mining	23
	Field Guide	32
4	Hard-rock Mining	35
	Field Guide	43
5	Mining Equipment	49
	Field Guide	63
6	Roads and Transportation	77
	Field Guide	93
7	The Blacksmith Shop	99
	Field Guide	107
8	The Assay Office	113
	Field Guide	127
9	The Women	133
10	The Towns	155
	Field Guide	163
11	Lodging: Log Cabins	165
	Field Guide	177
12	Lodging: Company Boardinghouses	183
13	Lodging: The Telltale Clues	199
	Field Guide	226
14	Cemeteries: The Last Chapter	247
Appendix A – Glossary		252
Appendix B – Approximate Patent Timetable		254
Appendix C – Mining Museums and Mine Tours		255
Bibliography		269
Index		277

x

FOREWORD

Coloradans and visitors have long prowled the state's ghost towns — which actually out-number the live towns. From the abandoned cliff cities of Mesa Verde to the most recent mining town ghosts, Colorado's dead cities have long fascinated sightseers.

To guide locals and visitors alike, a subspecies of local literature has become something of a cottage industry. Muriel Sibell Wolle, the longtime art professor at the University of Colorado, set the pace for this genre of guidebooks. Her classic, self-published 1949 book *Stampede to Timberline: The Ghost and Mining Camps of Colorado* was picked up by Sage/Swallow Press. *Stampede* has now galloped through some twenty printings and remains a perennial best-seller. Other ghost town guides include notable works by Robert L. Brown, Sandra Dallas, and Perry Eberhart, among dozens of others. Nearly all of these books are similar town-by-town listings.

Beth and Bill Sagstetter's book is different. Whereas other books tell you how to get there and give you a town history, *The Mining Camps Speak* tells you how to enjoy and appreciate the ruins you will find. In other words, this is a unique, helpful supplement to more conventional guidebooks. It also reaches beyond the boundaries of the state to embrace all the Western mining districts.

Beth and Bill Sagstetter, who once worked as a writer/photographer team at *The Denver Post,* have also collaborated on *Side by Side: A History of Denver's Witter Cofield Historic District.* That book sold out within three months. Since 1963, Beth and Bill have toured most of the mountain mining ghost towns. Both greenhorns and veteran ghost town prospectors should enjoy this book. They take you on a hair-raising stage coach ride, to a noisy company boardinghouse at dinnertime, panning for gold in an icy stream and behind the closed doors of an assay office.

The Sagstetters introduce you to everything from burros to tin cans. Beth and Bill — whose name appears on over twenty patents — have made it their business to precisely identify and date tin cans. For Beth and Bill, and for readers, an old can of coffee can be a most revealing clue, especially if it has been recycled as a shadowgee (candle lantern). The Sagstetters will lead you into the West's golden and silvery past for a close look at the ruins, showing you how to tell if the shambles is an assay office, blacksmith shop boardinghouse, mill or saloon.

The Sagstetter's love of anthropology, history and travel has flowed into numerous articles and the crackerjack book you hold in your hands. You will not find anything else like it. It is a gracefully written, handsomely illustrated guide to greater enjoyment and appreciation of ghost towns. These towns, like the Sagstetters, have a lot to say.

— THOMAS J. NOEL

June 3, 1997

PREFACE

For years we felt disappointed when we visited ghost towns and there seemed to be nothing left of them. And then one day we toured one with an old hard-rock miner. From a site we thought was empty, he was able to read an entire tale. And although he was of a different time and a different place than that camp, he could still recreate for us a story that had gone on there. We were spellbound. After years of visiting ghost towns, we thought we had seen it all. Yet right beneath our noses was a whole new aspect of mining camps to explore. We haven't been the same since.

The purpose of *The Mining Camps Speak* is to provide you with a companion for your ghost-town explorations like that old-time hard-rock miner. It is also the purpose of this book to be a backcountry resource. The information it contains will help you enjoy your outdoor experiences all the more. In it we have included all the rules and etiquette you need so you can relax, knowing you are not in violation of the law.

This book is not about the famous people of the West. You won't find stories about Butch Cassidy and the Sundance Kid, or about the time bank robbers were hung in the town square. Or about the fistful of miners who struck it rich. Rather, this book is about the ordinary folks who settled the West. These are the forgotten heroes, who represent the vast majority of people who came here. They have left us a legacy, one we often take for granted in our outdoor travels. Yet their accomplishments are all around us. *The Mining Camps Speak* will help you recognize this history in our midst and understand it.

Is this book for you? It is if you have ever looked at an old mining-camp site and wanted to know more. It is if you love to visit places considered remote in the twentieth century and retain a sense of awe and wonder that some intrepid souls were already hard at work here in the nineteenth century. It is for all those folks like us who have passed a rude log cabin along the trail and wondered, What went on here?

But this book requires an experienced backcountry traveler. It requires a person who knows that in the wilderness one is responsible for oneself. A person who knows to bring plenty of water, to bring a poncho or waterproof coat. This person carries some survival gear and a small emergency kit in a day pack or fanny pack. He wears heavy-duty hiking boots or shoes. He takes a compass and maps and, most important, he knows how to use them. In other words, he comes prepared. He doesn't take any needless risks, because he knows if others have to rescue him, they put their own lives in danger. He is cautious and travels with a companion. He also knows to **Tread Lightly!**® and he causes minimal impact to nature while on his backcountry excursions, whether on foot, mountain bike, or four-wheel drive or however he chooses to travel.

LEAVING A GOOD IMPRESSION

Travel and recreate with minimum impact.

Respect the environment and the rights of others.

Educate yourself, plan and prepare before you go.

Allow for future use of the outdoors, leave it better than you found it.

Discover the rewards of responsible recreation.

Beyond backcountry experience, using this book also requires a person who is sophisticated in her approach to what she finds. For example, this person can appreciate a field of wildflowers without picking them. This sophisticated explorer knows there is no gold buried in the walls of an old cabin, or nuggets lying in the trail. She is not a treasure hunter or a souvenir hunter. Nor is she interested in recreating a museum atmosphere with "museum rocks": She is satisfied with being awed at the privilege of witnessing a vanishing heritage. If she wants a memento, she photographs it. If she is looking for "art," she uses the experience to inspire her own artistic creation: An artist might paint a picture of the site, a musician write a song about it, a poet write a poem about it. But she does not remove anything from the site as a memento.

We are not scholars and do not mean to present ourselves as authorities on old mining camps. We are only interested backcountry travelers who have spent a lifetime exploring the backcountry and then searching the archives, and we would like to share our findings with you. The techniques in this book should not be interpreted as a sure road to immutable fact. An intriguing piece of debris might only be a recently discarded item from a passing tourist, for example. But this book does offer likely scenarios of events that could have happened. Think of it as offering rule-of-thumb or ballpark information. Scholars will eventually be able to provide us with those immutable facts we crave. But until then, we can use the techniques presented here to find out some fascinating, if imprecise, information about what might have happened. And have fun doing it!

ACKNOWLEDGMENTS

Writing a book is a grand adventure. You are exploring unknown territory. You desperately need good information like maps and compasses and experienced guides. And you sometimes have the great good fortune to meet up with enthusiastic fellow travelers — folks who share your passion and contribute immeasurably to the journey. We would like you to meet some of our fellow travelers, people and organizations that not only made this book possible, but made the journey an unforgettable experience.

It was a pleasure working with the Bureau of Land Management, who graciously established a set of workable visitation guidelines that backcountry travelers can live with. Dr. Rick Athearn, especially, spent many hours reading the manuscript, contributing ideas and valuable expertise. Because of the "map" they provided, *The Mining Camps Speak* is a *responsible* book.

We also thank the Tread Lightly! organization for allowing us to include their message. The Tread Lightly! program has had a profound impact on outdoor recreation since it was launched in 1985 by the U.S. Forest Service. We are proud to be a small part of that. The Tread Lightly! organization can be reached at (800) 966-9900 or E-mail tlinc@xmission.com.

On behalf of all who are interested in Colorado and Denver history, we want to thank Dr. Tom Noel, the extremely popular professor of history at the University of Colorado at Denver. He has done more for local history than probably anyone else. Thanks for taking the time from your busy schedule to read the manuscript and for your astute comments.

Mining historian Robert Spude of the Mining History Association joined with Rick Athearn to act as our compasses, guiding us through mining lore, keeping us on course.

They carefully read the manuscript and checked it for accuracy. Because of their work, *The Mining Camps Speak* has authenticity.

There are several fellow writers who have already walked this path before us, and who generously shared their knowledge with us. First is Clive Cussler. Many people don't realize how much he quietly, behind the scenes, gives back to the writing profession. Thanks for reading the manuscript and your comments. Ken Jessen is a trailblazer who also took much time to share with us what he has learned. Silvia Pettem has tread this way before and took time from her deadlines to speak with us. There is no more generous a group than writers; we feel blessed to have had the opportunity to cross paths with all of you.

Erik Swanson, curator of the Cripple Creek District Museum, holds a special place in our memories of this journey. He opened many doors for us. The South Park City Museum of Fairplay, Colorado, graciously allowed us to photograph their tin can collection. The Western Museum of Mining and Industry in Colorado Springs, Colorado, let us photograph the assaying process. By throwing open their doors to us these organizations have made it possible for us to share this knowledge with you.

Bill and Sue Knous of Railroad Memories in Denver are folks who not only contributed immeasurably to the journey, but also made it fun. The Knouses used their considerable skill in locating old archival photographs and rare out-of-print books and found "impossible" items for us. The travel chapter owes much to their keen insight and knowledge of railroads.

The tin can chapter evolved because of three people: Vere Wiesley of Scottsdale, Arizona, a retired executive with American Can Company. John D. Burroughs of Barrington, Illinois, a retired chemist for the same company. Robert Seifert of the Kuner-Empson Company of Brighton, Colorado. These men were able to confirm what we were seeing in the field and in the patents regarding tin can technology. They were able to answer many of our nagging questions.

Our guides on this expedition into the past were experts in their fields. They took us back to a bygone era and educated us. Retired miner Ed Van Westenberg walked with us through the ghost town of Alta, Colorado, and explained to us what we were seeing. The seeds for the book were planted that day. John Talbot is a retired assayer and spent months in the summer of 1996 patiently teaching us about the ancient art of assaying. Harrison Cobb, author of *Prospecting our Past,* spent time with us on milling. Blacksmith Jim Miller drove half way across the country to meet us in the ghost town of Animas Forks, Colorado. He taught us how to see ghost towns through the eyes of a blacksmith. Retired miner Harold Thompson related his experiences as a hard-rock miner during the depression and gave us a treasure trove of never-before-heard stories. His wife, Alice Thompson, shared with us a woman's side of the story. These people taught us how to "see" what we had been unable to see before. Without any one of them this book would not exist today.

Two informal groups of people were our fellow travelers on this grand adventure. The first group began as a Colorado History class and field trip that we taught. At ghost town sites, we were asked very intelligent questions by the class members. Questions we could not answer at the time. Questions like: What happened here? What is that object and what did it do? In our search for answers, this book was born. Since the first few classes, Rhonda Beck and Dan Crumb have ably led the group and it has flourished under their leadership for a dozen years now. We are grateful to Rhonda and Dan for encouraging us to test our ideas in this context. We also thank the group members: Edward Eugene and Beth Allen, Sharon Crumb, the Gresham family — Bob and Eileen and their children Josh and Rebekah — Eric Rindahl, Bud and Jacklyn Witman and Jeff Thurnau. They took time from their busy lives to read the manuscript and then met us in the mountains to "test-drive" the ideas and see if they were workable.

The second informal group also has years of ghost town experience behind them. They took a ragged manuscript and implemented the field guides in the backcountry. Because of them we were able to test our concept of field guides for ghost town history and see if they were usable. The group members are: Denis Payne, Gary Shoe, John Sterling, Will Loechel and Bill Johnson.

The enthusiasm of these groups for the book, their input, and their desire for intelligent backcountry travel have helped make *The Mining Camps Speak* the unique book that it is.

Several booksellers took the time to point the way for us. We would like to thank Donna Hudgel of Trails West Books, Pat Walsh of the Tattered Cover Bookstore, and Stephanie of Barnes and Noble.

Geoffrey T. Bleakley generously offered valuable information and much help on the Wrangell-St. Elias National Park and Preserve in Alaska. And Jane Haigh provided expert advice on the Yukon-Tanana Historic District in Alaska.

Finally, thanks to folks like John and Margie Grimsley who introduced us to old-timers we needed to interview. Their voices are how the mining camps speak today.

Thanks to all of you who helped to make this expedition into the unknown such an memorable experience. Hasn't it been a grand journey?

1

THE LANGUAGE OF
THE MINING CAMPS

All mining districts have a mysterious family resemblance.

— Albert D. Richardson, *Beyond the Mississippi*

 Have you ever passed an old deserted log cabin along the trail in a historic mining district and wondered, What went on here? Who were the people who came here? When did they build this old cabin? What were their lives like?

Or have you ever struggled all day to reach a famous old ghost-town site, and when you finally arrived there was little or nothing left? Maybe you felt the same disappointment we have felt when we were greeted with an empty grassy field.

Perhaps you've spotted huge, rusting antique mining contraptions in precarious perches on your backcountry travels, and thought, If only these rusted hulks could talk, what stories they could tell!

The fact is, ghost towns do speak. There is much they can tell us across a century of time: Stories about what people were doing here and roughly when. Stories about nineteenth-century life in a wilderness. Stories about mining and all the peripheral industries it attracted.

The vast majority of the time we will never know the name and date of birth or other specific information about a particular character. Or about an incident. Or the name of a site. We must continue to rely on history books for that. But still, we can know something about why people came here, roughly when, and make some educated guesses about what dreams brought them here. We can know something about the work they did.

Most sites still have something to say even if all that remains is an overgrown field, but the information is in their own special language — a coded message, in the form of clues. But

Rusted contraptions such as this old boiler dot the back country in historic mining districts. There is much it can tell a person who understands the language of the mining camps.

to hear it, we must learn the language of the mining camps; we must decipher the code.

In a way, animal trackers do the same thing. They look for clues — like a tuft of fur on a branch or a paw print in the dirt — that tell them what animals passed this way. An expert tracker knows the wildlife and their habits, their scat, and their tracks. Olaus Murie who wrote Peterson's *Field Guide to Animal Tracks,* was so experienced that he could tell not only what animal had made a track, but also its approximate age, what it last ate and if it had experienced a good year or a bad year.

The clues left behind at a ghost town have a story in them, too. Take the time we found an old, rusted gallon-sized tin can at a mining-camp site. This one had been reworked: Someone had made a wire handle that held the can on its side, instead of upright. An inch-round hole had been punched in the under-side of the can beneath the wire handle. Imagine our awe later when we learned that a candle fit in that hole. The can was a makeshift candle-lantern. When the can was still new and shiny, the candle flame would reflect off the inside bottom of the can and shine out the open top, creating a beam of light much like a modern flashlight. The can protected the flame from the wind and allowed it to stay lit as it was being carried.

We were enthralled! What this said to us was that the old-time miners were resourceful and used plenty of ingenuity when finding ways of lighting the darkness.

It told us something about their everyday lives as well — that their sources of light were sometimes unreliable, and that they frequently had to improvise. It might also imply there was a lack of goods like lamps or lamp oil, making even discarded tin cans valuable resources. According to Bill Stark, interviewed in *The Way it Was* by David Bachman and Tod Bacigalupi, these jury-rigged tin can candle-lanterns were called shadowgees. We find shadowgees often around old sites.

Sometimes the clue could be a standing building — there are a few that remain intact across the American West. These are picturesque and weatherbeaten and make wonderful photographs. Rejoice if you should find one. But the fact is, a standing building is not necessary for understanding what went on at a site. Do not despair if you find a seemingly "empty" site, with only a pile of boards or the outline of a log structure in the grass. With some practice, you'll be able to read such sites, to put together an intriguing story even if all that's left is bits and pieces.

But what you need to get started is a field guide, one like the popular nature guides for bird identification. A nature field guide similar to what a beginning naturalist might use, but one for human history in the American West. A book you can refer

These candle lanterns were called shadowgees, and were made from tin cans. The one on the left is typical. But every now and then we find one that is special, like the shadowgee on the right.

Sites like Rexford, Colorado, above, need not be disappointing just because there are no standing buildings. Indeed, this site had a wonderful story to tell us.

to so as to identify clues. You are holding that book in your hands. *The Mining Camps Speak* should be used just like a field guide for naturalists.

An old mining-camp site is like a footprint from the past. But besides these nineteenth-century "footprints," people also left behind paper trails, in the form of journals, diaries, and oral histories. These are not found at the sites, of course; they are found in libraries and archives and in antique books. We have scoured these sources to get a feel for who the folks were who peopled these sites, why they came here, and what their dreams were. The information we pieced together is addressed in various chapters.

What is a mining camp? For the purposes of this book, any old deserted mining sites — large or small, with buildings standing or not — are classified as mining camps. So are the towns that supported them and that are now classified as "ghost towns." We use the two terms interchangeably. But the mining camp must be inactive. Mines that are still operating are off-limits no matter how historically interesting they might be.

Peppering the American West, tucked into forgotten places are thousands of old mining sites. Keep in mind that the techniques of this book work best (especially for beginners) in remote, little-visited sites. Popular ghost towns with relatively easy access, are more difficult to read. Overvisitation, squatters, and misguided clean-up efforts garble the message that might once have been there.

Instead of seeking the well-known, well-traveled sites like Caribou and Animas Forks, Colorado, consider remote side canyons off the main trails. Look for the thread of a little-used trail. Or, historic trails shown on U.S. Geological Survey (USGS) topographical maps that today are all but forgotten just might lead to a little-visited site. The sites that will have the most to say, that are the most exciting to visit, are those that were inhabited for a relatively short time, perhaps a couple of years, and once they were abandoned were never reinhabited again. They will be tucked in remote or forgotten areas off the main trails and rarely visited by picnickers or campers. One example is Rexford, Colorado. You won't find any photogenic standing buildings there, but it speaks with a clear, straightforward voice that is a delight to decipher.

Powers of Observation

Again taking the lead from nature field guides, it is critical that you develop your powers of observation. Without observation, nothing follows.

But how do you develop a keen sense of observation if you weren't born with it? You train your eyes to see those important details. Looking for colors is a good place to start when you arrive at a site. Against the dark earth, the moldering wood, the rusting metal, white is a color that will jump out at you. Also look for the glint of glass. If there are the remains of buildings, look around the perimeter of each foundation for clues as to what went on in this structure. For example, finding antique household debris indicates that the structure was probably used for lodging.

Shapes are another clue. Sometimes equipment ages to the color of the earth. In such a case, look for geometric shapes: Geometric forms occur rarely in nature — they are a giveaway to human activity. This is also a valuable technique when studying the "empty" grassy meadows that are the sites of ghost towns. The foundations of old buildings are usually square or rectangular and those shapes can sometimes be spotted in the bushes and grass at "empty" sites. At times these will be outlined with stones, at other times they might merely be a depression in the soil. Check around the outline of these foundations.

Look any object over carefully. Is it whole, or is it a part of something? Is it a piece of mining equipment or a tin can? A shard of china, or a piece of bone? For example, say you find a whitish disc-shaped walnut-sized object as in the accompanying illustration. From having read the assaying chapter, you would recognize this

5

These walnut-shell-sized objects are called cupels and are part of the assaying process. Finding them at a site implies assaying was performed there.

object as a cupel. You would then know that assaying was probably performed at this site.

Is there any writing on this object? Maybe an embossed date or patent number? If so, the patent number timeline in Appendix B will help you date it approximately. Or is the name of the company that manufactured it on the object? Sometimes the writing on the object will help you identify what it was. Take your fact-finding another step further — Was this artifact made in a sophisticated or ingenious fashion, or is it rather crude? Has this object been reworked to serve a different function? We have seen some rather ingenious examples of reworked objects through the years. Everything from rusted boilers used as culverts to old powder kegs used as chimneys. And don't forget those shadowgees we mentioned earlier.

Then ask yourself, What does the presence of this object imply? The implications are on three levels. First, there are those for today. Ask yourself, What does this mean now? For example, once we were on an old trail when we spotted rusting tin cans spilling down the mountainside to the trail. When we studied the trash carefully, we realized this was antique household debris. Because it was common for old-timers to throw their trash downhill from their cabins, the implication today is that there would be a site uphill from the trail hidden in the trees. We followed those tin cans uphill as though they were footprints. And they led us to a forgotten mining camp buried in the trees, hidden from the trail. It was completely untouched, just waiting to be rediscovered.

In the case of discovering faint traces of an old forgotten road, the implication today is that a site might lie at the end of it. These old deserted roads required too much effort to build with wagons and hand tools for them not to lead somewhere.

Then there are past implications. Take the example of finding that shadowgee. Its presence suggests that earlier light sources were unreliable, because we often find shadowgees at sites that had electricity. It also suggests that the people who made them were highly creative in finding ways to light the darkness.

Then there are the personal implications. What does this artifact or site say about the people who lived or worked here? Sometimes this can be the most fun of the entire process. Take for example the time we discovered a shard of Sevres china beside a rude log hut in what is a remote wilderness even today. A hundred years ago this would have been unspeakably far away from anywhere. Yet somehow there appeared in the trash heap a shard of an expensive French china teacup saucer. Who would have brought such a fragile object to such a primitive place? Just visualizing the transportation of such a delicate thing to such a far-flung place brings to mind an incredible journey. And who would have delighted in using such an unpractical thing when a tin cup would have served the purpose just as well? We can't help but think that we would have liked this person. What would finding a shard of Sevres china say to you?

Exploration Etiquette

Before you begin your explorations of ghost towns and mining camps, you need to know the guidelines for acceptable behavior.

It is your responsibility to make sure you are on public land. If an area is fenced or if there are no-trespassing signs posted on it, it is private land, and you must have permission to visit it.

Be very careful. Old sites can be extremely dangerous. We have seen building debris hide an open mine shaft. Never even think about entering a tunnel or shaft. The unsafe air and gases that accumulate in tunnels have killed some curiosity seekers. In addition, there are hidden shafts and flooded tunnels. Even the shoulders around an open pit can be dangerous because the dirt is unstable and can give way under a person unexpectedly. Take our advice and stay away from any underground workings. There are so many, much safer mysteries to explore at grass level.

VISITOR ETIQUETTE AT HISTORIC MINING SITES

by Dr. Rick Athearn, Bureau of Land Management

As we visit historic mining locations, we should remember that we are always a guest here, and not the owner of the property. There is no such thing as an "abandoned mine" or town. Someone owns the property, be they a private citizen or the government. Therefore, it is protected from theft and destruction by law.

In the case of sites known to be on public lands, they are protected by numerous laws. Places in national forests, national parks, BLM lands, state lands, county or city lands are all subject to protection from damage or destruction under the law.

By treating each historic site as a special place that is still "owned" by someone, it becomes a matter of courtesy to behave the same way you would if you were in a friend's home. Would you take artifacts from your friend's or neighbor's house? Would you steal items from the garage or backyard?

Of course not. So the same principle applies to visiting "abandoned" mining towns and sites. When enjoying a historic mining location, remember to leave only footprints and take only photographs. You simply should not remove property that is not yours. You should also take your trash out with you, so the next person to visit can enjoy this place too.

Some of the most important information that can be gained from a historic site is in the architecture and archaeology. If a building is vandalized, data is lost. If a trash dump is dug up, the scientific information contained in it is gone forever. That's why it is critical to leave things the way you find them.

Here are a few etiquette tips that are useful when visiting historic sites:

■ Standing wooden structures are very fragile. They can be severely damaged by removing wooden parts from them. They are also extremely vulnerable to fire. Never smoke in or around a wooden building. Never remove wood ("barnwood") from a building.

■ Historic trash dumps, outhouses, pits, and surface scatter can be scientifically valuable. Never dig up dumps, pits, or outhouses. Doing so not only damages the scientific value of the site, but it is almost always illegal.

■ While using metal detectors might be fun, picking up artifacts or digging them up is not only destructive to the scientific value of the resource but is also likely illegal.

■ Take out the trash you bring in. Nothing spoils a visit for the next person more than to have aluminum cans, plastic wrappers, and other trash spread around a historic site. If you bring it in, take it out.

At the fascinating site above, fallen boards hide an open shaft. Be very careful in your explorations.

■ *Don't be a vandal. Vandalism is one of the worst things you can do to a historic site. Painting graffiti on buildings ruins them forever. Carving your name in the wood destroys the site for other visitors and degrades the quality of the site. Taking a four-wheel-drive vehicle and pulling down buildings for fun not only destroys our heritage but is illegal. Shooting interpretive and directional signs only ruins everone else's visit and destroys property. Leave a place as you found it. Would you do the above things to your own home? If not, then treat a historic place as you would your house.*

It is important to note that the above behavior is, in general, illegal. Whether you are on private or public property there are trespass and destruction laws that protect private lands. Equally, theft and destruction laws provide civil and criminal penalties for damaging federal, state and county/city properties.

By thinking ahead, planning your visit, and simply showing a little courtesy for others, you can help preserve and protect our fragile historic mining sites.

Companion Books

When we travel, we have been known to carry as much as ninety-two pounds of books: old mail-order catalogue reprints; books on assaying, blacksmithing, history, mining; trail guides; reprints of diaries and journals; and atlases. *The Mining Camps Speak* will take the place of many of these references for you. But there are a few books that could enhance your mining-camp experience in conjunction with this one:

The Sears, Roebuck Catalogue (reprint from 1897: Chelsea House Publishers, New York) and the Montgomery Ward Catalogue #57 (reprint from 1895: Dover Publications, New York) are both paperbacks and available through your favorite bookstore. These two reprints of turn-of-the-century catalogues help us identify items we don't recognize. Gadgets that were widely known and used a hundred years ago and might have been immediately recognizable to our great-grandparents, draw a blank with us when we see them. It's not unusual for us to spot an object at a mining-camp site and be able to find it or a similar one in one of the catalogues. Mail order was sometimes the only way to get certain items to a remote mining camp; people could even order food from them. Keep in mind that there were many mail-order houses besides these two, so an item you find may or may not have come from these sources. But at least you will know what the object was, what it was used for, what it cost in its time, and an approximate date for its manufacture.

The Mining Camps Speak will not give you directions to particular mining-camp sites. For that you might want a trail guide that will give you directions to a specific place. Most of the sites given as examples in this book can be found in any one of the existing trail guides. Besides giving directions to the site, these guides usually also give some historical information about that particular site. Once you are there, *The Mining Camps Speak* takes over. It will guide you around the site, and it will make the places you visit even more meaningful.

However, you do not need to own a trail guide in order to use *The Mining Camps Speak*. If you happen to be on a mountain trail and pass a deserted log cabin, then *The Mining Camps Speak* works just as well by itself.

The following chapters each take a structure or piece of mining equipment typically found at a mining-camp site, or an aspect of the life there. They give background on how the item or custom evolved from about the time of the California gold rush in 1849 until about World War I. This information holds true across the American West, whether the mining camp is in California or New Mexico or Montana or South Dakota, or even the Klondike. Just as certain plants and animals are indigenous to certain areas, so are certain structures common to a mining camp. The mysterious family resemblance mentioned by Albert Richardson allows us to understand what we see at an old mining-camp site.

In some cases, a chapter is followed by a Field Guide which will help you put the chapter's information into action at a site. The Field Guide gives you tips on what to look for and on what clues are associated with what structures. This book and the accompanying field guides will help you fit the objects you spot at deserted mining-camp sites into an overall picture of nineteenth-century life and mining. You might even be able to answer for yourself the question, What happened here?

Sometimes you can find objects that you encounter in the backcountry pictured in old catalogues. This advertisement is from Harpers Weekly, *Sagstetter collection. The old cookstove below is near Ouray, Colorado. Note the iron rods that hold the oven door in place and the crossed bars on the door.*

2

THE MEN

A prospector lives in hopes, and dies in
some old cabin.

— Hutch Stevens, in *The Restless Longing:*
A Prospector's Story

 It's a long, straight valley, like a finger pointing to Uncompahgre Peak. Near what would be the last joint of that finger valley sits the Silver Jack Mine. There is no reason to think a mine should be here: a report from the old state mine inspector implied that valuable-ore indications in the area were a little tenuous.

But here, deep in a wilderness area, sits a developed mine anyway. Stout log buildings scattered on the mountainside are still weathertight and occasionally used by hunters and backpackers. In their midst is an unusual screen-covered springhouse for food storage. Just building the trail in to this site alone represented a huge undertaking. The builders even went so far as to build an impressive dam on the creek. We had seen nearby settled towns that were smaller than this deserted mining camp. And all of it was the tangible remains of some man's dream.

Punctuating the grassy areas between the buildings are large rusting hulks of equipment. We studied the pieces of equipment and discovered we were looking at what might be called a "mill-in-a-box." These were parts of a potential mill brought all the way to this remote place, deposited on the ground, and then never assembled.

These miners were so confident they would find a vein that they had bought a mill and transported it to the site. Such brash enthusiasm, such confidence, such optimism still touches us today across all the years, and we are swept up in it. How could you dislike people with so much verve and energy as to build a small town based on a slim promise? And then, like many others, after so much energy had been expended toward the dream, their hopes were dashed when they never found the anticipated vein.

Above is the Silver Jack Mine in the San Juan Mountains of Colorado. It, and other mines like it, illustrate how enthusiastic and hopeful the prospectors were, sometimes without good cause.

But what's truly amazing is not that this mill-in-a-box exists in the wilderness, but that we have found other mills in the same unassembled condition at other old mines. Who were these men who were the miners? Who dreamed dreams and lived on the hope they inspired while they built that dream? There is an old-fashioned word used in accounts of that time to describe these men: *Sanguine*. You don't see that word used much anymore. It means cheerful, optimistic, confident, and vigorous. Warm and lively and energetic. And it was infectious. Even crusty newspaper editors of Horace Greeley's stature were not immune to it. Only sanguine men such as those who built the Silver Jack Mine could have taken on the settling of the West.

Mark Twain described them in *Roughing It:*

> It was a driving, vigorous, restless population in those days. It was a *curious* population. It was the *only* population of the kind that the world has ever seen gathered together, and it is not likely that the world will ever see its like again. For observe, it was an assemblage of . . . *young* men . . . stalwart,

muscular, dauntless young braves, brimful of push and energy . . . the strangest population . . . that ever trooped down the startled solitudes of an unpeopled land.

Some of these stalwart young men trooped west searching for a little adventure before they settled down. Anyone who had run afoul of the strict Victorian conventions, like young Frank Crampton who later wrote the book *Deep Enough,* could get a fresh start in the West. Others, who perhaps were rather sickly, went west searching for health. The Reverend John Steele, in his book *In Camp and Cabin,* described it: "But with all the toil and exposure, there is something invigorating in this mountain air which sharpens the appetite and promotes health."

But the vast majority of these men were tired of being poor and came west looking for a chance at a better life for themselves and for their families. George Groh, in his book *Gold Fever,* quoted from letters by Melvin Paden: "Jane i left you and them boys for no other reason than this to come here [California] to procure a littl

This mill-in-a-box was transported into the wilderness to the Silver Jack Mine and then never erected into a mill. Parts of a would-be mill lie scattered on the site, like the cog wheel on the left, and are being overgrown with vegetation. The two grinders below, a fine grinder on the left, and a coarse grinder on the right, sit there still today after the better part of a century.

property by the swet of my brow so that we could have a place of our own that i might not be a dog for other people any longer . . . i think that this is a far better country to lay up money than it is at home, if a man will tend to his business and keep out of licker shops and gambling houses."

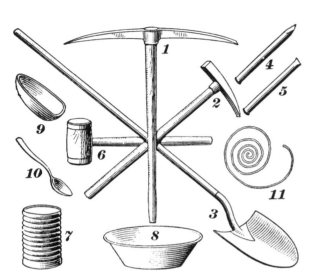

This was the typical outfit recommended for beginning prospectors by Arthur Lakes in his 1895 book, Prospecting for Gold and Silver in North America. *Numbers one and two are identified as picks. Three is a long-handled shovel, four and five are hand drills. Six is a heavy hammer, and seven is blasting powder. Eight is a gold pan, nine is a horn spoon. Ten is an iron spoon and eleven is fuse. Sagstetter collection.*

Men rushed to the American West from all parts of the globe. They were Chinese, American, Italian. They were Irish, English, German, and Finnish. They were former slaves. And although they spoke different languages, looked different, worshiped differently, and practiced different customs, they shared two things in common: They wanted a chance at a better life, and they knew zilch about mining.

No one knows how many men wound up discouraged and returned home. Because we don't know exactly how many rushed west in the first place, we will never know what percentage turned around and rushed back. But it was probably a large proportion. Deaths on the trek west thinned the number, as did death from disease upon arrival. Just as the mills did, these factors acted as filters, or classifiers, allowing only a special type of man to stay. This man was the "Honest Miner" that we find referred to in the literature of the time. This type of man set the tone for what the West would be and helped establish the Code of the West. He thrived on the independence and camaraderie even if the life was hard. He was the man who built the Silver Jack Mine and all the mines like it.

The Honest Miner

Because life in the nineteenth-century West was difficult at best, it tended to reduce men to a common denominator. Their essence, if you will. One could not take the measure of a man by the way he looked. The man standing next to you might be the territorial governor or a ditchdigger. Doctors, sheriffs, saloon keepers, lawyers, stable hands, and miners all looked pretty much the same. And even if you were a minister or a blacksmith by trade, you probably did a little prospecting on the side.

The result of all this was that a man might be a stranger to you, but he would still seem familiar in the way he looked and acted. Say a stranger showed up at your camp in the mountains. You'd treat him with the utmost hospitality even though he

Note how these men are dressed — the wide-brimmed hats, the tall boots, the guns on their belts. One smokes a pipe. From William Thayer's Marvels of the New West. *Sagstetter collection.*

was bewhiskered, mud-splattered (or dust-covered, depending on the season), and deeply tanned, like everyone else. For all you knew, this man might be the Earl of Crawford.

This same stranger sharing your campfire would be dressed very much as you were. He undoubtedly covered his shaggy hair with a hat, either a slouch hat or a variation of the Mexican sombrero. Because of all the mud, he wore tall heavy boots. Baylord Taylor commented at the time that even after cities like San Francisco

This very famous scene depicts prospectors inspecting specimens of ore. This particular version of this scene is from William Thayer's Marvels of the New West. *Sagstetter collection.*

became civilized and other articles of clothing were becoming commonplace, substitutes for the boots and hats were never settled upon. Perhaps that's why they became symbols of the West.

And it didn't matter whether you were in Nevada, Idaho, or Washington, this man across your hypothetical campfire was probably wearing a coarse shirt, perhaps wool. It might well be blue — but one color it was sure *not* to be was white. He wore pantaloons (today we've shortened that to "pants") of a heavy fabric like corduroy or denim. It was during the California Gold Rush that Levi's jeans were developed. And as likely as not the pants sported patches on them and were tucked into his tall boots. Vests were common.

Although the stranger's belt sagged with a bowie knife and gun, you would not feel threatened by his presence. You knew he was basically an honest fellow, though there were exceptions to this assumption. For example, in the early days, a man left tools at a place to show newcomers that this spot was claimed. One foreign traveler commented that unattended tools would not last overnight in other places. Also, because of a lack of storage facilities, bales of goods sat stacked outside buildings, unmolested. No, you knew the worst thing this stranger might do was to try to sell you his mine.

The man in the flickering light of the campfire would be hale and hearty and excited about his latest find. Sanguine. Invariably, the first thing two gold rushers would do upon meeting was to enthusiastically trade rock specimens, lick them to rid them of dust, and then eyeball them carefully. Then they'd exchange hearty congratulations and maybe a slap on the back before handing the specimens back. This ritual would undoubtedly be performed at your campfire.

Being a typical honest miner yourself, you'd insist on sharing your dinner of beans and sowbelly (a kind of bacon) and flapjacks with him. But you'd split your last crust with him if it's all you had. And if this man were down on his luck, you might send him on his way with a twenty-dollar gold piece. He might reward your generosity with a few (probably worthless) shares of stock from his mine. "Westering" men deservedly had a reputation for generosity, even to the point of extravagance. It became a part of the Code of the West. When you struck it rich, you would treat your buddies in the saloon and make gifts of money to any folks in town who'd ever done a favor for you. A man who was stingy would have a tough time getting along in the West.

In this cheeky take-off on the scene on the facing page, prospectors examine a specimen the size of a watermelon! From an old mining stock certificate vignette. Sagstetter collection.

But that generosity was also a curse. Of the handful of miners who ever struck it rich, most were dead broke again in no time. They would have systematically disposed of their money by drinking and gambling and giving it away.

After dinner, you'd both linger around the campfire and undoubtedly smoke a pipe. If you had a whiskey flask, you'd share a gulp or two and maybe empty it. Drinking played a big part in the mining West. You'd eagerly trade the latest news — western folks were always nearly desperate for news, any news. Afterward, you might swap a few tall tales. These men seemed to enjoy a story more for its entertainment value than for its truth. For this reason it's best not to take the stories of lost mines or the stories of how a prospector discovered his mine too seriously. Making ironical statements was also a favorite campfire pastime. The more rollicking and irreverent the humor, the better.

But one thing you would never hear around this hypothetical campfire was complaints. These men were cheerful, almost to a fault. Visiting Englishwoman Isabella Bird commented: "The men are so easy to live with, they never fuss, or grumble, or sigh, or make trouble of anything." Remember the words to "Home on the Range?" "Where seldom is heard a discouraging word," no matter how tough the conditions. That song expresses an important character trait of early settlers in the West.

Another thing that wouldn't happen around that campfire was bragging. That was one way to set an honest miner's teeth on edge, and the boaster could count on being the brunt of practical jokes and ridicule. Putting on airs of any kind disgusted the miners. And the top hat became a symbol of everything they hated. Mark Twain wrote: "If a man wanted a fight on his hands without any annoying delay, all he had to do was to appear in public in a white shirt or a stove-pipe hat, and he would be accommodated." Unfortunately, this revulsion for the trappings of privilege also extended to mining experts. This condemned the gold rushers to making many unnecessary mining mistakes.

You would not be welcomed around the campfire, however, if you were Chinese. And if you were Native American and approached the campfire, you'd probably be shot. Anyone of Spanish descent would also experience a less than enthusiastic welcome. These early western men were suspicious, and language barriers increased the misunderstandings.

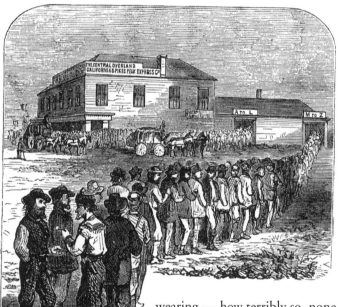

Long lines at western post offices as pictured in Richardson's Beyond the Mississippi. *Sagstetter collection.*

Nineteenth-century westerners rarely mentioned loneliness. But they were obsessed with the mail. Early accounts go into great detail about waiting in line for days at a post office. Some people even sold their places in line. The time the stagecoach arrived in town or a steamer arrived in the harbor was the high point of the day. Hometown newspapers also came by mail, and they were read and reread and passed around until they were tattered. Ovando Hollister went so far as to blame some of the later wildness of the mining camps on not enough letters from home: "But the delay [in mail delivery] was wearing — how terribly so, none can know but those who have felt it . . . Often the want of [letters] is the sole cause of [a young man's] falling into bad habits. It leaves him sick at heart, and inclines him to recklessness." This sounds suspiciously like loneliness.

The Prospectors

As mining grew and the West changed, the honest miner evolved into the prospector and the hard-rock miner. A prospector was a seeker — always searching for a new mine. A loner and a wanderer, probably unmarried, he worked for himself with only his burro as a companion, or maybe in partnership with another prospector. A hard-rock miner worked underground for a mining company. He was active in groups and organizations. There was always a lot of overlap between the two groups: A prospector might go to work as a hard-rock miner for a few months in order to grubstake his next prospecting expedition. Prospectors frequently hired themselves out for the winter months. Every hard-rock miner knew he worked for a man who had struck it rich, and he might well do a little prospecting on his time off.

But whether a man was a prospector or a hard-rock miner, he was looking for that ancient symbol of wealth, gold. (And later, silver.) Long before recorded history gold was considered valuable. Humans discovered early that gold will stay pure no matter what is done to it. That's what is meant when scientists call it "chemically inert." It will not rust or tarnish. It will not dissolve in salt water over a millennium, or even in acid. It doesn't shatter, it just flattens. It is malleable and easily worked with primitive tools. And it is heavy. It's this heaviness that enables prospectors to find it and retrieve it from nature. Gold is attracted to mercury (quicksilver), and this also aids in its recovery.

Miners' hand tools, as illustrated in Arthur Lakes' Prospecting for Gold and Silver in North America. *Sagstetter collection.*

Once mining went underground, it was no longer a one-person operation. Developing a mine became an extremely expensive proposition. Roads had to be built to the site and buildings constructed. Boilers had to be hauled in. Shafts needed to be dug and hoists installed. Maybe a mill was needed and a power source had to be arranged for. Basically, a small town had to be built, and usually in a remote place. This called for big money, for capitalists and investors, from the East or from Europe.

A prospector was not in a position to develop a mine except in small ways — just enough to keep his legal claim from lapsing. The prospector found promising sites, which he then patented with the federal government. Then his job became selling that claim to a capitalist.

An honest miner tended to be just that, honest, but with at least one glaring exception — when it came to selling his mine. No trick was too low down or underhanded to be used on some unwary mine buyer, especially if it enhanced a prospector's chances of selling his mine. He would do anything and everything in his power to try to make his mine appear as rich as Croesus. This included salting the mine. Salting a mine is similar to salting a steak, you scatter a few grains of high-grade ore (from an outside source) around your mine to raise the assay and thereby increase it's overall value. One early technique for salting a mine was to use a shotgun and fire gold dust into the walls of the tunnel. Later, as this ploy became well known, other, more sophisticated salting techniques were developed.

The salting could take place at the mine itself, or it could take place after the ore sample had been taken. You might salt the ore sample and send it on its way to the assayer for testing. Or you might attempt to bribe the assayer. Obviously, buying or selling a mine was a very tricky business. Suspicion and cynicism were the most important traits in a mine buyer.

You could trust an honest miner with all your worldly goods. You could trust him with your wife or daughter. And, indeed, when you worked together, you trusted him with your life every day. But if you were interested in buying his mine, this same man was not to be trusted.

As we visit the old mining-camp sites today, we try to picture these men who built them. At the remains of old buildings, we remind ourselves of their camaraderie and hearty sense of humor, the way they dressed and their dreams of a better life. We spot the clues as to what they ate, where they slept and what work they did, and know that we are seeing the remnants of their robust time here. It is at these times that we can almost hear the chuff-chuffing of the now stilled rusting mining contraptions. And almost hear the men's laughter among the rustling of the aspen leaves. And for a brief moment we stand at a window in time and boldly look in.

3

PLACER MINING

Digging for gold is about the hardest way on earth to obtain it.

— Albert Richardson, *Beyond the Mississippi*

 Pictures of the typical old-time prospector showed him with his burro loaded with supplies, headed to parts unknown. But what did a prospector do? How, exactly, did he go about finding gold? And is that what the gold rushers were doing?

What the prospectors and the gold rushers were searching for was "loose" gold, gold that was not imbedded in rock. This was gold that had weathered away from an outcropping and had gradually rolled downhill and found its way into stream bottoms through the eons. This gold was called free gold, or *placer* (pronounced *plasser*). The process of recovering this gold from stream beds is called *placering*.

There are several different types of placering. One way is to use a pan. Gold panning was the perfect setup for an individual or a couple of buddies working in partnership. It didn't require expensive tools or a huge investment of money, just a pick, shovel, wheelbarrow, a dab of mercury, a gold pan, and a lot of hard work. The techniques of panning could be learned quickly, although it did take some practice. Gold panning is probably the oldest method of finding gold. Mention of it goes back as far as ancient Greek legends. And it's a method that is used all over the world.

Say you are an experienced prospector. How do you start your search for gold? You begin by panning in geologically promising areas. It is with the gold pan that prospectors discover a place worthy of more intense exploration. First, you must be able to recognize a likely spot on the river for placer gold when you see it — say, at a place where the current slows, or at a sandbar. A typical rushing mountain stream moves so fast it washes everything downstream, including gold. It is only when the water slows down that the heavy grains of gold settle out.

This version of this famous gold panning scene is from Alaska and the Klondike Gold Fields *by A. C. Harris. Sagstetter collection.*

Through the millennia, gold granules, being among the heaviest minerals, sink all the way to the river's rock bottom. Knowing this, you'd begin digging in the sandbar or maybe on the curve of a stream, and you would continue digging all the way down to bedrock, panning all the while. You might have to dig a hole twelve to fifteen feet deep before you'd approach the lowest level. If there were any gold there, the deeper you dug, the more gold you would encounter when you washed it in your pan. And your pulse would quicken. Finally, when your shovel struck bedrock under or beside the river, you'd scour the rough depressions and natural potholes looking for gold.

You were lucky indeed if, nestled in a crack or crevice, was a tiny pocket of free gold that you could scrape out with your knife. The gold would be in the form of flakes, fine dust, or perhaps a nugget or two if you were fortunate. This was the moment a gold rusher had hoped for back home perhaps a year or more ago. This was the reason he'd crossed the continent. This gold could make his dreams come true.

But it would take a lot of it. An experienced man, working steadily, might be able to pan fifty panfuls in a ten-hour working day. If someone else was doing the digging, he might be able to do as many as a hundred pans a day. This amounted to moving about half a cubic yard of gravel.

You would need to have found at least one ounce of gold dust (at the time of the California gold rush this was worth sixteen dollars) in those fifty to a hundred pans or you wouldn't be making your expenses — which were outrageously high in a booming mining camp. Perhaps a third of the gold rushers did not make this minimum wage, according to Albert Richardson. And you would be sure to file a claim on that site for yourself to keep anyone else from panning there. But sooner or later the gold would give out. Then you would move on.

GOLD PANS

Kind.	Dimensions, Inches. Diameter x Depth.		Weight, Each.	Price, Each.
Steel, polished	12¼	x 2	1 lb. 2 oz.	.50
Copper	12¼	x 2	1 lb. 6 oz.	2.00
Aluminum	12¼	x 2	8 oz.	1.25
Steel, polished	16¼	x 2⅜	1 lb. 12 oz.	.50
Copper	16¼	x 2⅜	2 lb. 3 oz.	3.00
Copper bottom, steel edge	16¼	x 2⅜	1 lb. 14 oz.	3.00
Aluminum	16¼	x 2⅜	14 oz.	1.60

An advertisement for gold pans in the 1912 Mine and Smelter Supply Catalogue. Sagstetter collection.

GOLD PANNING

Panning is a lot harder than it might seem. Because water is needed to pan for gold, it is also wet work. Someone digs and shovels dirt and gravel from the banks or the bottom of a creek into the gold pan. This gold pan has a flat bottom and wide shallowly sloping sides. If you are the person doing the panning, you crouch as much as knee-deep in an icy mountain stream with the gold pan. The pan is filled with dirt and gravel. Then you submerge the filled pan in the creek and stir the contents with your hand around and around, removing the unwanted rocks and pebbles. You twist the pan from side to side and tap it with the heel of your hand, the purpose being to make the heavier material sink to the bottom. Then you swirl the contents of the pan, allowing the lighter material to wash over the edge. Just when your hands are good and numb, you have to swirl with the most finesse or you will propel the gold over the rim of the pan along with the worthless material. More water is added, and the pan is swirled some more, until there is only concentrate left. Gold, as the heaviest mineral, would be the last to wash out, and if it is present, it will be in the concentrate. Then you give the pan a final swirl so the concentrate remains in the angle of the flat bottom and sloping side of the pan in a streak, and you eyeball it carefully.

If there are gold specks in the concentrate, they do not glitter or sparkle in the light. In its natural state, gold is not as showy as iron pyrites (fool's gold) or mica. Gold has an unblinking, steady gleam to it. And if you bite it or hammer it it will flatten, but it won't shatter. Iron pyrites sparkle, are gritty to the bite, and shatter. If you wish to touch the gold specks, you use your knife blade. If you touched the gold with your finger to remove it, the natural oils from your hand would cause the gold, if it were very fine, to float and be lost with the worthless matter in the pan.

Recreational panning is allowed on some public land. But it is always best to check locally at the nearest ranger station. Using a power washer or portable dredge is not considered a recreational activity and requires a permit. If an area is fenced or if it has recently been worked, it is undoubtedly private. Panning there is considered at best trespassing, and at worst claim jumping!

Dr. Ben H. Parker Jr., world-famous geologist and an expert in gold placers has said, "The old time prospectors didn't find it all." Sizeable nuggets have been found as recently as 1990. But most panners today are lucky to find a couple of dollars worth of gold in an afternoon of panning.

Many mine tours and mining museums offer gold-panning lessons. Appendix C gives you information about some of these. There is also a gold-panning club, and every year it sponsors a gold-panning contest.

A good gold panner is hard to beat for thoroughness. He can find the most minute amounts of gold imaginable. Panning is still done today for prospecting and sampling. But the gold rushers wanted gold on a commercial scale, and panning is tedious and slow. They quickly came up with ways to speed up the panning process. One of these was the rocker.

The rocker looked much like a baby's cradle — a box mounted on curved runners. The box was kept rocking, and dirt and gravel were shoveled into the top of the "cradle." Water was added to wash the material over a metal sheet perforated with holes. The smaller, heavier material dropped through the holes and down onto something like rough fabric or canvas, which captured most of the gold. The bottom of the rocker had slats that formed riffles, irregularities that simulated the rough bedrock stream bottom. Any gold not captured by the canvas would be captured by the riffles. With a rocker, one man could wash perhaps two cubic yards of gravel and dirt in a ten-hour day.

Above, a cradle or rocker, as pictured in the International Correspondence Schools Reference Library *at the turn of the century. Sagstetter collection.*

Sluicing

In the summer of 1939, John Talbot and his friend Charles Godfrey went to Alma, Colorado, to try their luck at placering. Godfrey knew the area well; he and his father had worked there as hard-rock miners. The Alma area had been worked since the Colorado gold rush in 1859. But because there were no jobs to be had during those Depression years, Godfrey and Talbot figured that if they made enough to pay their expenses, they were ahead.

The technique they used was not much changed from that of the gold rushers. After they found a promising spot on the river by panning, they constructed a forty-foot *long tom,* which is a wooden sluice. Their long tom had three sections, and each wooden channel had a different slant, and therefore a different rate of flow. The top portion, approximately twenty to twenty-five feet long, was used to carry the water to the lower portion. During the gold rush, some valleys would be crisscrossed with long toms.

Godfrey and Talbot shoveled gravel into the long tom above the riffles, and water running through it washed the material down the wooden course and over the wooden riffles. The rate of flow slowed near the bottom, where the angle was

Sluice boxes crisscrossed entire valleys during the gold rush. This one is from the International Correspondence Schools Reference Library, *volume 155. Sagstetter collection.*

shallower, and washed over coarse, bristly mats. The coarse gold was captured behind the riffles and the fine gold in the mats near the bottom of the sluice.

To their surprise, they were able to average six dollars a day between them with gold selling at thirty dollars an ounce. This was at a time when, if a job was available at all, it might pay one or two dollars a day. "We were shoveling from daybreak to dusk, with time out for lunch only," said Talbot. They also lived much like the original gold rushers before them. They stayed in an old deserted cabin that they had cleaned up and repaired. It was part log, part planks. And they ate groundhog [marmot] stew. This they ate every single day, for every meal, until after a couple of weeks they could barely gag it down. "The meat was very fatty and rich," explained Talbot. "Other than the groundhog stew, it was a very successful summer."

This still is the way prospecting is done. A prospector starts with his gold pan. He works several sites along promising streams. Once he finds "color" (gold) in his pan, he might switch to a rocker or a long tom to move more dirt and gravel. If the site is rich, he will find more gold the deeper he digs, because the weight of the gold causes it to settle to the lowest point. But experienced prospectors have always known that the gold had to gravitate to its resting spot in the stream from somewhere else. Somewhere uphill. And that place is the source of the gold.

The prospector takes his gold pan and advances up the stream, panning all the while. When he stops finding gold in his pan, he knows he has passed the spot the gold came from. Then he backtracks until he finds the exact place where the gold originated. A good prospector can pinpoint this spot with amazing accuracy. From that point he moves up the mountain looking for a likely gold-bearing outcropping, typically of quartz. When he finds this place, he files a claim on it.

The men below are hydraulicking, as pictured in the International Correspondence Schools Reference Library, *volume 155. Sagstetter collection.*

Technically, at this point, hard-rock mining begins.

Hydraulicking and Dredging

California gold rushers found ways to placer on a commercial scale. Hydraulicking was one of these. Some astute gold rusher had the idea of turning a hoselike device on the gravel banks of rivers to speed up the sluicing process. Then no digging was necessary. The hose sprayed water under high pressure on the banks, which dissolved under the force. The water and gravel were captured in long toms and washed in the usual fashion.

Hydaulicking required a huge amount of water, and not all sites were viable for this reason. Elaborate dams, long ditches and flumes, and, sometimes, extensive wooden pipelines were developed to accommodate the voracious need for water. Hydraulicking left terrible scars on the landscape and buried towns such as Parkville, Colorado, the first Summit County seat, in their own mineral waste.

Dredges became popular around the turn of the century. These were "floating concentration mills," self-contained flat-bottomed scows that carried all the equip-

The bucket-line dredge like the one above was the most popular type of dredge in the American West. This one is from the International Correspondence Schools Reference Library, *volume 155. Sagstetter collection.*

ment necessary to process the gravel and remove the gold that was in it. On board were washers that separated the dirt from the gold and gold-saving devices such as tables, sluices, riffles, and amalgamating plates.

A dredge dug a shallow pond in the gravel riverbed, and that is what it floated in. Buckets scooped up the gravel and brought it on board. The dredges usually ran on steam power, although a few were electric. When the dredge had worked the gravels near it clean, it would need to be moved to dig a new pond.

Probably the most common type of dredge in the American West was the bucket-line dredge. The bucket-line dredges had a series of buckets strung in a line that did the digging. Then there were dredges with a shovel that performed the digging.

Today there is rarely enough left of the old dredges to be able to glean much information from them. You almost have to know that you're looking at a dredge to recognize it. In the 1960s, when we first became interested in the ghost towns and mining camps, finding the remains of an old dredge in a scooped-out pond was not

uncommon. But through the years they have become more and more scarce. Only a few remain across the American West, particularly in Oregon and Alaska.

Fifty-five years later, John Talbot is headed back to the old mining districts for another summer of recreational placering. This time he has a small, commercially made sluice about four or five feet long. At its bottom, outdoor carpeting captures the gold, instead of the "welcome mat" material he and Godfrey used in 1939. But other than that, what he does will be much like what the California gold rushers did in the 1850s.

Why he and other modern prospectors do it is much more difficult to answer. Hope has a lot to do with it. "Hope is a prime word in mining," says Talbot. There's always the chance of discovering a sizeable nugget. He may never come home with that gold nugget, but he will undoubtedly find some "keepsake" gold — that is, gold dust or flakes that he will save in a vial. "I would never sell it," he explains. And if he ever found that prize nugget, "It would go to a museum."

Today there is usually very little left of most dredges. This one is a surprising exception near Tincup, Colorado.

31

The above site is along the Swan River near Breckenridge, Colorado. Nearby are some intriguing remains, pictured below. Could they possibly be what is left of the dredge that created these dunes?

Miners of early placer diggings left few remains behind. Because the placers eventually gave out, accompanying buildings were generally of a temporary nature, like tents or crude log cabins. Whole towns that had been devoted to placer mining were vacant as early as the 1860s. But sometimes what has remained is the "lay of the land." Gravel fanned out in symmetrical dunes such as those above is a telltale sign that dredging was done here, even if there is no trace of the dredge itself. The gravel dunes lie along rivers.

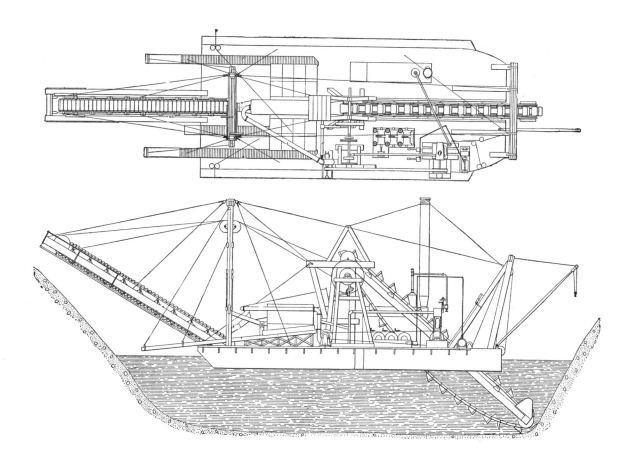

At the top is a plan for a bucket-line dredge, and below it is an elevation. *The International Correspondence School Reference Library* explains that the barge is squared at one end, but catamaran-shaped at the other. The remains of the dredge on the right clearly show this arrangement, indicating it was probably a bucket-line dredge. Finding a dredge in the condition of that on the lower right is very unusual.

The remains of this dredge lie on the Swan River, near Breckenridge, Colorado.

CAUTION:

NEVER *go underground in an old mine in any circumstances. Do not attempt to descend a shaft. Do not enter a horizontal tunnel (adit). It is extremely dangerous, and it's unnecessary. What went on underground can often be determined by what's left aboveground. If you are curious about what it's like underground, we urge you to visit any of the mine tours listed in Appendix C.*

4

HARD-ROCK MINING

The only chance [a miner] had of getting into heaven was to start a gold rush there.

— Richard E. Lingenfelter, *The Hardrock Miners.*

Hard-rock miners were a different breed from most prospectors. In hard-rock mining the gold and silver are encased in rock, as opposed to placering, where the gold has been weathered away from the surrounding rock. Among miners, gold and silver are considered the glamorous ores. A hard-rock miner working in the Western precious-metals mines in 1890 was a man at the top of his profession. He was highly paid, and although he worked for a mining company, he remained somewhat independent in that he probably had a mining claim or two of his own. He was an expert with explosives. He could recognize the difference between valuable ore and barren rock at a glance in flickering candlelight. He was as skilled as a sculptor with a clumsy three-hundred-pound Burleigh drill.

You would immediately recognize a hard-rock miner on his way to work, even though you did not know the man personally. On his head would be an early version of a hard hat called a *hard boil.* This was a felt hat that had been boiled over and over again in a resin until it was almost as hard as a modern hard hat. His clothes verged on raggedy. Tom Morrison, in *Hardrock Gold,* said, "The mine is the graveyard of old clothes." A loose woolen shirt and overalls were popular, and these would be wrinkled and splattered with clay. On his feet would be hobnailed boots or "India Rubber" boots. And most telling of all was that his clothes would be spattered with candle drippings. At a small mine, his pockets and the tops of his boots might be stuffed with dynamite and a coil of Bickford fuse.

This man was not as burly and big-chested as you might imagine. Although he punched holes in solid granite with hand tools everyday, he used skill, not brute strength. At every opportunity, hard-rock miners let gravity move the rock for them.

These hard-rock miners prepare to go to work. Note each of them has fresh candles from the box in the foreground. Nearby are their miner's lunch pails. We can roughly date this picture as before the turn of the century, since carbide replaced candles about then. These are the faces we envision as we visit the ghost towns today. Sagstetter collection.

Clenched in the man's calloused hand would be a symbol of the hard-rock miner: the miner's lunch pail. This ingenious device was brought from Cornwall by immigrant miners. There were two shapes: round and oblong. The old Sears, Roebuck and Montgomery Ward and Company catalogues both list "Miner's Lunch Pails" and mention how many trays each model contained as well as the number of quarts each pail held. The bottom of the pail was filled with tea or coffee. Above this was one or sometimes two trays. One tray would traditionally be reserved for a *pasty.* This was a mixture of meat, seasoned potatoes, and vegetables neatly tucked inside a pastry shell. The pasty was affectionately referred to by the miners as a "letter from home." The other tray might be for dessert. The top of the pail was a lid, and in the center of this lid was an upended tin cup.

As soon as the miner arrived at the work site, he hung the wire bail of the lunch bucket from a nail, and under it he placed a lighted candle. The candle slowly heated the tea, which, when hot, steamed the pasty. By *croust,* a Cornish word for "lunchtime," his meal was warm and the tea or coffee was hot.

He might well greet you with a foreign accent or language. Waves of immigrants from different countries swept through Western mining camps at different times. Miners from Cornwall, Italy, Ireland, and the Austrian Empire were in turn attracted by the high wages. Each group tended to stick together. Native-born U.S. residents made up only about a fifth of hard-rock miners in the last half of the nineteenth century. Of all the hard-rock miners, the Americans were the most restless. It was the American miners who made up the ranks of the "tramp miners" who wandered the mining districts, seldom lighting for long in one place. Woe to the mine manager when a rumor surfaced about a new strike in another district: He might lose most of his workers overnight.

Dinner Pails.
Each.
44935 3 quarts. $0.17
4 quarts. 18
5 quarts. 25
Oblong Dinner Pails.

Above is the miners' lunch pail as pictured in the Montgomery Wards and Company catalogue of 1895. Reprinted here with permission from Dover Publications.

The hard-rock miner's greeting to you might be with a wheeze or cough. The early machine drills belched a terrible dust that slowly destroyed a miner's lungs. The disease is called silicosis and ultimately led to the miner's death. Silicosis left a man very susceptible to pneumonia, the leading cause of death in a mining camp. Harold Thompson, who worked as a hard-rock miner during the Depression, said his shift boss had blue lips and coughed up blood on occasion. Thompson could always tell when the shift boss was coming, for he could hear him puffing up the ladder long before he arrived. Later a stream of water was introduced to the machine drills, lessening the man-killing dust.

The hard-rock miner was a gregarious man, and he probably belonged to the Oddfellows, Elks, Freemasons or other fraternal groups. These organizations were well represented in the western mining camps. The hard-rock miners formed strong labor unions that were very active.

It's very unusual to find the remains of lunch pails at a site today. Below is one of those rare exceptions.

If you were a mining newcomer, you could expect a little teasing. As mentioned earlier, a sense of humor in the West was a must. How a person reacted to a gentle "hazing" determined how he would be treated in the future. Underground, a newcomer could expect to be sent looking for nonexistent tools like a "shaft-stretcher," a "rock bender," a "sky hook," or a "left-handed wrench." If he accepted this as good-natured fun and was a good sport about it, he was accepted into the group. If he could give as good as he got, he earned respect.

Hard-rock mining is dangerous, uncertain work. A man risked his life every day he went to work. As a result, the hard-rock miner was a superstitious man. For example, women were not allowed underground, for this was considered bad luck. Underground, the creaks and groans of the settling timbers, the plink of dripping water, the opaque blackness beyond his candle flame, was fertile ground for his imagination. The *Tommyknocker* was created to help explain the inexplicable. Tommyknockers were gnomes said to inhabit the underground workings of a mine. These short little men came from England with the Cornish hard-rock miners. If, in the shadows beyond his candlelight, a miner couldn't find a tool he had laid down, he blamed it on the Tommyknockers. If the flickering light played tricks on his eyes, the Tommyknockers were deceiving him. Like the miners themselves, the Tommyknockers were pranksters. But the Tommyknockers, if a miner listened to them, also warned him of imminent danger.

For example, Harold Thompson told of a time when a new man on the job had just plunked himself down to eat lunch when a handful of dust and gravel rock peppered his "hard boil." He was tired and hungry and went on eating. Thompson pointed out to him that "a big boulder always follows dribble rock." The new man tiredly got up and moved. He had no more than settled into his new seat when a huge rock thundered down and smashed onto the exact spot where he had been sitting. Cornish miners would have said it was the Tommyknockers who had warned him with the "dribble rock."

A Day in the Life

A hard-rock miner's shift began with descending the shaft. This was probably the most dangerous part of his day — coming and going. Before modern safety equipment, this might have entailed standing on the rim of the bucket while grasping the rope. A miner's hands and feet could be smashed as the bucket glanced off the rock walls; therefore, he had to remain alert. With him he took three candles — enough to last for a ten-hour shift — and a bundle of sharpened, tempered drill steels, a hammer, and his lunch pail.

In the early days, a miner rode on the edge of the bucket when coming or going from the shaft. This was extremely dangerous, of course. This scene is from William Thayer's Marvels of the New West. *Sagstetter collection.*

Once he was underground, the shift boss directed him to a particular area of the mine to work. Using a lantern, he made his way to the rhythmic clang of hammers and drills in the background, stepping aside for mule-drawn ore cars. In the nineteenth century, mules were the preferred form of power underground. They pulled a string of one-ton ore cars that were mounted on small-gauge rails. Getting a mule down a mine shaft to the underground workings was a difficult proposition. First the animal had to be blindfolded to calm it. Then its hooves were bound together. That way, if it were to panic, it wouldn't batter itself to death on the walls of the shaft. Then the mule was secured in a sling and lowered down the shaft tail end first by the hoist. Once a mule was in the mine's workings, it stayed there for life. A mule that remained underground for years would eventually go blind. Accommodations for the mules below ground level were blasted from rock. The stable had to be well ventilated, which meant blasting an air vent. Hay and oats and straw needed to be hoisted in and manure out. And the stable had to be constantly maintained by a stable hand.

The men above are double-jacking. From an old stock certificate vignette, Sagstetter collection.

Once the hard-rock miner found his work site, his job was to drill holes in the rock to hold the sticks of dynamite. In the old days drilling was done by hand with a set of drill steels of varying lengths. The starter steels were short and slightly bigger round than the longer drills. As the hole got deeper, the shorter drill steel was replaced with a longer steel. The miner struck the end of the steel with a four-pound hammer while turning the steel slightly. This was called *single-jacking* when he worked alone. *Double-jacking* involved two miners alternating using an eight-pound hammer while turning the drill steel. At the end of a shift, the rock face would be pock-marked with holes. Using hand tools, this could take an entire ten-hour shift to accomplish.

The men below are single-jacking. From International Correspondence Schools Reference Library, volume 149. Sagstetter collection.

When each hole was deep enough, perhaps three feet, the miner cleaned out the rock dust with a special long-handled "spoon" and inserted the stick of dynamite in the hole. A rat tail of fuse hung from each hole. Then he cut the fuses to differing lengths so that the dynamite would detonate at slightly different times and in a designated sequence. This allowed the miners to count the blasts as they went off to make sure that all the dynamite detonated. A leading cause of death among miners

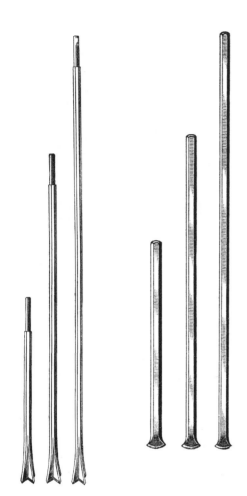

The drill steels on the left are machine drills. On the right are hand steels. They have a chisel tip on the end. From the International Correspondence Schools Reference Library. *Sagstetter collection.*

was to accidentally drill into undetonated dynamite left over from a previous blast, called a *misfire.*

When all was ready, the miners lit the fuses and left the area. If the number of expected blasts occurred as anticipated, the miners called it a day and left for home. Noxious fumes and clouds of dust would fill the work area after the blast, and it would be uninhabitable for a while. The next day they would *muck* (shovel) the blasted rock into ore cars and start drilling again. At larger, well-ventilated mines, the work area could be cleared in the time it took the miners to change shifts, and the new shift could begin mucking when they arrived.

Highgrading

The term *highgrade* means rich ore. A mine that had highgrade ore was very rich indeed. The term can also mean a particularly rich piece of ore, like a gold nugget. But through the years the term highgrade also began to be used as a verb. To *highgrade* means to filch a rich piece of ore from the workings underground. This a larcenous miner would smuggle out in his lunch pail. Highgrading became a serious problem for mine owners, though only in gold mines, and then only in those mines where the rich ore could actually be seen. There were plenty of gold mines where the direction of the lode could only be determined by assaying because the gold was not visible to the eye. In these mines, highgrading was not an issue.

Highgrading was not a problem in the early days of the gold rush but became so later on, when mines were owned by big corporations and absentee investors. It became a commonplace way for a hard-rock miner to supplement his salary. A small gold nugget could be worth a month's salary to him and his family. And the practice was condoned in the community. Highgrade ore was readily accepted as payment for bills by shopkeepers. Frank Crampton said that even the girls on the line accepted it as payment for their services. But the most common destination for highgrade was a less-than-honest assayer. An assayer had all the tools necessary to melt the rich ore down into untraceable gold bullion. Gold ore is recognizable —

These men use machine drills. We can see these are early "widowmaker" types because there is only one hose — for the compressed air. From the International Correspondence Schools Reference Library, *volume 149. Sagstetter collection.*

an experienced geologist or mine engineer or hard-rock miner could tell by looking at it what mine it had come from. So it was important not to get caught with the highgrade in its original form.

If a man were caught with highgrade from a particular mine, he almost never was convicted for it. Because highgrading was accepted in the community, no jury of a miner's peers would convict him of engaging in it.

In placering, more gold is found the deeper one digs, then finally, at bedrock, the richest discoveries are made. Early hard-rock miners thought the same would be

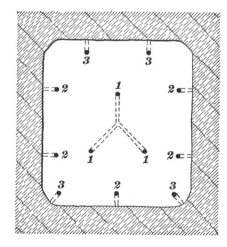
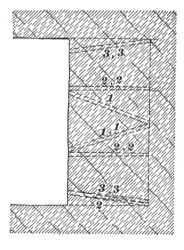

Holes in the rock face were driven in a certain pattern that caused the rock to shatter in a predetermined way. The dynamite was fired in numerical order: first, numbers one, then twos, then threes. From The International Correspondence Schools Reference Library, *Sagstetter collection.*

41

true in lode mining. But the opposite proved to be the case. In lode mining the veins almost always become *less* rich as the mine deepens. This made it extremely difficult for a mine to turn a profit. It is also one reason there were so many mining towns that became "ghosts."

EXPLOSIVES

Blasting powder was packaged in metal kegs like the one above, right. The most popular size weighed about twenty-five pounds. Black Powder was used before dynamite was invented in 1866. But it continued to be used well after the turn of the century for smaller jobs. It was still for sale when the above advertisement appeared in the Keystone Company's 1923 The Mining Catalog. On the top left is an embossed lid to a powder keg. Because it reads "powder," we can be assured what it originally contained. Note that the lid was cut off the keg, more than likely to reuse the keg body. Powder kegs were often reused, ranging from simply being turned on end as a stool, to below, as a chimney in a sod roof.

EXPLOSIVES

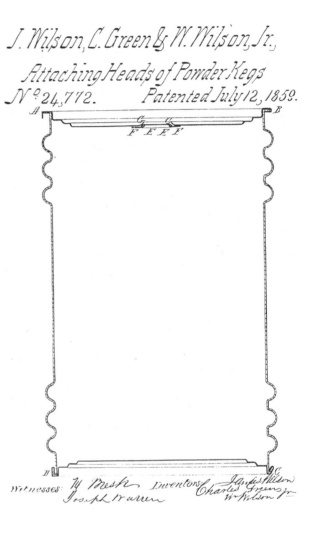

J. Wilson, C. Green & W. Wilson, Jr.,
Attaching Heads of Powder Kegs
Nº 24,772.   Patented July 12, 1859.

Witnesses: W. Mesh   Inventors Charles Green
Joseph Warren   James Wilson
                              W. Wilson Jr.

We suspected when we found the above embossed lid that it might have been part of an old powder keg — because of the large size of the rusted tin can, and the opening for pouring out the contents. Armed with the patent date, we looked the patent up and found that it had indeed been a powder keg. The patent on the right was issued to three men in Wilmington, Delaware. Many powder companies were located in Wilmington. The patent date, July 12, 1859, is the earliest date we have ever encountered.

By the way, if you discover an object with a patent number or a patent date on it, it is a very easy matter to look up the original patent. Patents are issued by numbers which are assigned sequentially on the date they are granted. So, if you have a patent number or date it's easy to look up. There are patent document files in every state, usually located in the capital city of the state. We understand that patent information is also available on the internet. If you just have a patent number and would like a quick "ballpark" date, check the Approximate Patent Timetable in Appendix B.

CARBIDE CANS

The 25 Pound Drum with Large Screw Top is an Economical, Convenient and Very Popular Package

The advertisement on the above right appears in the Keystone Company's 1923 The Mining Catalog. Sagstetter collection.

Carbide was also packed in a keg. Note how much it looks like a powder keg. The probable carbide can above left, had a screw lid that we often see at mining camp sites. We are not always sure which can we have found unless, like the one pictured on the right, the can actually says what it contained. The size pictured in all three pictures is the most typical size of carbide can we see at sites. A carbide can tells you that the old-timers at this mine were using carbide for lighting instead of candles. It also gives you a rough timeline for the mine, in that carbide was not in use until after the turn of the century. In the field look for the rusted corrugated sides, and the very large size with the screw-on lid.

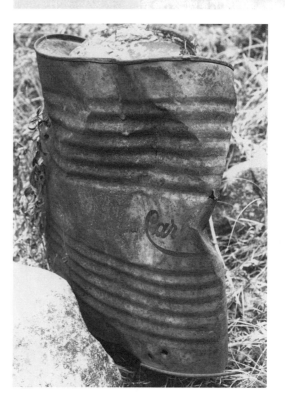

45

AIR COMPRESSOR

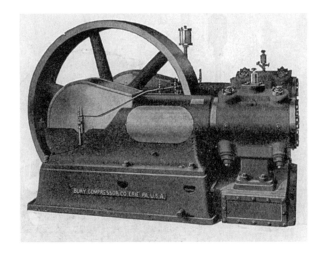

Above is an air compressor at an old site. On its side is embossed "Ingersoll Rand Co., New York, Imperial Type 10." On the left is a brand new Bury brand air compressor as pictured in the 1912 Mine and Smelter Supply catalog.

An air compressor tells you the miners were using machine drills underground, as opposed to hand drills. Mines with air compressors had a certain level of capitalization, because it was very expensive to purchase equipment like this and transport it to a site. Machine drills were used as early as the last quarter of the nineteenth century, but only at the larger mines. Look for embossing, like the one below which reads "The Ingersoll Drill Company, New York." This would be an air compressor.

STEAM ENGINE

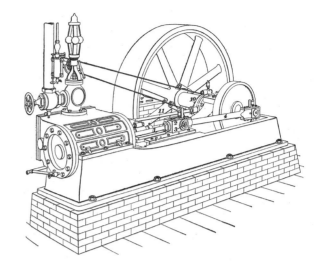

Note how much these old steam engines looked like an air compressor. The steam engine on the above left is from the 1912 Mine and Smelter Supply catalogue. The above right is described as a "common type of simple slide-valve steam engine" in the *International Correspondence Schools Reference Library*. Old flywheel pumps like the one pictured below also looked similar to air compressors, but we have never seen a flywheel pump in the backcountry, only in museums. When in doubt, it is probably an air compressor. Sagstetter collection.

FLYWHEEL PUMP

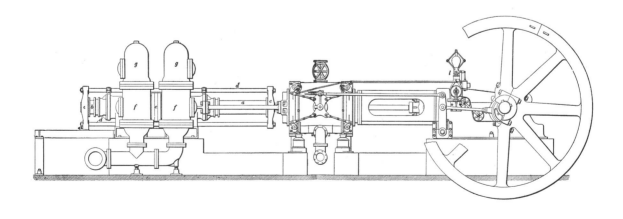

5

MINING EQUIPMENT

If ghost towns do indeed have a language, then the
mining equipment is the verb "to be."

 White trunks of aspen trees lined both sides of the trail like a colonnade.
The pale columns were topped by Day-Glo aspen leaves, their color so
intense, so nearly fluorescent, that they could practically have glowed in the
dark. Above them, silhouetted against the cobalt sky, loomed the dark
outline of an old head frame.

Sometimes the only thing that remains at a ghost-town site is a few hulks of antique mining
equipment. Rusted now, and sometimes even in pieces, they arouse questions in us. What
was this? What did it do?

There are certain pieces of equipment and buildings that were necessary to mines or mining
camps. Knowing their purpose makes sense of the jumble of buildings and old equipment
that characterize the sites today. If we were to follow a hypothetical load of ore making its
journey from underground, we would directly or indirectly encounter much of the equipment that we see today and many of our questions would be answered.

The first structure our load of ore would encounter would be the head frame. At one time
the head frame was one of the most recognizable structures associated with a mine or
mining camp. The head frame was the support for the cable, (or, as they called it at the turn
of the century, wire rope) that descended the vertical or steeply inclined shaft. Perched on
the very top of this headframe was the *sheave* (pronounced *shiv*) *wheel.*

The head frames we encounter today in the backcountry are wooden. They are also in ruins
— very few remain standing. They look like just one more jumble of wood, except for the
sheave wheel. The sheave wheel is recognizable by the deep groove in its rim, which guides

Sheave Wheel

On the right is a steel head frame. It is from the International Correspondence Schools Reference Library, *volume 148. Sagstetter collection.*

the wire rope. Finding a sheave wheel today serves to identify what was once the head frame.

Not all sites had a shaft. Some (usually smaller) mines had a horizontal *adit* (tunnel) instead. Building an adit was generally less expensive than digging a shaft, erecting a head frame and buying hoists and the boilers to run them. The adits (tunnels) were typically dug at a slight angle so as to drain the mine.

A head frame suggests the presence of a hoist. The old rusted hoist is often still visible at mine sites; its drums and operating levers make it an obvious piece of mining equipment. Hoists come in all sizes, from those so large as to have their own separate building, to a simple hand winch for prospecting work. Everything needed underground came by way of the shaft and hoist. Sharpened drill steels, dynamite, even the miners themselves. It would be the hoist that lifted our hypothetical load of ore from the underground, and it would be the hoistman who was in charge of accomplishing it.

The hoistman was a special breed of miner. He held lives in his hands every time the miners went down into or up out of the mine. He operated thousands of dollars' worth of expensive equipment. A moment of inattention on his part could not only cost lives but also could shut the mine down until any problem he caused was solved. This spelled hardship for the families of the miners. Therefore, the hoistman had to be an extremely dependable, nondrinking man. He was generally paid more than a hard-rock miner and he was usually hired from the ranks of the hard-rock miners.

Such a man is Harold Thompson. During the Depression he worked as a hoistman at the London Butte Gold Mine in Alma, Colorado. Harold Thompson started his career underground as a hard-rock miner. Then later he was tapped to run the hoist.

The International Correspondence Schools Reference Library *identifies this as a direct current hoist, very high tech at the turn of the century when this book was published. Sagstetter collection.*

Just one powerful turn-of-the-century boiler could power all the equipment at a mine. Here is an entire bank of them, from the International Correspondence Schools Reference Library. Sagstetter collection.

Thompson had a depth indicator to help him locate the five different underground levels of the mine. He had to be careful not to pull the brake lever too hard, or it could jam the bucket in the shaft and stretch the cable. Part of his job was to keep an eye on the boiler gauges.

Boilers

The hoist at the London Butte was run by a steam boiler. "The steam was very powerful," explained Thompson, "more powerful than diesel or gas." This one boiler powered everything at the mine, including heating the boardinghouse.

"If you hoisted muck all morning," Thompson continued, "then you had to clean out the clinkers from the boiler at noon." Clinkers are a byproduct of coal burned in a boiler. It is like ashes, but larger and hard as rock, though much lighter in weight than stone. Clinkers would collect in the firebox under the boiler and clog the vents so the fire couldn't breathe. We sometimes find clinkers strewn around old mining camps today.

Of all the equipment in all the buildings left at old mining-camp sites, the huge rusted boilers are among the most recognizable. At one time, many of these boilers would have been surrounded by fire bricks. But today most old boilers are bare, the old fire bricks having crumbled or disappeared. The most common type of boiler we find is called a tubular boiler. The tubular boiler was so popular at mining camps, that it was the only mining boiler offered for sale in the 1912 Mine and Smelter Supply Company catalogue. Tubular boilers are so called because they had long tubes running the horizontal length of the interior of a cylindrical body. The body of the boiler held water. A fire was built beneath the body in a special place, and the heat and smoke were drawn through those long tubes, heating the water on their way out the smokestack. One such boiler could run most every piece of equipment necessary to operate a mine, just as at the London Butte.

All of this equipment was necessary just to lift our hypothetical load of ore from the ground. After our load of ore was hoisted from the shaft by the hoistman, it was dumped into an ore bin. Ore bins were sturdy structures built to take a beating and to hold enormous weight. Indeed, the ore bins are sometimes the only structures to survive today. The ore bin could be freestand-

Today old boilers dot the backcountry of historic districts, looking much like this one near Dumont, Colorado. The rows of holes in its face identify it as a tubular boiler. Below are the remains of a smokestack, after it has been crushed by time.

Above, an ore bin, often the only structure left standing at sites.

Below, mills were typically built in descending stair steps on a hillside. The underlying structure can often still be seen today, even at millsites that are in ruin, like this one.

ing, or it could be a part of a building, say a tram house or a mill. Here the ore was stored until it was time for it to continue on the next leg of its journey, often this would be to a mill.

Mills

If you were the owner of a small mine with low-grade ore, a mill might be a good investment. It was so expensive to transport ore that only the highest-grade ores could pay the freighting costs. But a simple concentration/amalgamation mill could take a low-grade ore and separate enough waste rock from it to increase the value four to six times. Then the mine owner was only paying shipment for this concentrate, which was perhaps 25 percent of the original amount. Often, this process made the difference between a mine being profitable or not. Therefore, in places where there was a combination of low-grade ore and difficult, expensive transportation, as in Colorado, the remains of mills dot the backcountry in historic mining districts.

A mill mimicked what nature did, except that what took nature eons to deposit on the bottom of streambeds, a mill could process in a few hours. Just as in nature, the early mills relied on gravity as the force for moving the rock through the mill system. Therefore, most mills are found arranged in descending steps on the slant of a hillside. Also like nature, water washed the pulverized rock through the millworks. Therefore, early mills were almost always situated near a dependable water source.

If you were a millman with practical knowledge, as opposed to a university education, you could, at the turn of the century, order a simple mill from a catalogue. One of these was the Mine and Smelter Supply Company catalogue of 1912. This catalogue had everything the millman needed to construct a simple working mill. The specifications included even the nuts and bolts. A mill that was constructed from a catalogue might well be like the Sound Democrat Mill which lies outside the ghost town of Animas Forks in the San Juan Mountains of Colorado. Very few original wooden mills are standing today. They are wrecked or have been salvaged. The Bureau of Land Management (BLM) believes the Sound Democrat Mill to be the only standing stamp mill on public land in the United

States. In 1991 the BLM undertook, along with the National Park Service, to stabilize the old mill. As part of the project, they produced the Historic American Engineering Report (HAER No. CO-69), by Robert L. Spude and Frederic J. Athearn, which is well written and beautifully photographed.

According to this report, the Sound Democrat Mill was originally constructed in 1905 and 1906 and was remodeled in 1909. It employed techniques perfected in the late nineteenth century and was probably a little old-fashioned even at the time it was built. On our first trip to the Sound Democrat Mill — before the report had been produced — we noticed the bolt collars were embossed with the patent date of May 10, 1904, and October 29, 1907, and we suspected it had been built around this time.

The details of the Sound Democrat's construction are not known. But it was a simple stamp mill for ore amalgamation and concentration, and was built by a practical millman. It is the type of mill that could have been constructed from a catalogue. The Sound Democrat is an example of the small stamp mills that were commonplace in nineteenth-century mining districts.

The Sound Democrat Mill has at its top a tram terminus. Here the ore was dumped from the hanging ore buckets of the aerial tram into an ore bin. These ore bins are

The Sound Democrat Mill. It is the type of mill common in western mining districts, and the type of mill ordered up from an equipment catalogue.

55

TYPICAL AMALGAMATION/CONCENTRATION MILL

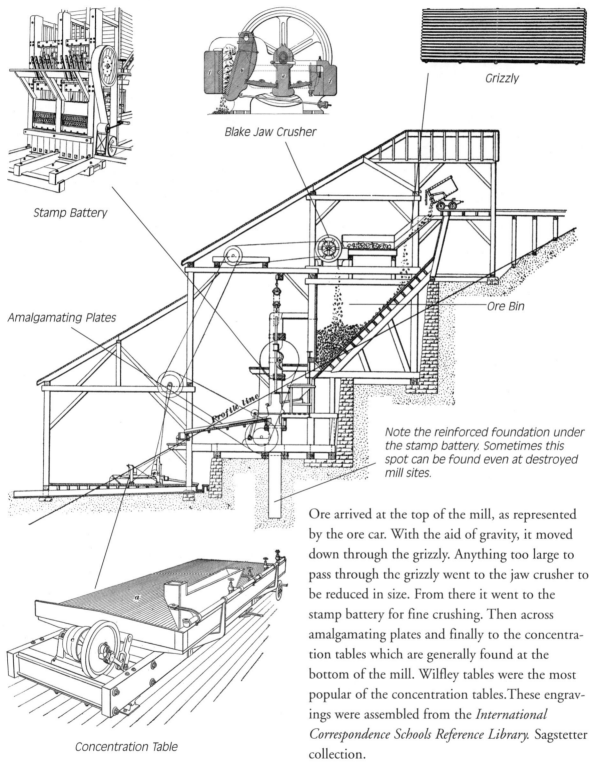

Grizzly

Blake Jaw Crusher

Stamp Battery

Amalgamating Plates

Ore Bin

Note the reinforced foundation under the stamp battery. Sometimes this spot can be found even at destroyed mill sites.

Concentration Table

Ore arrived at the top of the mill, as represented by the ore car. With the aid of gravity, it moved down through the grizzly. Anything too large to pass through the grizzly went to the jaw crusher to be reduced in size. From there it went to the stamp battery for fine crushing. Then across amalgamating plates and finally to the concentration tables which are generally found at the bottom of the mill. Wilfley tables were the most popular of the concentration tables. These engravings were assembled from the *International Correspondence Schools Reference Library.* Sagstetter collection.

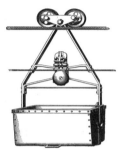

The tram terminus at the top of the Sound Democrat Mill. The tram buckets are gone now, but they would have looked much like the one below. More on aerial trams in the chapter on transportation.

common at the very top of a mill. The ore bin usually held enough ore to last the mill several days, for it was expensive to start and stop a mill. So the ore bins held enough to keep the mill running in case the mine shut down for a few days. The ore bin has a slanted floor that slides the ore down next to a gate.

Also near the top of the Sound Democrat was a water tank. The wooden staves that made up its sides are gone today, but the metal hoops that secured the wooden staves are still there, stacked loosely on the wooden base. Water tanks were typical equipment at mill sites. Water was stored for the same reason as ore was — a mill couldn't operate without water. The water tanks generally sat on the ground and not directly on the foundation of the mill building itself. This is because the constant vibration created by the stamp battery could jostle the water and eventually the constant wave action could pull the building apart. A water tank would be near the top of an old mill structure.

On the far left is a wooden water tank advertisement from the 1912 Mining and Scientific Press magazine. On the near left are the remains of a similar water tank at the Sound Democrat Mill.

Mills contained two sections, for grinding and recovery. The grinding sections were at the top of the mill. The recovery sections were located in the lower part of the mill building.

Grinding Section

From the ore bin, ore tumbled through a screening device — the grizzly. Anything that did not fall through the grizzly went on to the first step in the grinding section of the mill — coarse grinding. This was done by a rock breaker.

The most famous of the rock breakers was the Blake Jaw Crusher. But other brands existed — the Dodge for one. The cast-iron crusher is a distinctive piece of equipment, making it easy to spot today. Two sturdy belt wheels flanked the sides of the Blake, and these can often still be seen even if the crusher is in pieces. The crusher at the Sound Democrat is the Samson brand, but it is in pieces. A rock crusher reduced the rock to morsel size.

Our ore, now crushed, tumbles down for fine grinding. At the Sound Democrat and many other old mills, this was done by a stamp battery. Stamps were the heart of such a mill. Heavy iron shoes (the stamps) were lifted by a cam wheel and then dropped on a small amount of ore. The stamps reduced the rock to the size of sand or smaller. The noise the stamps made was deafening. The ground shook with each drop of a stamp, and the constant vibration could shake a building apart. For that reason, the stamp battery was

On the right, a Samson brand rock crusher like the one at the Sound Democrat Mill, as it looked new, in the 1912 Mine and Smelter Supply catalogue. Below, as it looks at the Sound Democrat Mill today, sans parts.

usually placed on its own foundation, separate from the main building foundation. Sometimes today we can ascertain where the stamp battery sat in a ruined site by looking for its separate heavy-duty foundation.

Stamp batteries were in use as early as the 1849 California gold rush, and they remained in use until as late as the 1930s. Today, ball mills and rod mills typically have replaced the old stamp mills. But stamp mills were once so important that the number of stamps determined the relative size of the mill. For example, the Consolidated Virginia Mill in the Comstock District of Nevada was a sixty-stamp mill during the 1860s. The Sound Democrat is a seven-stamp mill. By comparison, down the road at Animas Forks, the Gold Prince Mill had one hundred stamps.

As our finely ground ore leaves the stamps, it is screened to assure uniform consistency and then is washed down to undergo the recovery phase of the process.

Recovery Process

The recovery parts of mills differ from mill to mill and in the gold rushes the recovery method was sometimes a secret of the millman. Here they experimented with everything they could lay their hands on to remove the metal from the ground rock — including herbs and tobacco juice.

Today there are many different recovery processes. Which one is used depends upon the character of the ore. At the Sound Democrat and many other old mills, amalgamation was used. Amalgamation was the most common technique for gold recovery during the nineteenth century. Amalagamation is an ancient technique known as far back as ancient Rome, and uses mercury to remove gold from ore. Gold is affected by very few substances but mercury is one of them. Gold is attracted to mercury and readily combines with it, or "amalgamates."

This old advertisement in the Mining and Scientific Press *shows a five-stamp battery with amalgamating plates. The plates are not to scale, however. They were actually much longer.*

To do this, millmen extended platforms down from the stamp battery. These were called plates. According to the Mine and Smelter Supply catalogue of 1912, these plates were about four and a half feet wide and eight feet long and copper-covered. The old-timers would coat these plates with mercury. Gold that had been ground and freed from its surrounding rock by the stamps would combine with the mercury on these plates. Then, the substance that had formed, called amalgam, would be removed from these plates.

On the right is a Wilfley table, upside down now, at the Sound Democrat Mill. The disc next to it with the star design is also pictured on the Wilfley table below from the International Correspondence Schools Reference Library.

After amalgamation, the residue of crushed rock and water would be washed across concentrating tables to collect anything missed by the amalgamating plates. Concentration tables are about the size of a pool table, and the linoleum-covered tops have a series of shallow riffles. The table was mounted at a slight tilt and then was gently shaken by mechanical power. Any metals, being heavy, were caught in the riffles, and then captured in a bucket. The worthless rock, being lighter, washed across the riffles and away to the tailings pond.

The most famous of the concentration tables was the Wilfley table. Arthur Wilfley discovered that different metals actually sorted themselves out on the shaker tables

Richardson describes this picture as a "quartz mill" in Idaho in his book Beyond the Mississippi. *Amalgamating pans are shown on the second level up from the bottom. The year was 1865.*

The remains of amalgamating pans at a ruined mill on the Alpine Loop in the San Juan Mountains of Colorado. Below is a diagram of an amalgamating pan from the International Correspondence Schools Reference Library.

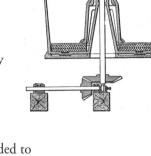

in a particular order. Watching a Wilfley table in operation, you can actually point to a particular streak of ground ore and identify it as gold, silver, lead, and so on. We have often seen old Wilfley tables embossed with patent dates from the 1890s still in use at mines today. At old mill sites we often find the remains of concentration tables. They may be upside down and in pieces, but they are unmistakable. They are invariably at the bottom of what used to be the mill building. Such is the case with the Sound Democrat.

Sometimes we find at the bottom of old mill buildings remains of amalgamating pans. The ground ore and water from the stamp battery was added to mercury in these pans to facilitate amalgamation. Amalgamating pans were not listed for sale in the 1912 Mine and Smelter Supply Company catalogue, and thus were probably out of favor by then.

About the turn of the century the cyanide process of recovery became popular, cyanide process could recover much more gold than did earlier methods. The crushed ore pulp that comes from the stamp batteries is placed in vats of a weak cyanide solution to soak for several days. The cyanide dissolves the gold. Later, the gold is filtered from the cyanide. The remains of a mill building with many large vats at the bottom level could have been a cyanide mill. The cyanide recovery process is still used today.

Sometime in the 1920s the flotation recovery process became popular. In this process, certain mineral particles attach to bubbles and float, while others sink. We associate many troughs with square wooden cells at the bottom level of the mill with the flotation process.

Any gold bullion from our hypothetical ore that would have been retrieved by the Sound Democrat Mill would be sold to the U.S. Mint. The concentrate would be sold to a smelter, such as the one below advertised in the *Mining and Scientific Press*.

EQUIPMENT FIELD GUIDE

EMBOSSING AND NAME PLATES

Any writing on equipment also speaks. Take it beyond the obvious name and place and ask yourself what this *implies,* as we discussed in chapter one. For example, on the above left is a huge boiler that sits high in the San Juan Mountains of southern Colorado. Yet it was built in Erie, Pennsylvania, by the Erie City Iron Works, more than a century ago. Its presence here suggests that the impact of the western gold rushes reached way beyond the boundaries of the West itself. That boilermakers in Pennsylvania were touched by the discovery of gold and silver, just as surely as someone living in the West. On the above right is a name plate that reads, "Fraser and Chalmers, Chicago." Below, the words "Rogers Joplin" are embossed on this mining equipment. Most sites contain something embossed with a faraway place name.

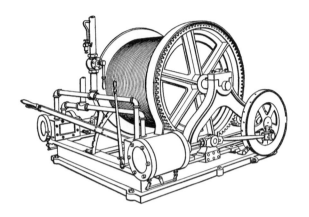

Hoists are easily identified by the drum that the cable wound around. But be careful! The presence of a hoist suggests that a shaft is nearby. The hoist on the left is identified by the *International Correspondence Schools Reference Library* as a portable hoist that was steam-driven. It states "portable hoists are made with drums up to six feet in diameter" and that they were "self-contained, easy of erection, and suitable for small mines, shaft sinking, and prospecting work." The hoist below appears to be a portable hoist of approximately the same turn-of-the-century era as the one on the left.

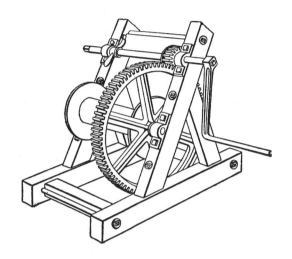

The International Correspondence Schools Reference Library identifies the hoist on the right as a crab winch. It says they were popular because a heavy load could be hoisted with little effort on turning the handles. Double-geared crabs, like the one shown below, "will permit one man to hoist a ton or more with little exertion."

The 1912 Mine and Smelter Supply Catalogue identifies this as a horse-powered hoisting whim. "The operations of hoisting, dumping and lowering can be performed with the horse in constant motion. Readily knocked down for muleback transportation." It was offered for sale by itself or as part of their "Prospector's Outfit." Below, left, is how it appears in the *International Correspondence Schools Reference Library,* and shows the wood lever that the horse propelled. On the lower right is how it is today, in the backcountry.

Coarse Grinding

BLAKE JAW CRUSHER, THEN.

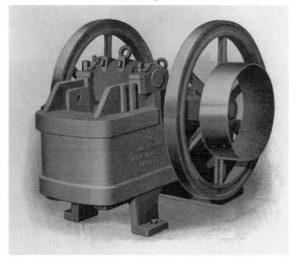

BLAKE JAW CRUSHER, TODAY.

On the left is a Blake Jaw Crusher as it looked new in the Colorado Iron Works Company's Catalogue No. 10B of 1908. Above is how it typically looks at a site today.

The ore had to be ground up first. The coarse grinder, or primary grinder, was located near the top of the building, under the ore bin and the grizzly. Any ore that was too large to pass through the grizzly went to the jaw crusher to be reduced in size. The Blake Jaw Crusher is the most common type of coarse crusher we encounter at ruined mill sites. Others include the Dodge Crusher and the Samson brand. The Blake Jaw Crusher had a larger capacity than its competitors, according to the *International Correspondence Schools Reference Library.* But the Dodge Crusher had the advantage of crushing to a finer and more uniform size.

DODGE CRUSHER

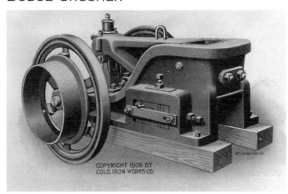

Above is the Dodge Crusher as it appeared in the Colorado Iron Works Company's Catalogue No. 10B of 1908. On the right is a Samson Crusher in the Mine and Smelter Supply Catalogue of 1912.

SAMSON CRUSHER

67

Fine Grinding

STAMP BATTERY, NEW

STAMP BATTERY, TODAY, FALLEN

Stamp mills crushed the ore with a heavy metal piston dropped on the ore. The piston was lifted with a cam. Parts of all of these are often visible at old mill sites yet today. On the left is a stamp battery for sale in the Mine and Smelter Supply catalogue of 1912. On the upper right, an example of how stamp mills look today. Below, the Huntington mill crushed ore with centrifugal force. On the lower right is a picture of the Huntington mill as it appeared in The Mine and Smelter Supply Company catalogue. On the lower left is how a Huntington appears in the field today.

The fine grinder, or secondary grinder, crushed ore to sand size. The *International Correspondence Schools Reference Library* states that the gravity stamp battery was "the best of the fine-crushing machines." They were simple to construct and to operate. They were cheap compared to other systems. They were particularly well suited to mines that were located in remote places. Perhaps that is why we see their remains so often in the backcountry today.

HUNTINGTON MILL

Fine Grinding

ROD MILL

The rod mill was so called because long heavy metal rods were inserted into the interior along with the ore and these rods did the crushing. It was also called a tube mill. The rod mill on the above left is from the Colorado Iron Works Company catalogue no. 10B. It is described as being fifteen feet long with a diameter of forty-five inches. On the right above is a tube mill as it appears today at a mining camp site. The Mine and Smelter Supply Company said, "The tube mill is the cheapest in first cost, lowest in maintenance expense, simplest in construction and lowest in power consumption." Below is a cone mill. These mills used heavy steel balls inside the enclosure to crush the ore, instead of rods.

So much of the mill was devoted to grinding the ore because a uniform size was critical to the recovery processes. The heaviest metals would sink in water and would arrange themselves according to weight, but only if all the particles were the same size. Oversized particles would sink because of their larger size. Therefore, we find many devices that were designed to crush and re-crush, with screens to size the particles.

BALL MILL

Fine Grinding

CRUSHING ROLLS

This roll crusher is as pictured in the Colorado Iron Works Company catalogue no. 10B.

In general, crushing rolls were the fine crusher of choice when the ore needed to be ground to a very specific size, not too large, not too fine. According to the *Internal Correspondence Schools Reference Library*, this was the preferred fine crusher when ores were to be roasted or sent through a jig system. They were based on the principle of an old roller crusher that originated in Cornwall. Crushing rolls could be dismantled into sections for mule-back transportation.

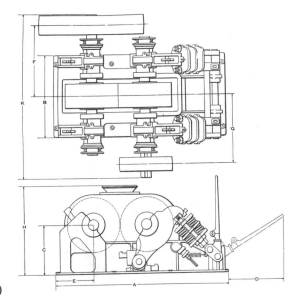

On the left is the plan of crushing rolls from the Colorado Iron Works Company catalogue no. 10B. Below is a unit that was part of a mill-in-a-box in an extremely remote area today.

CONCENTRATION TABLES

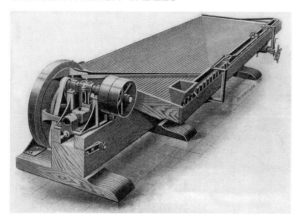

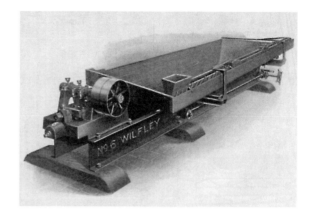

Usually located near or at the bottom level of the mill were the concentration tables. Above is a Wilfley table, the most popular of the brands of concentration tables. On the right is the heavy-duty Wilfley with a steel frame. We have actually seen some old Wilfley tables, their 1890s patent numbers still evident, in use today. The tables were set up at a slight cant, and water and ore pulp ran over the linoleum top and riffles. A motor shook the table slightly, and the various metals arranged themselves naturally along certain riffles. At destroyed mill sites we often see the remains of old Wilfley tables — sometimes they're covered with debris or in pieces, but they're still there. Below are concentration tables at old mill sites. Their linoleum covers are still intact and some of the wooden riffles are still in place.

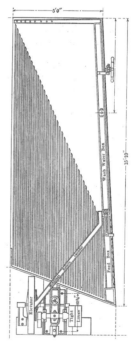

Recovery Process

AMALGAMATING PANS

Above is a diagram of an amalgamating pan from the International Correspondence Schools Reference Library. *Below left is an illustration of an arrastra from* Richardson's Beyond the Mississippi.

Amalgamating pans were based on the principles of a simple arrastra. Mercury and ore pulp were placed in the pan. Mullers (grinding apparatus) ground the ore and mercury mixture. The grinding action facilitated amalgamation. Below left is an arrastra. These were primitive but effective devices, and indeed were sometimes the first type of mill to be erected in a new gold rush area. Ore was placed on a paved circle, and heavy grinding stones were dragged over it. Mercury was added to the ore for amalgamation. A horse or mule powered the operation. Below right are the remains of an early arrastra near Buckskin Joe, Colorado.

ARRASTRA

Richardson, Beyond the Mississippi

Recovery Process

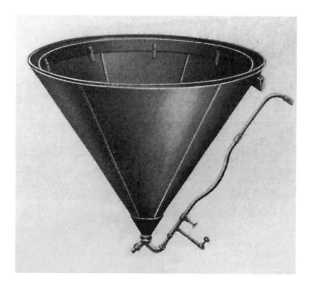

Both the picture above and below are from the Mine and Smelter Supply Company catalogue. Sagstetter collection.

The Mine and Smelter Supply Company refers to the above as a "Callow Settling and Pulp Thickening Tank" in their catalogue. It measured eight feet in diameter and eight feet in length. We often see these at old mill sites in the backcountry. Experts tell us they were part of the flotation process. Below, the Akins classifier measured 45 inches in diameter and 13 feet long. The spiral rotated in a tilted trough, pulling oversized pieces of ore up the incline and back for regrinding. Ore not captured by the spiral moved to the next step of the recovery process.

AKINS CLASSIFIER

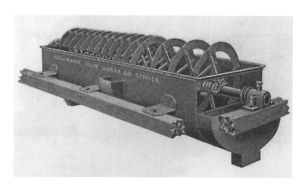

Recovery Process

SCREENING DEVICES

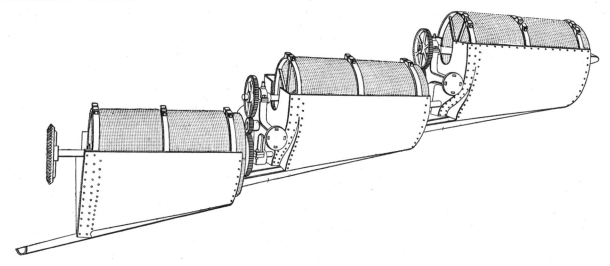

The revolving screens above were called trommels. We often find them at sites since sizing the ore was so critical a step in the operation. The impact screens below were another way to accomplish the same thing. The above illustration is from the *International Correspondence Schools Reference Library.* The catalogue picture on the below left is from the Colorado Iron Works Company catalogue.

IMPACT SCREEN

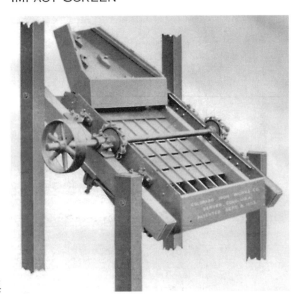

Recovery Process

HARTZ JIG

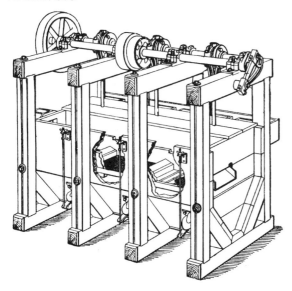

The Hartz Jig agitated ground ore in water as part of the flotation process. The final miscellaneous piece of equipment is the Challenger Ore Feeder, below. An ore feeder regulated the flow of ore to the fine grinder and can sometimes be seen between the coarse grinder and the fine grinder. We often see them at old mill sites. Both the above example and the one below are from the *International Correspondence Schools Reference Library.*

ORE FEEDER

6

ROADS AND
TRANSPORTATION

Sometimes you traveled in a wagon, at other times in a sleigh, and sometimes you were forced to walk. You had to push the wagon or the sleigh to help the fagged horses up the slippery hills, and by way of change you spent hours digging the almost smothered horses out of the soft snow or mending broken harness with rope, twine, or wire. It was the last straw on the camel's back to have to pay seven dollars for the privilege of riding on the stage.

— The Reverend J. J. Gibbons, *In the San Juan.*

 We were on a major route through an old mining district and thought we spotted an old trail paralleling the main road. In fact, modern thoroughfares of today often retrace the routes of the old mining roads. It's common to see old stagecoach roads or railroad beds engaging and disengaging from major roads. We were intrigued. Was this really an old trail, or just a figment of our imaginations?

There was only one way to find out — walk it. We were rewarded around the first bend with stone cribbing shoring up the road edge. This was man-made, there was no doubt. Old roads such as this were difficult to build with hand tools, horses, and wagons, so they usually led somewhere. We knew we could look forward to the destination.

But the journey along an old road is an adventure in and of itself. You never know what you might encounter along an old trail. First, there are the wonders of the early road builders. Many old roads have corduroy in boggy spots, some of which dates back to the time the road was built. Looking carefully, we have found wagon ruts worn into rocky spots along old trails. *Snubbing posts* imbedded in the rock along steep sections of a trail are common. These posts were used by the old wagon drivers when going downhill. They tied a rope to the back of the wagon, then wound it around a snubbing post and helped to lower the wagon down the steep sections of the road. Otherwise, the horses could be run over by the heavy wagon they pulled.

Scattered along old roadbeds are also bits and pieces of the past, such as hardened, blackened strips of old leather or rusted metal pieces of harness or saddle. Bits and pieces of the cargo that traveled a road sometimes can be found, too. Once we encountered a pile of ore that had fallen from an old wagon. Another time, as we hiked one trail with a modern

The smashed freight wagon had been painted a cheerful shade of school-bus yellow and maroon.

blacksmith, he found what looked to us like a rusted horseshoe. He identified it as a mule shoe. Then, in Sherlock Holmes fashion, he went on to describe the mule that had lost it so long ago: It was not a large Missouri-type mule but had been medium-sized. The shoe was from his right rear hoof, and the blacksmith pointed to where the old-time blacksmith had altered the shoe to correct the mule's faulty gait.

The old trail we hiked now was a shelf road etched into a cliff wall that traversed the heads of gulches. Far, far below, we spotted something that looked like a piece of equipment — cogs perhaps. We decided to check it out and descended the gulch. To our great surprise, we found an old freight wagon, smashed to bits.

In many respects it was a typical freight wagon of its day: It had wide, sturdy wheels with steel tires, and thick wooden spokes which radiated from keglike heavy-duty hubs. A wagon such as this could have weighed as much as four thousand or five thousand pounds empty. The most popular freight wagon of its day was the

Below is the mule shoe we discovered along the trail.

Studebaker wagon, built in South Bend, Indiana. We carefully turned over several pieces of the wreck, looking for some indication of the wagon maker, and encountered our biggest surprise of all. This wagon had been painted a cheerful school-bus yellow and dark maroon, not colors we would have imagined on a freight wagon.

We knew there was a story to this wagon accident. A story of what it was hauling and where. A story about what happened the day it

crashed. A story about what happened to the driver and the mules or horses. Unfortunately, we will probably never know it. But a story we *can* know is about freighting in the old days.

Pack Trails

Transportation was a critical issue for a mine owner. It didn't help a prospector if, after years of looking, he discovered a rich vein only to find out the mine was inaccessible. His vein could be extremely rich — but it was worthless if he couldn't get the ore to the nearest town, or supplies up to his mine. And how *do* you move heavy, cumbersome equipment like boilers and air compressors to remote sites? It was these transportation problems that kept mining-camp prices so high and goods so scarce. Transportation, or the lack of it, touched every part of life in the early American mining West. Transportation ran the gamut from packing burros and mules on narrow pack trails, to using freight wagons on wagon roads, to aerial trams, and all the way to railroad spurs at the largest mines. Relics from all these modes of transportation crisscross the backcountry in historic mining districts.

If you were the owner of a small remote mine, a pack trail might be the only means of transportation to it. Mules and especially burros were your best bet to pack goods in and ore out. Even after the railroads came to remoter areas, animal power was still used to get supplies and ore to and from the railheads. Draft animals were still

Burros were kept in herds such as this one, from the International Correspondence Schools Library. Sagstetter collection.

used for this purpose as late as the 1920s. Where beasts of burden were used for transportation, there were ten times as many animals as people.

The savvy little burro became a symbol of our mining West. Here was a compact animal that could haul a hundred pound load on a tiny thread of a trail. Burros were usually herded from behind in a loose band, with some bands numbering in the hundreds. They are smart enough to naturally walk single file on dangerous, narrow sections of the trail. They can live on practically nothing — grass, sagebrush, cactus, or even garbage, so you don't have to carry food for them. But they aren't above snatching your own dinner over the campfire if you aren't careful, or even chewing your favorite saddle if you leave it unattended. They also don't sweat and suffer as much as mules and horses do in the desert heat. They are friendly, and a burro made a better companion for a lonely prospector than a dog. But they are noisy, and their obnoxious bray earned them the name Rocky Mountain or Washoe (depending upon the location) Canary.

They are also survivors in difficult terrain. Prospectors, when they left the district, frequently just abandoned their burros. But burros thrived so well in mining country on their own that they became pests around the towns. So much so that a legend sprang up that burros never died. "I admit they are hard to kill," said Reverend George M. Darley in *Pioneering in the San Juan:* "A baby burro fell from

Mules were tied in strings such as this one. In this picture a continuous length of cable is being transported. To do this they had to coil the cable from animal to animal. From the International Correspondence School Library.

Much of the old equipment we see today in the backcountry was hauled to these unlikely sites by mules, such as these pictured in Leslies Illustrated Newspaper *of 1879. Denver Public Library, Western History Department.*

the top of a cliff 60 feet in height, into the Gunnison River and was not in-jured. . . . Another one packed with flour fell 200 feet; the weight of the flour turned the burro heels up, and, striking in the snow, his life was saved."

A mule train was another possibility for a small-mine owner. As a small-mine owner, you might stockpile your ore for months and then, a few times a year, hire a mule skinner to haul it out for you to the nearest railhead. Mules could carry more than burros — from 150 to 220 pounds. Mule skinners said that heavily loaded mules could wear out a set of shoes in ten days of slipping and sliding down those narrow granite-studded trails.

Mules had to be fed and cared for. They needed hay and grain and a barn and someone to tend them. On pack trails they also needed to be tied together and strung in a line. A mule skinner on a horse led the procession with a lead line. The lead mule wore a bell. Mules had to be placed single file on narrow trails. Although

they required more care and more investment, they were more versatile than burros. Mules could be used as pack animals on trails, or hitched to wagons on roads or ore cars underground.

Wagon Roads

A horse or mule could pull much more weight than it could carry on its back. A horse that could carry only two hundred to four hundred pounds on its back could draw three thousand pounds on a level surface. Therefore, a wagon road was a good investment if the output of a mine could justify the expense.

A good wagon road of those days did not resemble the graded, gravel roads of today. Freighter Dave Wood said in *I Hauled These Mountains in Here:* "The roads were bogs of mud when they were wet, blankets of dust when they were dry, and traps of glaring ice and drifted snow all winter." Stumps jutted up in some places, boulders in others. The roads were rutted and tilted out toward the cliff edge. And heavy-duty freight wagons did not have springs on them. Hitting one of the many bumps could flip the driver and sometimes freight or passengers right out of the wagon and onto the ground. This also insured that a freight wagon needed a lot of blacksmith work to keep it on the road.

The heaviest of the freight wagons carried ore shipments and had very high sides. Often two wagons were hitched together to haul exceptionally large loads. The advantage to this was that when a steep section of trail was encountered, the wagons

could be unhitched and the team used to pull each wagon up, one at a time. In the earliest days oxen were used because they were able to pull the heaviest loads — a team of eight could pull as much as 100,000 pounds, according to Dave Wood. An outfit such as this could haul huge loads, but it was slow and cumbersome. For this reason, freight wagons always had the right of way on narrow mountain trails.

The last leg of the journey to equipment's final resting place was the most difficult part. This old photograph illustrates a novel approach to moving a boiler and a hoist to a difficult site. Denver Public Library, Western History Department.

David Wood said: "More than anything else people wanted speed in those days. If you could cut a seven day trip to six days, you worked magic, and people didn't hesitate to pay for it. It was not 'How much?' but 'How fast can you do it?'" Therefore, mules (and sometimes heavy draft horses) became the preferred animal power because, although they could not haul as much, they were a lot faster than oxen.

Freight teams generally left the mining towns early in the morning for the trip to a mine, and returned in the late afternoon. In *The Way it Was*, people who lived in the towns recalled hearing each morning the jingling mules' bells, the clattering of wagons, and the swearing of mule skinners as they left. When the thermometer registered below zero, the steel tires on the wagons made a sound on the ice and snow that was like a clap of thunder and could be heard five miles away. At the snow line the load was shifted from freight wagons to sleds.

Going downhill in the mountains in an old freight wagon was dangerous at any time of year. Those early friction brakes were primitive and unreliable. Sometimes freighters dragged a log behind the wagon to help slow it down. Sometimes they

Lake City! Telluride! Rico!

AND ALL POINTS IN THE SAN JUAN.

SAN JUAN STAGE LINES

Carrying the U. S. Mails and Passengers and Express from Dallas to Telluride, and all intermediate points, also from Sapinero to Lake City. Close connections made at Sargent's with Western Stage Line for Ames, Ophir and Rico.

ASK FOR THROUGH TICKETS AT ALL D. & R. G. RAILROAD OFFICES.

LARGEST FREIGHTING OUTFIT IN THE WEST

Forwarding and Freighting by thoroughly equipped teams to all the above mentioned points.

Consign all freight in care of David Wood, via Dallas for Telluride, Placerville, San Miguel, Rico, Ophir and all points in San Juan; via Sapinero to Lake City, Capital City and Mineral Point.

DAVID WOOD,
PROPRIETOR,
MONTROSE, - - COLORADO.

Wholesale Dealer in Flour, Hay and Grain.

This advertisement appeared in the November 1889 Denver & Rio Grande Railroad Timetable. Lettering on the stagecoach reads "San Juan Stage Lines." The freight wagons in the background are hitched together and read, "Magnolia Route." Of course this is an example of their robust sense of humor. The San Juan Mountains of south-western Colorado are anything but balmy. Bill and Sue Knous collection.

"snubbed" it, as described on page 77. In the winter they wrapped chains around the sled's runners to slow it down. But sometimes a big wagon would get away from the freighter, and there was no stopping it until it hit bottom and was smashed to smithereens, just like the one we encountered.

84

Riding the Stage

People also needed to be transported in those days. Even after the railroads were established, a stagecoach would be the only alternative from the railhead to the diggings. Stagecoach travel had a reputation for being hair-raising almost from the days of the California gold rush. Frank Marryat wrote in *Mountains and Molehills* in 1855: "No one knows what a waggon [sic] will undergo, until he has mastered Californian trails and gulches."

If you wanted to get to a mining town in the 1880s, you planned as much of the trip as possible on the railroad. But railroads didn't make it to the most remote mining towns, even after the turn of the century. Therefore, at least part of your journey would have to be accomplished by stagecoach. That thought was enough to make a seasoned traveler's blood run cold.

Your trip would begin in a civilized enough manner: Waving goodbye to friends and family from the platform of the ultramodern mode of transportation of the day — a first-class railroad car. Even the least expensive railroad cars of the time had upholstered seats, so you could be assured of comfort. The railroad cars were heated by a small stove in winter and were comparatively dust free in summer. There was no mud to contend with on iron rails. The ride was so smooth that you could enjoy an elegant dinner in the dining car while the train was underway. And the speed! It averaged perhaps twenty or thirty miles an hour. The conductor in his snappy uniform was there to respectfully take care of any problems that arose. There was no doubt that railroad travel was a civilized experience. It would be with regret that you say goodbye to the train at the nearest railhead to your destination. Here you would spend a restful night in a fine hotel, if there was one.

This particular version of the famous stagecoach scene is from Thayer's Marvels of the New West, *Sagstetter collection.*

It is early the next morning when the stagecoach rumbles into town. You are considerably cheered when you discover that the stage line has sent a Concord stage. The Concord was considered the best coach of its kind, and the most comfortable. Concord stages were built with leather thoroughbraces that ran from the front of the body toward the back to hold it in suspension. This caused a rocking motion. Some people preferred the rocking sensation to the bumps and lurches of a spring wagon, but in other people it inspired motion sickness. But because you like the big red Concords with their yellow wheels and running gear, you think perhaps this will not be as difficult as some stage trips after all. As you mount the steps, the U. S. Mail pouch is placed under the feet of the driver. Late-arriving passengers tumble into the coach and ontop of it until there is humanity in every possible nook, cranny and perch.

There is no snappy uniform for the driver of the stagecoach, of course. His clothes are dust-covered and mud-splattered. His attitude is gruff, not at all respectful of the passengers. In fact, stagecoach drivers had a reputation for being eccentric. They were well known for being irascible and cocky. Each was the undisputed boss of his rig and king of the road. At the stage stops drivers were treated like visiting royalty. Their language was rough enough to be shocking to the lady passengers. And they barked orders at the passengers, very unlike the polite conductors on the train. But even so, the most sought-after seat in the coach is the "shotgun" seat next to the driver, and everyone vies for it. When journalist Ernest Ingersoll reserved the shotgun seat of a stage coach in 1880 while writing *The Crest of the Continent,* the stagecoach driver had to keep it free for him with the help of a stout stick.

At first four horses are hitched to the coach, and although they may not be pedigreed, they are well-kept and lively. The driver snaps his whip, and the stage lunges forward fast enough to jerk your neck. The rig will average about eight to ten miles an hour on the straightaway. There are no bridges to speak of in the new mining areas, so the stage must ford the creeks and rivers and ravines. Each time the coach dives down a riverbank, the swing of the thoroughbraces exaggerates the motion and your stomach is left up on the road. One horrified old-timer, knowing how beloved newspapers were in remote mining camps, told of a stagecoach trip where the driver flung a stack of newspapers into the mudhole for traction when the wheels of his stage became stuck in the mud.

Inside the coach the seats are narrow, and you are crowded into awkward contortions by so many other passengers jammed in the interior. Frank Marryat in 1855 described bewhiskered miners sitting next to the windows who "squirted their [tobacco] juice at passing objects on the road with astonishing accuracy."

The first stage stop is reached about noon. You shake off the dust that covers every inch of your person and attempt to clean up a little. Frenchman Louis Simonin described a stage stop in 1867:

> A basin and a pitcher of water awaits you, with soap and a towel that turns without end around a roller. You will find mirrors, combs, brushes of all kinds, even toothbrushes, fastened by a long string, so that everyone may help himself and no one carry it off. You would laugh in Paris at these democratic customs; here they are accepted by all and even wel-

Stagecoaching in the Sierra Nevadas. From Richardson's Beyond the Mississippi. *Sagstetter collection. Note in the bottom left corner, there is a mule-drawn cart. Is it sprinkling water on the road to keep the dust down?*

comed, unless perhaps the toothbrush, which is regarded with a suspicious eye.

You settle down to an indifferent meal of stale coffee, bacon, beans, and biscuits or flapjacks. It is a menu that will be repeated at each stage stop along the way. Mean-

87

while, the four horses are replaced with six. And instead of a comfortable, if crowded, Concord stage, they are pulling a strong uncovered spring wagon with wooden seats. Some of the passengers grouse that they have been deceived by leaving town in a Concord that is replaced with a clattering wagon at the first opportunity. But the reality is that the Concord stage is too top-heavy for some of the upcoming mountain roads.

Now the road becomes rougher. Those boulders and mudholes and stumps that litter the roadway are dangerous hazards for a heavily loaded ranch wagon hurtling along at top speed. But the driver and the horses know the road intimately, and they fly through the obstacle course at an unnerving pace. It is enough to turn a passenger's hair to white. It is the slow-moving ox-drawn freight wagons that enrage the driver more than anything else. He heaps upon those freighters terrible epithets as he demands, and then seizes, the right-of-way.

Up, up into the mountains you wheel, and now the wagon is on a narrow shelf road that tilts outward. Suddenly the wagon lurches to one side and all the passengers are pitched to the cliff-edge side of the wagon. It leans dangerously close to the edge, and the driver orders all passengers to the safe side of the wagon. The men hang on the outside of the wagon, holding it on the canted roadbed like a sailboat as the driver urges it forward. Fortunately, no one is lost this time. Sometimes passengers and cargo were tossed entirely out of the wagon. Reverend J. J. Gibbons was once pitched right out of a wagon and over a cliff. Fortunately, it was in the winter, and he fell into a snowdrift and escaped without injury. (Stagecoaches did turn over on occasion. One worried father threw his two young children out of an overturning coach and into a snowdrift, safe from the falling coach and the thrashing, terrified horses.) Before you reach the top of the hill, the exhausted horses have slowed down to a walk. The driver orders the passengers to get out of the wagon. Now everyone must walk to the top of the hill.

But the ride down the other side! Albert Richardson described it best in 1865:

> Down the narrow, winding shelf-road our horses went leaping at a sharp gallop. It is a thrilling ride; for at many points, a divergence of six inches from the track would send the coach rolling from five hundred to a thousand feet down the mountain . . . Here is the ideal of staging. For weeks afterward, one's blood bounds at the memory of its whirl and rush. Twenty-four in the coach, with six horses, galloping down the Sierra Nevadas, along a winding, narrow, dizzy road, at *twelve miles an hour!*

The pace doesn't slow down until the final moment, when the coach lurches to a stop at your destination. Not surprisingly, there is a crowd present to greet the stage. The arrival of the stagecoach (or in seaside towns, the arrival of steamships) is the high point of the day. With the stage come interesting people in the latest fashions. They bring with them news from the towns along the way. And of course the stagecoach has the U.S. Mail. You have arrived in town in time for dinner. You are sweaty, dirty, and tired. Your clothes are wrinkled and soiled. And recalling how you had arrived in the last town after a day on the train, you wonder how long it will be before the railroad can reach this remote mining town.

Aerial Trams

Roads were not the only way to traverse the back country. T. A. Rickard wrote that aerial trams spanned "the intermountain spaces like great spider webs." An aerial tram was an expensive improvement possible for only the richest mines, in the most remote mountain terrain, but the system was cost-effective compared to roads and railroads. Aerial trams began being used in the 1890s and remains of these systems dot the backcountry to this day.

An aerial tram worked by gravity. Heavy ore-laden buckets traveling down the cable, pulled up the lighter buckets loaded with supplies. Sometimes there was enough power left over to run a small piece of equipment off the aerial tram. Everything necessary to run the mine was sent up to it on the tram: dynamite and coal, groceries for the boardinghouse, hay and grain for the animals, iron track for the tunnels. Sometimes two cars would be hitched together and a mine timber lashed between them.

The International Correspondence Schools Reference Library *describes this aerial tram scene as in Wardner, Idaho. It operated by gravity with enough power left over for some hoisting.*

Old aerial tram towers like this one on the right dot the backcountry of historic mining districts. Below, an ore bucket dangles yet today. It is an example of a two cable system.

Even people made the trek up to the mine in dangling ore cars. It took a cast-iron stomach to make a trip over an aerial tram. The loud clickety-clack and the rumble of the ore being dumped from the full ore cars would assault your ears as you entered the tram house. As you clambered over the side and awkwardly found a place to stand, the operator would warn you about keeping your head down near the support towers. Sometimes people were killed as the buckets passed the towers. And then your stomach would take flight as the bucket swung out into space. The tram cables lifted high over the topography of the land, staying way above the valley floor and then swinging close to the mountainsides again. The view of the valley below, the wind in your face, the lurching of the bucket over the tram towers was an unforgettable experience for even the most jaded of travelers.

The most common type of aerial tram system we have seen is the Bleichert two-cable system. As the photograph on the left shows, an ore bucket rode on one wire rope and was towed by another.

Stables

At the site of Rexford, Colorado, there sat the remains of an intriguing lone building. It sat away from the other structures, seemingly banished from the cluster of town buildings. Inside, it was an open room. If it had ever had a roof, it was long gone now. One of the most puzzling aspects of the structure was the "window." On the back wall a section of a single log had been cut out, leaving a slit. There were no other attempts at windows. We contemplated the possibilities of what this building might have been, but nothing seemed to fit. There was no debris around the building that might give us a clue as to what went on here. Then we spotted the remains of a long low structure along one interior wall. It was an open V-shaped trough-like structure that ran the length of one wall. It took us a moment to realize that this was a manger! The building had been a stable. In the days when most of the transportation was by animal power, there were likely to be more animals than people in

The manger in the Rexford stable.

91

The stable at Carson, Colorado. The wide, notched doorway on this end might have been for a freight wagon.

mining camps. The remains of stables are everywhere in the old mining districts. Once we found a small camp of only two log structures — one of which turned out to be the stable.

At the ghost town of Carson, Colorado, we saw a different configuration. The barn there still had its roof and was in surprisingly good condition. It was divided into six individual stalls, and there was one space on the end, probably for a wagon. Perhaps these were the components of a typical freight outfit that made the trip to Carson: six mules or horses and one freight wagon.

The interior of the stable at Carson had individual stalls. It is unusual to find a stable of this size, and in such good shape. The stable at Rexford, Colorado, is much more typical.

TRAIL FINDING

Historic mining districts are crisscrossed with historic trails that were once stagecoach roads, railroad beds and pack trails which have become the hiking trails of today. All along these trails are traces the early travelers left behind. If you find yourself on one of these trails and follow it, you'll find it connects sites easily and directly that would be difficult to get to otherwise. The old trails usually lead somewhere. The trail on the left is an old stagecoach route that runs next to a highway. The trail below connects a series of remote mining camps. If you look carefully, you can see the wisp of the trail off in the distance.

ROAD BUILDING REMAINS

Look for the remains of when the road was built. Sometimes it has been the dry stacked stone cribbing or the remains of bridge abutments over creeks that have cued us that we were on an actual man-made road and not just a game trail. Above left is an example of a corduroy road. These were typically used in boggy, muddy places. The example shown here is a modern restoration, but original corduroy still exists. Above right is an example of an old wooden culvert of the type we sometimes see on old roads, although this particular example is draining a mine. All these harken back to when the road was originally built, and the problems encountered by the road builders, below. (From *Harpers Weekly,* Sagstetter collection.)

TRACES OF DIFFICULT PASSAGE

As you travel the old trails watch for indications of difficult passage along the old roads. For example, old snubbing posts as in the picture above. In this case they had used old drill steels imbedded into the rock along the trail. We see this quite often. Below, bolts in a rock wall next to a trail and drill holes suggest problems of some kind.

TRAIL DEBRIS

As you travel the old trails watch for interesting debris from the old travelers, such as the mule shoe mentioned at the beginning of the chapter. Above is an embossed lid to a can we found along a trail. It reads "Frazer Axle Grease." Besides the snubbing posts discussed earlier, there are often other indications of travel along the trail, such as bits of black, gnarled leather and rusted metal fittings from harnesses and saddles. Below is possibly the remains of wagon ruts in the rock on an old trail. We followed this old trail for miles into the backcountry to an old mining camp.

STABLES

A stable can look like any other log cabin, as the stable above at Rexford shows. The dead giveaway to a stable is the remains of a manger. This typically ran the entire length of one wall at one time. But today there might be just the *suggestion* of a manger — rubble along one wall, more pronounced in the corners.

Most remains of stables we encounter were not divided into separate stalls, but rather consist of an open area. We have often wondered if this was how burros were housed — as a herd, and not in individual stalls. Usually these buildings do not have windows, and if they do there aren't many. Doors are often wide and low.

The stables were typically located away from the living quarters because they were smelly and fly infested. It's unusual to find mangers as intact as those below. Note the vertical boards in the **V** of the mangers, sometimes they are the only distinguishing factor left.

7

THE BLACKSMITH SHOP

As there is a great amount of mining going on throughout the country, first-class sharpeners of miners' tools are in great demand, and likewise receive high wages.

— Holford, *Twentieth Century Toolsmith and Steelworker.*

 The flattened building lay near the entrance to a mine tunnel. Like playing cards, its four walls lay fanned out as though the building had been dealt a losing hand and had folded. Pieces of corrugated tin from the one-time roof peppered the downhill slope of the mountain. The vague square outline in the dirt where the building had originally stood told us it never had a plank floor and had been a small building. There was no trace of any antique household debris, which told us this building probably hadn't been used for lodging. We didn't hold much hope for deciphering its story.

We scrutinized the building debris, looking for clues. Downhill from the building we spotted a galvanized hood, the type that frequently hung over blacksmiths' forges. Near it we picked up one board that was about two feet long and that had been carefully cut into the shape of a teardrop. A tabletop? A part of some kind of chair? Someone had put considerable effort into the piece — all along the outside edge of the piece were nail holes, and some of the tacks were still in place along the perimeter of the board. Then it hit us that this was an end piece of a bellows! Could this building have been a blacksmith's shop?

We searched around for a few more corroborating details. We were about to leave when we spotted a bundle of drill steels lodged against a bush. The bundle had been neatly secured with a length of wire. It looked as if it might have rolled away from the collapsed building. Checking the chisel tips of the drill steels, we recognized these as hand tools. To confirm this we saw that the back ends of the drills were slightly flattened where they had been hammered. Now we were convinced that these were hand tools. Also among the drills was a long-handled spoon used to clean rock dust from drill holes. We will never know for sure

Above are the remains of a bellows that we saw that day. Below the photograph is an engraving of a bellows as it appeared in the Mine and Smelter Supply catalogue.

what this building was, but we are willing to bet it was probably the blacksmith's shop.

Iron forging is an ancient profession. No one knows exactly when the first warriors took up iron swords and shields and triumphed over people with bronze weapons, but certainly blacksmiths were already respected by the time of Christ, because they are mentioned in the Bible. Medieval nobility retained the best blacksmiths to make them suits of armor and chain mail. Later, blacksmiths were able to fashion firearms from a hearth, a hammer, an anvil, and a lump of iron.

Blacksmiths were also toolmakers. The blacksmith had the distinction of being the only craftsman who could make his own tools as well as the tools for all the other trades. For example, nineteenth-century physicians went to blacksmiths to have their surgical tools made. For centuries, if someone needed kitchen utensils, a steel tire for a wagon, a door hinge, a weapon, or a tooth pulled, he would go to a blacksmith. Because of this, implements made by blacksmiths are unique — no two are exactly alike. Therefore, even humble everyday forged articles seem works of art to our machine-age eyes.

Civilizations literally marched to the rhythmic beat of the blacksmith's hammer. Every village needed one. One clue as to how widespread blacksmiths were is in your local phone book — anyone with the name "Smith" or "Schmidt" probably had an ancestor who was a blacksmith or a silversmith, tinsmith or goldsmith.

And nowhere was a blacksmith more indispensable than at a mine. Blacksmiths shoed the horses and mules that pulled the ore wagons. They repaired the ore wagons and replaced their steel tires. They repaired broken equipment and occasionally could make a part for a mill that was out of order. Sharpening rock drills was the most difficult job for a blacksmith. The men who worked the forges at a mine were some of the best in their field. And they were well paid. At a time when hard-rock miners made three dollars a day, a blacksmith made four.

But the Industrial Revolution changed all that. As early as 1790, a nail-making machine was turning out square nails. This simple device marked the beginning of the end for the craftsmen who worked in the "black metal." By the time of the gold rushes of the American West, the blacksmith shop was slowly being replaced by the hardware store. More and more of what had laboriously been produced by hand was being mass-produced in factories. Then a person could actually buy a machine-made length of chain instead of having a blacksmith painstakingly make it up one link at a time. Even the blacksmith himself was buying the inexpensive factory-made hammers offered for sale in the mail-order catalogues instead of forging them himself.

The hand drill steels we found that day. Note the flattened ends where they were hammered. Hand steels had a chisel tip.

Although objects lost their artistic uniqueness, machine-made objects gained a much needed standardization. In former times, a blacksmith would hand-make a door lock, then the bolts that would secure it to the door. Then he would painstakingly craft the threads on the bolt, and then a nut that would fit the end of that particular bolt and no other. He would forge a wrench that would fit only that bolt. And finally, he would make a key that opened the lock. But after machine standardization, homeowners could choose among many machine-made door locks, nuts and bolts that were interchangeable, and one wrench would fit them all. Only the key retained its uniqueness. Just think of it!

Possibly a hand-forged wrench. Who was the man who made this wrench?

The man who made this wrench was a blacksmith, like the one below from Holmstrom's Modern Blacksmithing, *Sagstetter collection.*

THE SMITH

The final blow came after World War I, when working horses were rapidly replaced with trucks and tractors. By the mid-twentieth century the blacksmith was an endangered species.

The Blacksmith Shop of Old

If it were possible to step across the threshold of one of these old blacksmith shops and back in time a hundred years or so, what would you see? First of all you'd hear the ringing of the hammer and the huff of the bellows long before you opened the door. Then you would probably be greeted by a blacksmith whose face and hands reflected the sooty nature of his work. A leather apron protected him from being burned and from flying sparks. He would probably be wearing rather close-fitting clothes because loose-fitting clothes would be dangerous in a blacksmith's shop. On his feet would more than likely be heavy boots, because hot heavy weights could fall off his anvil and onto his toes.

The shop itself would also be sooty from the constant coal fire kept burning in the hearth. A window was a necessity in a blacksmith shop because daylight was needed to read the color of the metal as it heated on the fire. The different colors the metal turned as it was heating told the blacksmith when it reached certain critical temperatures.

The hearth would be located across the room from the door, so the drafts from people coming and going would not interfere with the fire. It was frequently placed in a corner. The base of the hearth might be something like a fifty-gallon oil drum or wooden cribbing, filled with stones. More recent hearths are filled with cement. Around this base might be leather straps to hang tools within easy reach. A hearth needed a hood and chimney stovepipe above it. Hanging next to this would be a rather large bellows suspended by chains and with a wooden handle that the blacksmith could pump with one hand. The nose of the bellows would be buried in a pipe in the side of the hearth that would transport the blast of air to the very heart of the fire. This air pipe was called the *tuyere* (pronounced *twee air*) or *tuy iron* (pronounced *twee iron*).

Perhaps about six feet from the fire and out in the middle of the room would be the anvil. This was usually mounted on a tree stump that had been buried in the dirt floor of the room, although sometimes these tree stumps were free-standing. Occasionally a blacksmith would build a base for the anvil from boards. This base provided a solid support that would not bounce when hammered.

Between the forge and the anvil would be a bucket or barrel containing water. In a mining setting in particular, there would also be a bucket for brine and a can of oil. The drill steels were dipped in one of these after the sharpening process to temper them. The character of the rock being drilled determined what was used to temper the drill steels. Around the perimeter of the room would be worktables or benches. With these might be many cubbyholes for storing nuts, bolts and small items.

The tuyere is clearly visible in this picture as a pipe that penetrates the sides of the barrel/forge. The snout of the bellows would be buried in the pipe, forcing air to the heart of the fire.

Below are the remains of the blacksmith shop at the Sound Democrat Mill, discussed in detail in Chapter 5. Note the stump, the barrel/forge, the rock cribbing that surrounded the fire. This is typical of what remains at an old blacksmith shop today.

THE BLACKSMITH'S JOB

by Jim Miller, blacksmith

The blacksmith possesses a knack for simplicity in his work even in the face of complexity. As a craftsman he maintains simple control over his material by minding the ancient elements of fire, earth, air and water. The basic elements are dictated to him by his profession. This knack resembles at times the skill of a priest.

When I heat metal I must mind the color of the steel as it takes in heat and I must mind the fire itself as the air blasts at the center of the "bloom." When I cool the steel, I must mind the speed of cooling and the direction the heat takes when leaving the piece.

Scribner's Monthly, 1879

Water cools hot steel quickly, dry lime cools it very slowly (brine, oil, and air cool at rates in between.) My coal is a particular type that lacks sulfur, but it is simply pure, clean earth and sparkles like black diamonds as it is taken from the earth.

A blacksmith in the mines of the American West was pragmatically familiar with his material and the logistics of his job. If the steel were used as a tool, he knew that it had been produced in open-hearth furnaces in Pittsburgh and responded to tempering. He knew his tool steel contained high amounts of carbon because it produced spectacular sparks as it burned. Technically, he might not have been aware that carbon and iron molecules arrange themselves into specific patterns as they heat and cool, which dictates the softness, durability or brittleness of the metal. Our blacksmith, though, being the priestly character he was, was intimately aware of this through his skill and intuition.

Remains of forge

Cubbyholes still containing nuts and bolts

This large device is engraved with "The Denver Rock Drill Company," and was a drill sharpener.

Workbench

Stump

The Blacksmith Shop Today

Today what we see at mining camps are the remnants of the blacksmith shop of long ago. Some parts of a blacksmith shop survive the ravages of time quite well. One of these is the stump the anvil sat on. Sometimes one can still be seen in the middle of a room, a dead giveaway to what the building originally was. And if you look closely at that stump, you can sometimes make out the outline of the anvil or the marks of the clamps or spikes that held the anvil in place. We have never seen an anvil still in place on top of a stump.

Less often, the remains of the forge can be found. Sometimes this will survive as a pile of stones in the corner of a log cabin. Every now and then a barrel hoop might be evident from the barrel of water that was necessary to douse the hot metal.

Usually the remains of the coal storage place can be found. Frequently there are little coal chips still present. Then, near the forge, there might also be a smaller box to keep coal in. This coal had to be kept wet, so the box might have a bucket over it or near it. (Wet coal performed better for the blacksmith's needs than dry coal.) But keep in mind that other buildings also needed coal for various jobs, so finding the remains of a coal bin doesn't unquestionably mean you have found a blacksmith shop.

Blacksmiths counted on a constant supply of iron. This would have been difficult at a remote mining camp where transporting heavy metal was expensive and waiting for it to arrive could take weeks. A blacksmith could recycle metal from just about anything. Therefore, no broken part, no scrap of metal was ever thrown away. It was usually kept in a scrap pile behind the blacksmith shop. Even if no scrap pile exists today, you can sometimes find bits of metal left where the scrap pile was at one time. Also, check the floor of the shop. Little rusted metal "crumbs" can sometimes be found on the dirt floor.

As indispensable as a blacksmith was to a mine, some mine sites do not have a trace of one. There are several reasons for this. Sometimes the shop would be located underground to be that much nearer to the workings. And some sites were never large enough to justify their own blacksmith. These small mines used a nearby independent blacksmith, or the small independent-mine owner might have sharpened the drill steels himself. One of those faceless log cabins you see along the trail might well have been the shop of an independent blacksmith who sharpened the drills for small nearby mines, fixed wagons, and shoed horses. This same blacksmith might even have worked his own small mining claim on the side. If a mine had a blacksmith shop, it's not unusual for it to be located very near the tunnel or shaft.

STUMPS

A surprising number of cabin remains prove to be old blacksmith shops. In this very typical scene, the stump in the center was our first clue that this had been a blacksmith shop at one time. Then, the pile of rubble in the corner and part of a bellows corroborated that fact.

A stump standing in or near the center of a cabin is a dead giveaway that a structure was a blacksmith shop. The stump was the base for the anvil. Often we can still see the impression the anvil made in the top of the stump, or like the picture on the left, there are the remains of straps or nails or other means to attach the anvil to the stump. At other times, there have been leather straps on the sides of the stump where the blacksmith hung his tools. Sometimes the stump is an actual tree stump like the one above, sometimes, like the example on the left, the "stump" was constructed from boards.

BELLOWS

Even after fans and blowers came into general use, some blacksmiths still preferred to use the old double-chambered bellows. We have often seen the teardrop-shaped wooden top and bottom pieces with tacks around the perimeters. We have never seen a bellows intact at a site. If you look very carefully at the photograph below, you can see the tacks around the perimeter of the bellows.

FORGES

Most often all that remains is the *suggestion* of a forge, like the piles of rubble above. Originally this might have been a square wooden box, filled with rubble. Or it sometimes was a fifty-gallon drum filled with dirt and rock rubble. This pile is usually in the corner of the building and today might have grass and saplings growing from it. We actually found a piece of coal the size of a potato in the rock pile on the left. The forge below left is as pictured in the 1923 Keystone Company's The Mining Catalog, although we have never seen a forge like this at a site. Below right is a forge made from cement. The pipe projecting from its left side is the *tuyere* where the bellows or fan would have been.

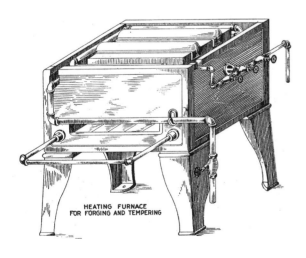

HEATING FURNACE
FOR FORGING AND TEMPERING

WORKBENCHES

Workbenches, wooden tabletops and cubbyholes are common to blacksmith shops. These are frequently located around the perimeter of the room. On the left is a tiny workbench with rusted pieces of metal and tools on it, in a tiny log cabin. More was on the dirt floor. Below is the fallen wall of the blacksmith shop at the Sound Democrat Mill, with all the workbenches and shelves still in place.

REMAINS OF TOOLS AND EQUIPMENT

A clue that an old building was a blacksmith shop is on the floor — it is usually dirt, not wood, because wood floors could catch fire from the flying sparks. Often we find little bits of rusted metal on the floor. Every now and then we are surprised to find old rusted tools like rasps and files like those on the left.

We rarely find a substantial piece of equipment like the Waugh Drill Sharpener made by the Denver Rock Drill Company on the right. This particular piece of equipment was advertised in the 1923 Keystone's The Mining Catalog, below, thus giving us an approximate date for this blacksmith shop. The catalogue said of the drill sharpener, "An ordinary blacksmith, working with Model 8, can easily make sixty perfect bits an hour or from thirty to forty perfect shanks."

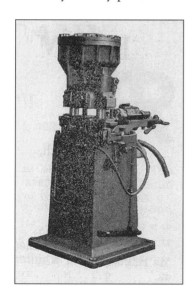

8

THE ASSAY OFFICE

We came to smelting establishments [their assay offices] disgorging red-
hot crucibles [outside onto the road, and] which took up half the road,
and compelled the teamsters . . . to turn out of the way.

— A. A. Hayes Jr., *New Colorado and the Santa Fe Trail.*

 Of the three buildings that once anchored this meadow to Glacier Peak, only one was partially standing. But it was a sorry mess. The one-story frame building clung to the edge of the meadow, seeming to lean against the fringe of pines for support. Its roof was peeled off, and one wall was missing. Because it looked as uninteresting as an oversized wooden packing crate, we had never bothered to explore it, even though we had passed by it often. To our surprise, this unlikely building was to become one of our most memorable finds. Those plank walls enclosed a classic assay office, the most complete we have ever encountered in the backcountry. Very little had been removed from it through the years.

Our first clue to the identity of the building lay just outside the door. There we found shards of crucibles and cupels. These vessels are used in the assay process, and we often find them strewn outside buildings in the back country. They suggest that the structure was used as an assay office.

Inside, we found the layout to be "classic" assay office: three rooms in a row, each opening to the next. Every room was skirted with wooden worktables and numerous shelves. The first room was usually the office. We studied the room that opened onto the trail. With its numerous shelves and a built-in desk-worktable, it would have made a passable office. We could picture bagged ore samples on these shelves and tables, waiting to be tested.

The center room was usually the "laboratory." We entered the center room and looked around. In this room was a cribbed stand that had been lined with metal. The rusted metal sheets had been made from large square tin cans that had been flattened out — the solder that had held the original tin can together was still visible. The is metal-lined cribbed stand

Even a sorry-looking building such as this can have an interesting story to tell. This one turned out to have been an assay office.

would have been an excellent base for an assay furnace. Nearby we found broken pieces of formed and shaped firebrick. We took a few minutes to fit some of the pieces together like a jigsaw puzzle. The shape of a double-chambered furnace began to emerge from the pieces. A rusted metal cover lying next to the firebrick had double D-shaped doors — a distinguishing feature of a muffle furnace. We placed the rusted metal cover over the reconstructed firebrick, and it fitted over them perfectly. There were several worktables and shelves in this room, too. We

A crucible, used in the assay process. Shards of crucibles and cupels (facing page) were scattered on the ground outside the door.

114

A cupel, made of bone ash, and part of the assay process.

could picture on them the apothecary-type bottles that were common to assay offices of that era, with labels for the frequently used liquid reagents.

The back room in an assay office was usually where rock was crushed and was the domain of the apprentice. In the back room we found a special stand made of two posts driven into the ground under the building. It supported a small worktable

Above, the rooms were lined with worktables.

On the far left, a stand, probably for the furnace, had been lined with tin cans that had been straightened out. If you look closely you can see the whitish solder still there. On the near left are the remains of an old assay furnace. It was in pieces and we pieced it back together like a jigsaw puzzle. Note the D-shaped door.

115

Above, support posts for the bucking board are buried beneath the building. Below it, a muller and bucking board from the International Correspondence Schools Reference Library.

top. We had read about special stands like this, called *bucking boards*, that served as a base for the *muller* (a grinding device) or a small rock crusher or for making cupels. The many shelves of this room would have held cupels and the molds for making them, and crates of crucibles.

If we still had any doubts that this had at one time been an assay office, these would have been dashed by our next discovery. Under a pile of debris in the corner of the last room was one side of a wooden crate. When we turned the wood slat over there was stenciling on the side. Carefully we brushed away a century's worth of dust and grime and held it up to the light to see what it once said. It read: Denver Fire Clay Co, Assayer Supplies. This is exactly the type of wooden crate that crucibles were shipped in.

The assayer was a very important man in a mining camp. The assayer was a burster of dreams or the maker of bonanza kings. A good report on a prospector's ore sample might mean the sale of a mine and a spree. Therefore, thousands of dollars changed hands on the basis of his tests to determine the metallic content of an ore sample. Every smelter needed an assayer. Every ore sample office needed one. Every mill needed one. Some mines where the gold in the ore was not visible to the naked eye particularly needed an assayer to determine the direction of the rich ore in a vein.

Along with these company assayers would be a few independent, or "custom" assayers. Prospectors needed to have the ore from their discoveries tested for its contents and they would take their ore samples to a custom assayer. A speculator interested in buying a mine would want his own tests run on the mine's ore. Smart mine owners did not rely upon the results of an ore buyer's assay. If they did not have their own assayers, mine owners had assays run by independent assayers to verify the ore buyers' test. Therefore, an assayer was a busy man in a booming mining camp.

In the early days of the gold rush era, an assayer might well have been trained in one of the prestigious European mining schools. Mining historian Otis Young states

One side of a wooden packing crate still had readable stenciling on it.

that in 1849 there were probably no assayers in the United States beyond those employed at the U.S. Mint. But by 1907 there were fifty-four assayers operating in Goldfield, Nevada, alone. Most of these men learned assaying by apprenticeship. No matter how the assayer came by his knowledge, he came from a proud tradition that originated so far back in human history as to be lost in time. The assayer was a well-respected man in a mining camp. The community considered him a scientist, and if he worked for a mine or mill he was part of the management team.

Assaying was hot, grimy work. If you stepped back in time and took an ore sample to an independent assayer to test, he might likely appear in the doorway of the log-shanty laboratory clad in overalls and a rough shirt and covered with rock dust.

Ernest Ingersoll in *Scribner's Monthly (1879)* described what you might see inside the door of this nineteenth-century assay office:

> In one corner of the cabin stands the assayer's small square brick furnace and his kegs of charcoal. Against the wall are fastened the shelves that hold his few tools, his bottles of acid and his knickknacks. Upon a heavy post, converted into a table for the sake of its solidity, rest his bucking-board and muller, and a similar post give firm foundation for his diminutive anvil, while close at hand hang the various sieves, samplers, tongs and so forth, which his business calls for.

Scattered about on the rough wooden worktables and shelves would be ore samples waiting to be tested. Most of the time these samples were bagged and tagged. Other

THE INTERIOR OF AN ASSAY OFFICE

From the International Correspondence Schools Reference Library, Volume 155.

This is one side of an assay laboratory. The floor is cement and the side walls are covered with sheet metal wherever there is danger from fire. The pulp weighing room is to the left of the partition against which the shelves carrying dishes is shown. The operator shows the proper position against which the shelves holding the muller when bucking samples. To the right of the bucking board is a pan for catching the rock coming from the hand-power crusher. As each sample is crushed it is turned on the bucking board, but previous to bucking the larger pieces of rock are reduced by the hand hammer shown leaning against the wall. This method of breaking samples greatly reduces the labor of bucking. Cupels, scorifiers, crucibles, and roasting dishes are kept in sight on the shelves, while the extra furnace muffles are kept on top of the cupboard; if, therefore, the assayer runs out of any such articles he is to blame. Back of the operator and against the wall the sieve used for sizing may partly be seen. On the left hand front corner of the table is a flat anvil on which the slag is broken free from the lead button and the button is also shaped. Boxes for holding slag and rubbish are shown beneath the table. All pulp samples are kept in order in the pulp room, as well as the fluxes.

This is the side of the room opposite the shelves. The furnace is heated by gas mixed with air. The blower is not shown distinctly, but it is revolved by the motor back of the operator. The furnace, which is of the muffle type, works very satisfactorily. The operator is seen taking a crucible from the muffle for pouring into the button molds on the bench. The button tray is seen hanging on the window box. The door to the furnace is on the bench back of the molds. The cylinder under the furnace is the chamber in which air and gas are mixed previous to being burned in the furnace. The hood above the furnace is for the purpose of drawing the hot air from the room up the chimney. Fresh air is brought in from the outside the building to supply the blower, as that air is not so rarified and can supply more oxygen for combustion per cubic foot. The dimensions of the furnace are such that it occupies a floor space of 5.683 square feet. It has a height of 57 inches, and weighs in all about 900 pounds.

assayers might keep samples in metal pans about the size and shape of a roasting pan. Nearby would be two scales — one for weighing ore samples as they came in, and a glass-covered, extremely delicate, scale to weigh the button of gold and silver resulting from the assay process. Over all the paraphernalia would be a thick layer of grit. To carry on a conversation with an assayer you'd have to shout over the roar of the assay furnace and the noise of rock being pounded.

The Assay Test

What went on behind the closed doors of an assay lab? Assaying seemed to us to be one part science, one part mystery. Assaying is a form of quantitative analysis whereby metal-containing rock is tested to determine its value. Quantitative means a substance can be measured, in this case by weight. There are two types of assaying: wet or chemical and dry or fire assaying. The fire assay is used only for gold and silver (and in the old days for lead), and is what was used almost exclusively in the American West. That is the process we will discuss here.

Scales for weighing ore samples.

Glass-covered, extremely delicate scale for weighing the tiny bead of silver or gold that resulted from the assay process.

John Talbot is retired now, but for twenty years he was an assayer in Colorado and Arizona. Talbot took us figuratively behind those closed doors by explaining to us — in simplified and nontechnical ways — what went on in an assay laboratory. Some things have changed since the turn of the century, but a gold rush era assayer would be able to understand and operate in a modern assay laboratory, and a modern assayer like Talbot would be able to operate a turn-of-the-century lab such as the one we found on Glacier Mountain, Colorado, if he were to go back in time.

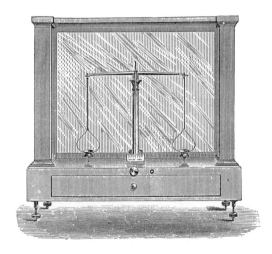

The typical assay process began when a mine or mill handed over to an assayer a bagged and labeled ore sample weighing as much as ten to twenty pounds. The assayer then gave this sample to his apprentice, who began breaking it with a sledgehammer. Then

The following
series of photo-
graphs were taken
at the Western
Museum of Mining
and Industry at
Colorado Springs,
Colorado. They
offer classes in
assaying and
graciously con-
sented to let us
photograph the
class. Eric Clements
was the teacher.
Left is the muller,
below is the
splitter.

the apprentice put it through a miniature jaw crusher. Finally he ground it with a bucking board and muller, which worked much like a pestle. After each crushing it was run through successively finer and finer sieves and screens until the rock was reduced to nearly a powder.

Then the apprentice handed the pulverized sample back to the assayer to begin his tests. Before beginning to crush the next sample, the apprentice cleaned all surfaces carefully so as to prevent inadvertently salting the next sample.

The assayer then put the sample through a device called a *splitter*. This divided the sample into three equal parts, called *splits*. One of the major concerns of the assayer at this point was making sure that the portion of the pulverized rock that ended up in the assay furnace was truly representative of the whole.

> The selection and preparation of the sample for assay may be called the "secret of success." It is the most important operation which the assayer has to conduct; and unless the sample be well taken his work will be useless . . . One portion may be very rich and another portion valueless, so far as the metal sought for is concerned. The sample, therefore, taken for an assay, must *always* be an *average* of all the ore. (Ricketts, 1880).

In the old days there were problems with different assays on the same ore sample achieving different results. This caused no end of hard feelings between the mine owners and the people they sold their ore to — the mills and smelters. The results of assay tests often varied. Even though the three splits came from the same original bagged sample, they were basically three different samples, no matter how meticulous one was in selecting them. The particles of free gold themselves could be of different sizes, and this would affect the outcome of an assay.

A system was developed a long time ago in which one split went to the ore seller's (the mine's) assayer, one went to the ore buyer's (the smelter's or mill's) assayer, and one was held to be sent to a third impartial assayer called an umpire to be tested in the event that the first two assays didn't agree. If the difference between the two assays was small, the two parties divided the difference. If the results of the two assays were wildly divergent, the third part of the sample was sent to umpire, who broke the stalemate.

Once the assayer was confident he had a representative sample, he then weighed a portion of crushed rock for the assay. This was also a very important step; a small mistake here on highgrade ore would be multiplied many times over, making it a very large error indeed. So, much care had to be taken when weighing.

The assayer measured a certain amount of the pulverized rock into a crucible. To it he added substances called *fluxes*. The majority of ores don't melt at temperatures achieved in assay furnaces. But if they are pulverized and mixed with fluxes, then heated in a furnace, the mixture readily melts. Different types of ores call for different fluxes or different amounts of the most common fluxes. Litharge (lead oxide), borax, and sodium carbonate are the three most common fluxes. It was also not uncommon to add niter (saltpeter), silica, potassium carbonate, lime and fluorspar.

After mixing the contents of the crucible thoroughly, the assayer thrust the crucible into a hot assay furnace. At a small independent assay office a small portable furnace might have been used.

Below, fluxes are added to the ground ore in the crucible. Note the apothecary-style jar. We often find shards of glass similar to this at assay-office sites.

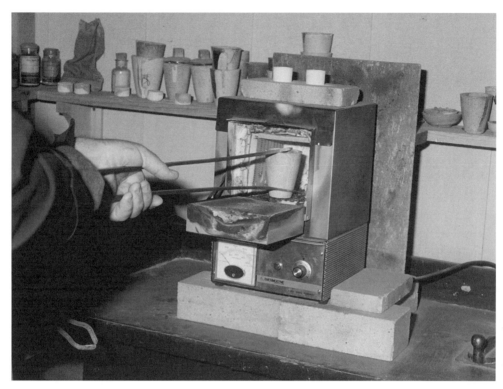

The crucible is thrust into a furnace for the smelting part of the process.

These were usually made from molded fire clay held together by metal straps. These typically had two chambers, each with a D-shaped door. Each chamber handled one of the two steps in the assay process. A large mine, a smelter, or a mill might have a large brick assay furnace held together by buck stays and tie rods.

This ore sample was fired for about a half or three quarters of an hour. This, the smelting stage, would be done in direct heat without oxygen. Gradually, the litharge (lead oxide) would give up its oxygen and become lead. When the crushed rock and the fluxes all melted, slag would be formed. A molten drop of silver/gold/lead sank through the slag to the bottom of the crucible. The assayer then retrieved the crucible from the furnace with a forked tool and poured the contents into a pointed-bottom mold. He could actually see the lump of molten silver/gold/lead slither over the side of the crucible and into the mold.

Pouring the melted contents into a mold with a pointed bottom.

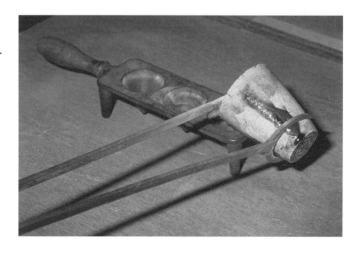

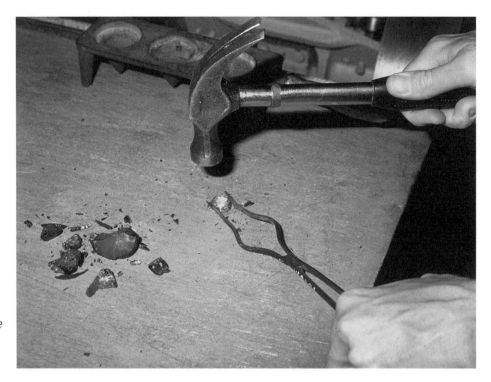

Shattering the glasslike slag, on the left, from the lead/gold/silver tip, held in tongs.

Again, the molten lead/gold/silver would sink through the slag to the bottom in the mold. When it had cooled and the mold was inverted, it popped out in the shape of a cone. The slag formed the largest part of the cone and was glassy-looking with a lead tip. The assayer then took a hammer to it and pounded off all the slag, leaving just the silver/gold/lead tip in the shape of a Hershey's kiss.

Placing the lead/gold/ silver tip in a hot cupel.

"An experienced assayer could tell a lot from the appearance of the slag at this point in the test. Occasionally colors on the surface of the slag hint at the content of the ore and how well it fired," says Talbot. "For example, if the slag was real black, it may mean that iron or manganese is present in the sample. If it appeared blue, cobalt might be present."

The second part of the assay process in the furnace is called *cupellation*. The assayer placed the cupels in the muffle and heated them. The metal tip from the smelting stage was dropped into the cupel and the furnace door left partly open to allow oxygen to flow over the cupels. The oxygen combined with the lead which returned to litharge (lead oxide). Someone in ancient Egypt discovered that bone ash had the ability to absorb litharge, and with that discovery the science of assaying was born. A cupel is made of bone ash and can absorb its weight in litharge. As the metal becomes molten once more, the litharge is absorbed by the cupel.

What is left is a bead of silver and gold called the *dore* (pronounced *dough-ray).* Sometimes this button might be no larger than the head of a pin. Just before cupellation is complete there may be a display of colors on the surface of the dore, then a flash of light called a blick. C. Beringer, in *A Text-Book of Assaying,* described it eloquently:

> The finish is easily recognized. The drops of litharge which in the earlier stages flow steadily from the surface of the alloy, thin off later to a luminous film. At the end this film appears in commotion, then presents a brilliant play of colors, and, with a sudden extinction, the operation is finished. The metal again glows for an instant whilst becoming solid.

Using needle-nosed pliers or forceps, the assayer removed the metal button. The cupel could only be used once. This explains why there are large numbers of cupels around probable mining-camp assay offices.

Then the assayer dusted off his delicate scales and carefully weighed the bead of gold and silver. He would subject it to one last procedure. After flattening the dore, he would dunk the button in nitric acid, which dissolved the silver and left only the gold. The gold would appear black.

John Talbot explains: "Unfortunately, debris somehow finds its way into the annealing cup, and may also show up as black specks or flakes. If these were weighed along with the gold, the assay result would be wrong. Annealing brings back the unmistakable color of the gold and leaves the debris black. Then, the gold can be easily separated from the debris and the true weight found."

The litharge (lead oxide) is absorbed by the cupel, leaving a silver and gold bead called the dore, below.

The bit of gold may be so tiny that it can only be seen with a magnifying glass. "Sometimes the only way I knew the gold was actually on the scales is because the scales were so sensitive, they would react to the tiny weight," says John Talbot. This the assayer would weigh to determine the amount of gold

in that original ore sample. The difference in its weight before and after the nitric acid bath would be the amount of silver that was present in this typical ore sample. "I could perform perhaps twenty or thirty assays a day," John Talbot remembers.

There are other tests an assayer had to be familiar with, like blowpiping and the scorification and inquartation processes. We won't go into them here. But we occasionally spot pieces of the paraphernalia for these other tests at probable assay-office sites. For example, it's not uncommon to find shards of scorifiers among the crucibles and cupels.

Working around lead and litharge all the time subjects assayers to lead poisoning. John Talbot says that it's not unusual for an assayer to have elevated lead levels in his blood. He himself has never had any noticeable ill effects from lead poisoning.

John Talbot recalled a time when there was one impatient millman who would show up at the assay office demanding the results of the tests long before it was humanly possible to have finished them. But Talbot and his fellow assayers found a way to get rid of him. They would bring out a beaker of ammonium hydroxide. The assayers were used to its powerful smell and no longer gagged and choked when its fumes filled the air. But that was not true for the millman. The fumes of the ammonium hydroxide would drive the pesky man out of the assay lab and back to the mill every time.

There was a reason that assay offices discouraged casual visitors. One method of highgrading was to attempt to deceive the assayer. If a person selling a mine could intercept the ore sample on its way to the assayer or while it was unattended in his lab, he could salt it, and increase its value artificially. An assayer had to be on constant alert. Probably for this reason more than any other, the work of the assayers has remained shrouded in mystery.

CRUCIBLES AND CUPELS

Crucible

Cupel

Remains of crucibles and cupels are a dead giveaway that assaying was performed at a site. Crucibles are made of unglazed, fired fireclay and come in many different sizes. Assayers would usually buy crucibles by the crate. They can be used several times. Cupels are made of bone ash and are used only once. An assayer would usually make his own cupels.

Assay Furnaces

PORTABLE FURNACES

We often find the remains of assay furnaces. Those pictured here are of molded fireclay bound together with wrought iron straps. These were considered small, "portable" furnaces, although they could weigh hundreds of pounds. The dead giveaway of an assay furnace is the D-shaped doorway. The fireclay is discolored on the inside of the furnace as in the photograph below right. Sometimes you can see the glassy remains of slag or other spilled liquids, now frozen in time. The engraving on the left is from the *International Correspondence Schools Reference Library.*

By itself, this would not have been enough to identify it as furnace remains. However, we discovered this outside the door of an obvious assay office. Nearby, there were pieces of fireclay.

Discolored fireclay

Assay Furnaces

COMBINATION FURNACE

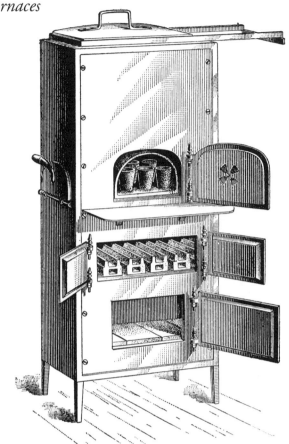

The furnace below was along the line of the one pictured on the right. If you look carefully you can see the D-shape of the two doorways outlined in the dirt. Also evident is the embossed place of origin in New York. The interior of the fireclay is discolored. Large furnaces like the one on the right had two separate furnaces, one for smelting and one for cupellation. The small portable furnaces had to do both in the muffle furnace, according to the *International Correspondence Schools Reference Library,* where this engraving is from.

Discolored fireclay   Remains of D-shaped doorways

129

Assay Furnaces

STATIONARY FURNACES

The *International Correspondence Schools Reference Library* identifies the engraving below left as a stationary three-muffle furnace. They were described as "built of red brick, lined with one course of firebrick. The walls are firmly braced with buck-stays and tie-rods." The chimney pipe in front was used to draw off the fumes and vent them to the outside. We have seen the remains of these furnaces fairly often in the backcountry, as shown by the photograph of the two-muffle furnace on the right.

130

MISCELLANEOUS

These photographs are from the same site. On the right is writing on the wall. If you look closely you can see chemical abbreviations — Pb for lead and Zn for zinc. If there are any standing buildings, always look for writing on the walls. More on this in later chapters.

Below is a different version of a bucking board. A long bolt running through it provides the extra stability that was required on a bucking board. On its top are pieces of fireclay, possibly from the assay furnace.

9

THE WOMEN

 In front of us lay the stark remains of a former frame building that now was just a nondescript pile of boards perched among the rocky crags. But it was proof nonetheless that people had been here — a place so difficult that it twisted trees and crushed buildings. What strength, what tenacity would it have taken to live here! But then we spotted the wind-tossed bonnets of columbines among the crags. Incongruously, delicate-looking wildflowers had ventured here, too, their presence providing a lace edge to the rocky cliff face and softening the harshness of the place.

Household debris peppered the downhill slope from the building remains. This led us to believe that the building had at one time been lodging. It was the sort of place you'd expect a few very tough hard-rock miners to have "bached" it. We nosed about the debris for a few minutes looking for clues. Spotting a shard of china, we eyed it intently. And there before us emerged an anomaly: a delicate white china shard with festoons of blue forget-me-nots along the scalloped edge. Try as we might, we just couldn't picture burly, hard-rock miners eating from frilly china like this. It bore the unmistakable mark of a woman. Could a woman have lived in this craggy place?

One lone clue such as this only makes for speculation. To get at fact, convincing corroborating clues are needed. But when you consider it, what could possibly remain after a century that would convincingly suggest a woman might have lived here? Old discarded corset stays? Shards of a fancy perfume bottle? An old-fashioned high-buttoned, high-heeled shoe? We have never found any of these items at a site, yet we know from the records that wives sometimes accompanied their husbands to places like this.

Above left, the doll's head we discovered that day, her painted features still visible. On the right, the baby's shoe, black and gnarled today, barely recognizable.

And then we spotted a piece of a hobnailed boot sole. When we studied it we realized that it was not just a piece of a sole, it was a tiny whole. This was a baby's shoe! As if to emphasize the point, nearby was a doll's head. It was made of china, and when we brushed away the dirt and grime, its pink painted cheeks were still visible. And now we had our convincing clues. If a baby had been in this windswept place, we felt quite certain that its mother had been here too. Not single miners but a family had lived in this difficult place! Just like columbines, the women *looked* delicate in their billowing skirts, bonnets, and lace-bedecked bodices. And their presence softened the rough edges of the wilderness. But they had to be as hardy and independent as wildflowers to survive mining-camp life.

Crossing the continent in a covered wagon was difficult and dangerous enough to kill a man. Yet it is awe-inspiring to consider that women somehow managed to make the trip in long skirts and corsets, with many of them pregnant. No one knows exactly how many men and women died during the trek West. Some early journals describe the Overland Trail as being nearly lined with graves. But any woman who survived that journey was well prepared for life in an early mining camp.

Just as many men headed west in search of new lives, so too did women. Any woman who wanted to escape Victorian restrictions or who yearned for a new life could get a fresh start in the West. Western women had more freedom and more independence than their eastern sisters. In the West, wives could own property in their own names; in the East only a single or widowed woman could. By 1910, ten percent of all homestead claims were filed by women. Divorce laws in the West were far more liberal toward women than were the eastern laws. It's not surprising that there were far more divorces in the West than in the East. Most of the western divorces were filed by women, and in the West women were far less stigmatized by divorce. And women first received the right to vote in the West decades before their sisters in the East. If a woman could survive the crushing physical labor, she might have a more independent life out West. Wildflowers might flourish in the West, but hothouse flowers would never last a season.

These women brought with them across the plains Victorian ideals about a woman's place, her proper role in life. Although the realities of living in a wilderness tempered these ideals, women in the West were still guided by the Victorian vision of womanhood. Harvey Green, in *The Light of the Home*, discusses how Victorians had assigned the job to women of "civilizing" men. Woman was the bearer of culture. Her sphere of influence was in the home. The home she created was a measure of herself as a woman and also reflected the social standing of her family. No wonder that many a young woman when faced with a rude log cabin with a dirt floor, sat down and cried her eyes out — daunted by the immensity of her task. And she was to accomplish this with

In this scene from New Colorado and the Santa Fe Trail *, A. A. Hayes, Jr. expressed typical Victorian admiration for this woman who remained so cultured as to ride sidesaddle "hatted and gloved" in the midst of such raw conditions. Sagstetter collection.*

few implements from civilization. This story perhaps illustrates it best:

> A man urged his wife to sell her Haviland china when packing for the Overland journey. To him it was a nuisance. But his wife clung to the china with despair on her face. Uncomprehending he finally allowed the china to be packed. The dishes were more than beauty — they were a tangible link to the refinements of civilized living that would be difficult to re-create in the "rugged frontier condition" that so attracted her husband (Riley, 1988).

In all the journals and diaries we read, we noticed that women seemed to be afraid of becoming barbarized by the wilderness. Women appeared determined at all costs to remain "civilized" no matter what the conditions. Young bride Keturah Penton Belknap, in getting ready for her overland journey to Oregon in 1848, reflected this when she naively wrote: "[I] have made four nice little tablecloths so am going to live just like I was at home."

A woman who arrived in an early booming mining camp stepped into a strange world. It was a man's world where women were so rare as to be curiosities. Dame Shirley in 1850s California reported that as she walked down the street one dog barked at her unrelentingly. The dog's owner apologized profusely and explained that his dog had never seen a woman before. In California, men paid one dollar for a look at two feminine items: a bonnet and a high-buttoned shoe. One woman with a baby on a stagecoach said that when a grizzled prospector got on at one stop and saw her inside he burst into tears because it had been years since he'd seen a woman or a baby. It must have been unnerving to be a woman walking down a street when suddenly all the doors would be flung open and the men inside the buildings would stand in the doorways and stare until she was out of sight.

It might have been unnerving, but it was not particularly dangerous. We read account after account of stagecoach robberies where the men were relieved of their valuables but the women passengers were allowed to keep theirs. One account from early Durango, Colorado, told how a band of horse thieves swept through a valley, stealing the horses of all the ranches except one. The owner of this ranch was recently widowed, and her husband was well known for his fine, well-bred race-horses. The outlaw band was eventually apprehended and at the trial the widow asked the thieves why they hadn't stolen her horses. Their reply: "We don't steal from a woman."

In the same area, one man had "brutally mistreated a woman," but the account does not say exactly what he did or who the woman was. His neighbors were so

A. A. Hayes, Jr. in New Colorado and the Santa Fe Trail *identified this as a stagecoach robbery. The "road agents" even robbed the furious stagecoach driver of fifty-seven of his hard earned dollars. The woman was separated from the men and was not robbed. She looks glum, he explained, because the robbers carelessly turned their backs on her but without a pistol she was unable to take advantage of the opportunity. Hayes assured his readers that a Western woman would have no qualms about shooting the robbers in the back.*

outraged that they formed a vigilante committee and hung him.

Most early women travelers negotiated their way through this male world without incident. In fact, they reported being treated well by western men. Isabella Bird traveled from California across the West in 1873 by herself. This forty-year-old upper-class Englishwoman reported that the men she met along the trail were friendly in what might have been considered a "free and easy tone" in other circumstances. Twice she went on excursions alone with men who were well known as "desperados." Both men treated her with the utmost respect and were gentlemanly in every way.

It was also customary for men to stop work with the arrival of the first woman in camp and take a day to throw together a rough log cabin for her. It was well worth their time. A woman in camp usually meant resources that were not available in an all-bachelor camp.

A Home in the Wilderness

A woman was barely out of the covered wagon when she launched herself into making a home out of a hut in the wilderness. She really had her work cut out for her. Usually her ingenuity and resourcefulness were all she had to work with.

The first thing that most women reported doing to their new homes was pasting newspapers to the inside walls of the cabin. Smart women recognized that this might be the only available reading material for months, and pasted the papers right-side up. Papering the dark walls lightened the room substantially. It also helped keep insects out of the living areas and served as insulation. But newspapers weren't the only wall covering. If a family could afford it and if it were available, calico was sometimes used on walls. We have often seen canvas on the walls of old cabins in the wilderness, especially on the ceilings. Later, brides like Harriet Fish Backus used blue building paper on her walls. Blue was a popular color at the time because it was believed that flies didn't like the color blue and would be repelled by it.

If she were lucky enough to have a board floor in the cabin, some semblance of carpeting would be in order. She would spread straw on the floor and then cover it with burlap. Harriet Fish Backus used blue denim on her floors.

Next, she might tackle the windows. Flour sacks were frequently used for making curtains, although we read of one woman who did a reverse Scarlett O'Hara and made curtains for her cabin from an old lace-edged petticoat. Flour sacks were also used for tablecloths, but the favorite material if it was available was oilcloth. Oilcloth was a waterproof cloth that to our twentieth-century eyes would look and act much like vinyl. On the table, any woman worth her salt placed a canning jar filled with wildflowers. Then, with a colorful handmade quilt on the bed in the corner, the place would be quite cozy.

If she had the resources, a mining-camp wife would personalize her cabin even more. She might line the open shelves on the walls with newspapers. This she would fold over the edge of the shelf so that it would hang down, and then she would cut designs in it or notch its edges — like a newspaper doily. Pictures on the walls might be cut from magazines, and even the colorful lithographed labels from cans of food might be used to decorate. The Victorian age was an era of "throws" — a fringed shawl draped artfully over a swell-top trunk could go a long way to civilize a drab cabin in the woods. It was also an era of knickknacks, which were supposed to be little treasures or souvenirs from a lifetime of travels, like a seashell from an

A careful study of this picture will show you a discarded doll, flowers on the window sill, and a small cage (for a canary, perhaps?) Also note the cabin in the background with a canvas tent for a roof, the miners' lunch pail in the father's hand. There is also a horseshoe above the door for luck. This picture was titled, "A Rocky Mountain Mining Camp" by artist W. L. Taylor, and appeared in the Ladies Home Journal *in March 1904. Sagstetter collection.*

ocean visit or a small Indian pot, for example. In a mining camp this practice might be suggested by a few interesting rock specimens. The newfangled photographs of friends and relatives were also popular. Books were treasured in a mining camp, and any books would be prominently displayed as a sign of culture and education.

The furniture in these cabins would necessarily have been sparse. A few homemade pieces might supplement what a family had managed to bring with them. A section of log, upended, might suffice as a stool. Or a rough chair might be made from bent tree branches. Most babies born in mining camps started life in cribs made from wooden packing crates. If they could afford it, a couple might splurge and buy a mail-order rocking chair. This furniture would have to be left behind on their

next move. Sometimes — especially in remote places — the furniture was sold with the cabin.

Keeping a canary was considered a genteel thing to do and many women had a small cage with a bird or two in it. Flowers were very important to Victorians, and pans of geraniums or moss roses were often a part of the home decor, provided a woman could keep them alive. A common sight was a miner walking home from his shift, his face blackened with Giant Powder and his overalls muddy, his lunch pail in one calloused hand and a bouquet of wild roses from the mountainside that he had picked for his wife in the other. Old-timers have reminisced that they could still see in their mind's eye the early log cabin homes with lace curtains and blossoming geraniums at the windows, sparkling glass lamp chimneys, and the smell of Arbuckles coffee (an inexpensive brand of ground coffee popular at the time.)

Note the interior of this rough cabin depicted in New Colorado and the Santa Fe Trail. *The chair on the right is handmade from sticks. They are using a fireplace for heat, cooking and light. Also note the knickknacks on the mantel. A cabin like this might well have had a dirt floor.*

Women's Work

Ideally, the Victorian woman was above the rowdy world of commerce, protected from the vile and sordid aspects of life outside the home. But what this actually meant was that the only respectable work she could do was housework, or variations of housework. So whether a woman was married or single, her work was pretty much the same. And if a woman were single or widowed or divorced, the only respectable means she had of supporting herself and her children was domestic: She could take in boarders, she could do laundry, cook, sew, nurse, or teach. In a mining camp a woman might do a little of each.

A woman in a mining camp found the fruits of her labors were eagerly sought and valuable. An early arrival in the Pikes Peak gold rush, Augusta Tabor, set up her laundry kettles over a campfire along a trail after a grueling day in the wagon. She put up a sign announcing her offer to wash the passing freighters' shirts for fifty cents. You could buy a *new* shirt for fifty cents at that time. But the freighters stripped off their shirts and got in line to take advantage of her offer. A married woman could make as much as her miner husband by taking in laundry or boarders.

Victorian Housework Wasn't for Sissies

In the earliest days of a gold rush, no roads or transportation meant few goods were available. And those that were available were wildly expensive. Anything you needed you had to make from scratch first. You'd like to read in the evening? You'd have to make tallow candles first. Want to clean your house? First you'd have to make the cleansers. Want a bath? You'd need some homemade ash pit soap, the making of which was a huge undertaking in itself, and to carry enough water from the nearby creek to fill a bathtub. Want a new dress? It had to be stitched by hand, and only after you had somehow managed to come up with a length of calico cloth. Even a simple cup of coffee was an ordeal. First you had to roast the coffee beans, grind them in a hand grinder, lug water from the creek, chop wood for the stove, and only then could you start making the coffee. Every single item in the house, every article of clothing, everything that was eaten, represented a huge amount of labor. Victorian women voted that the most time-consuming products to make were candles and soap.

Store-bought soap was available to most Victorian women after the Civil War. And the Industrial Age forged ahead in making many more products available by the turn of the century. But much of this would not have been available to early arrivals at a mining boomtown. A woman would have had to make many household items herself until roads and transportation made manufactured products as available to her as they were to women in the East. Then she would be able to buy candles or have coal oil (kerosene) lamps. She could buy cleansers and bar soap. And she could buy the Victorian equivalent of instant coffee — preroasted, preground coffee sold in tin cans.

Taking in Laundry

The most dreaded of all a Victorian woman's tasks was the laundry. Because in those days it was typical to have a bath on Saturday night, a person changed clothes once a week — on Sunday. Therefore, the laundry was usually done on Monday, earning it the nickname of "blue Monday." Tuesday was reserved for ironing.

Monday mornings were not for the faint of heart. As a Victorian woman on a Monday morning, you would face a grueling day's labor. Clothes reeked from being worn so long at a time when everyone was employed at hard physical labor. The clothes might even be covered with lice. For that reason you began the laundering process by thoroughly boiling all the garments. This entailed an exhausting ritual of lugging gallons and gallons of water from a well or nearby stream to the stove or campfire. Susan Strasser, in her book, *Never Done: A History of American House-work,* wrote that it took about fifty gallons of water for one boiling, one wash, and one rinse — which represented four hundred pounds of water for *each load.*

Then the clothes had to be vigorously rubbed against the washboard while you slathered caustic soap on. After being rinsed, each heavy woolen garment and soggy pair of canvaslike overalls had to be wrung out by hand. Then each water-laden load had to be lugged to the clothesline and hung up to dry. You'd have to return later to retrieve them. In the winter the clothes would freeze stiff. When you retrieved these frozen items, you'd shake them energetically, freeing and scattering the ice crystals, and the clothes would be more or less dry.

If a woman had any discretionary income at all, the job she hired out was the laundry. This freed up two full days a week for other chores, and she wouldn't have to hire additional household help. If a woman were supporting herself or a family, taking in laundry was the most lucrative, albeit physically exhausting, work she could do. One early pioneer in California was a former slave. She earned enough money taking in laundry to buy all the members of her family from their slave owners and pay their travel expenses to California.

Taking in Boarders

Men in mining camps did not particularly like "baching it." Under those primitive conditions, cooking and cleaning was a strenuous full-time job that miners would cheerfully pay to have done. A letter to the editor of the *Rocky Mountain News* from the new settlement of Breckenridge in 1860 read: "A few very respectable looking women have ventured over to see us. Send us a few more, as we need several boardinghouses started in this country." Another letter to the editor attempted to lure women there: "We have one lady living in Breckenridge and one on Gold Run; we would be glad to welcome many arrivals of the 'gentler' portion of the gold-seeking humanity, and can offer a pleasant country, good locations, and very peaceable neighbors as an inducement. The people are very orderly, and quiet here, except for an occasional lawsuit."

Taking in boarders was a way of earning money that didn't affect one's social status. In the East, and even among the wealthy, taking in boarders was a popular way to stretch the family income. A woman could take in boarders and still raise her children.

There were actually several different versions of private boarding situations. The Code of the West dictated that a traveler was welcome at any cabin along the trail. The householder was expected to take travelers in and feed them. To turn someone out might mean death to the traveler. But the traveler was expected to pay something in return — the going rate was about one dollar a day. This worked out well for both parties. A woman in a cabin along a busy trail could easily support her family or make as much as her husband did by taking in travelers.

Another version of the private boardinghouse situation was in established mining camps. Immigrants from various countries would take in boarders from their homelands. That way, a foreigner a long way from home would have a chance to speak his own language and eat the foods of his country. If this were the situation, the boarder was expected to work the same shift as the man of the house.

In the most typical boarding scenario, a young single hard-rock miner (or several) lived in a private boardinghouse run by a woman or a couple. After the original rush subsided he had a bed, but probably not a private bedroom. He took breakfast and the evening meal at the boardinghouse, and the woman of the house filled his miner's lunch pail with his lunch. This became known as the American Plan. At a dollar a day each, a woman with three boarders was earning as much as her hard-rock miner husband.

The European Plan was sometimes practiced in towns that were more established. A miner bedded at one place and ate elsewhere. Frequently, restaurants sold meal tickets good for a week at a time. This system was more popular on the West Coast, particularly in California and Nevada. It would not have been feasible at some of the remote mines.

Cooking and Sewing

Women did not make inroads into being camp cooks until after the turn of the century. But they did bake bread and pies that they would then sell. Sometimes a woman had a cow that provided enough milk for butter and cheese for her own use, and some left over to sell. Eggs, too, were a big seller. One woman was offered the princely sum of one dollar per egg by the gamblers in her town, but she refused to sell them at any price, for they were for her children. Anne Ellis's mother kept cows

From an advertisement in Harpers Weekly, *Sagstetter collection.*

and pigs in the mining camp of Bonanza, Colorado, in the 1880s. And most people there kept a vegetable garden, although this would not have been possible at all locations.

Sewing was a popular way for a woman to support herself. Looking at the multitudinous detail work on Victorian-era clothes — the tucks, the darts, the bustles, the trains, miles of lace edging and ribbons — and all done in tiny hand stitching, it is mind-boggling to consider the number of hours required to make one "average" dress. In those days, a dress was judged by the quality of the sewing on the inside of the dress. The first thing a woman did when she looked at a dress was to turn it inside out and carefully study it to see how skillfully it had been made. How carefully had the seams been finished, how straight were the "steels" that had been sewn into the many seams of the bodice, how tiny were the stitches? Treadle sewing machines became available only in the last quarter of the nineteenth century.

Even though some of the women in mining camps had never been to a big city in their lives, they still dressed surprisingly stylishly. *Godey's Lady's Book* and other women's magazines and mail-order catalogues kept them aware of the current fashions. The women copied the dresses in the pictures. One person said that the most stylishly dressed women would step from the most miserable shacks.

But dresses were only a small part of the sewing that needed to be done. In a mining camp, everything had to be made by hand, at least at first. The woman of the house made all the undergarments for every person in the family. Usually the underclothes were made from flour sacks, and in a large family there were never enough flour sacks to go around. If socks were available to be bought, German socks were considered the best. But in the early camps, socks were one of those items that were hard to get. A bachelor had to tear a flour sack into strips and wind the strip around his feet and ankles. These were called "California socks," so we have a good idea where this practice originated. Imagine the lucky man who had a wife who could hand-knit socks for him!

Teaching

For a young woman who wanted to leave home and travel to new places and support herself, teaching looked good. But she had to be able to afford to go to school and get a teaching certificate. Most teachers did not teach for long. Only single women were allowed to teach, so if a teacher married, she had to give up her job. And few teachers remained single long. The young schoolmarm who found herself in a mining camp would be besieged with suitors.

When a school was deemed necessary in a community, the families with children got together and created one by throwing together a one-room log cabin for that purpose. They divvied up the books they had among them. These would be the books the teacher used for teaching. Then they sent for a teacher.

In due time, a young woman arrived. This was probably her first teaching assignment. Whipping the crude arrangement into a functioning school must have been daunting, for teachers had little or no help, and no one to ask for advice. The teacher served as the janitor, including scrubbing the outhouse as well as bringing in a pail of drinking water for the students and chopping wood for the stove or fireplace. She was often the sole adult present and therefore responsible for any emergency, including medical emergencies. She was the principal, she was the disciplinarian, and she was the sole contact with the school district, the school board, and the state department of education.

And she had few resources to work with, perhaps just the books of local families — no maps or globes. She might not even have a real blackboard, but maybe only a piece of wood with black paint covering it. The children did not have much in the way of supplies, either. Paper and pencils in early mining camps were hard to come by. Children would normally expect to use a small personal slate blackboard to write their assignments. If the school was lucky, there was one slate per student.

Small schools wouldn't have the resources to pay even enough for the young teacher to have her own place, and she would board with the families of her students,

The Malachite, Colorado, schoolhouse. Photograph by Rick Athearn, BLM-Colorado.

rotating among them. Larger camps might have a cabin near the school specifically for the teacher to live in during the school session. At least the school sessions were mercifully short, some only three or four months long.

In a one-room schoolhouse, the students were all together, regardless of what grade they were in. The teacher focused on the oldest students, and the younger students generally learned from the older students. A student was ranked by what reader he was in. Readers were books that became progressively more difficult, and they ranged from the first reader to the eighth reader. *McGuffy's* readers were the most famous. After the student had finished the eighth reader he was ready for high school. Most students didn't go on to high school. A student was expected to learn in school just enough to be able to read proficiently, and to know enough math to run a small business, and to write just enough to produce personal and business letters.

Nursing

Just as some wildflowers have medicinal qualities, some women were talented nurses. And the diseases that swept through mining camps were formidable indeed: diphtheria, typhoid, whooping cough, smallpox, and pneumonia being the worst. Victorian women were armed with only a handful of various herbs and home-grown remedies, yet their cure rates were touted by their neighbors. Sara A. Gleason, in *I'd Do it Again* wrote:

> Our village was very fortunate in that we had two women, Mrs. Osgood and Mrs. Hagerman, who knew how to cure practically any disease or ailment. They were always ready to come at a minute's notice to those in need of help. . . . Sometimes when the type of sickness was too much for either of these good women, a doctor from a larger community was called . . . Frankly, I had more confidence in Mrs. Osgood.

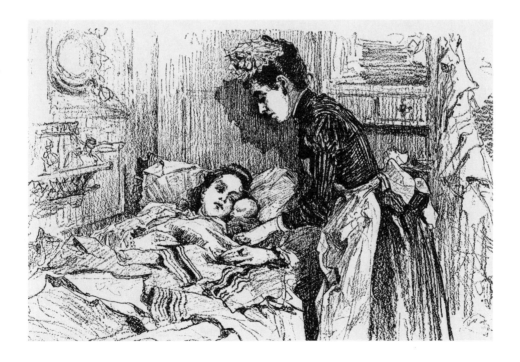

THE TYPICAL NINETEENTH-CENTURY HOME MEDICINE CHEST

What might a hypothetical Victorian woman's medicine chest contain? Each of a mother's children trudged to school with a smelly bag of asafetida hanging around his or her neck. Asafetida is a gum resin that smells strongly of garlic and was thought to ward off disease. A patch of chewing tobacco placed on a sore spot was as common as Band-Aids are today. Whiskey was used for medicinal purposes. It was handy for everything from childbirth to snakebite and was the first bottle to be brought out of the chest in times of sickness or injury.

Herbs which were brewed into teas were a necessity. Sage tea was good for high-altitude sickness, which was called "mountain fever." Oregon grape root brewed with rock candy, juniper and whiskey was considered good for the kidneys. Rose-root tea was considered gentle enough to treat babies, although we are not sure exactly what it accomplished.

Quinine and camphor were common to Victorian medicine chests. Petroleum jelly (Vaseline) was an important all-round household medication. Even turpentine and pitch plaster were mentioned often. Witch hazel was listed in the Montgomery Ward catalogue of 1895 and was said to be the "universal all healing remedy." Epsom salts and castor oil would have been familiar to most women. In addition, the well-prepared mother might have some of her favorite patent medicines on hand.

Aspirin was not a part of the Victorian medicine chest; it was developed about the turn of the century in Germany.

Even though a woman's medicine chest was sparse, a kind word and a gentle touch could go a long way toward curing a crusty old prospector whose contact with women in general was very limited. When a man lay dying a long way from kin it was a woman he wanted as a nurse. And we are told that as a man lay dying it was always a woman's name he called out.

One of the most important nursing jobs a woman performed was as a midwife. In those days women did not go to hospitals to have their babies. Hospitals were for sick people and accident victims and having a baby was considered a natural, healthy thing to do. But childbirth claimed many women's lives. In addition to all the diseases and accidents that befell nineteenth-century people, the women had also to survive childbirth. And not just one childbirth but many. If anything went at all wrong during the process, they simply died.

Women usually traded midwifing duties with a neighbor or a friend. Sometimes if a woman was exceptionally talented as a midwife, she might do all the midwifing in her area. Sometimes she would get paid a little something for this, sometimes not.

Once a woman's pregnancy progressed far enough to be noticeable, she went into confinement, for it was not thought proper for her to be seen in public at that time. As she neared her delivery date, she would have a small cardboard box with items in it ready for the delivery. In this box there would be some safety pins, string, clean rags, a bottle of Vaseline, hand-made receiving blankets, and some lovingly stitched baby clothes. After a woman delivered it was considered necessary for her to remain in bed about ten days.

Children

The only person childbirth was tougher on than the mother was the baby. One set of statistics claimed that a baby born in the 1800s had only a fifty-fifty chance of reaching adulthood.

But for the children who survived, many looked back upon growing up in a mining camp with fondness. One old-timer who grew up in Arizona recalled that one of the camp cabins was roofed with a red-and-white-striped canvas, giving it the look of a circus tent, much to the delight of the community's children. There were many things to do for entertainment: camping, hunting, swimming, and picnicking in the summer; sledding and skiing in the winter; horseback riding all year. The recitals and skits schoolchildren performed were a major source of entertainment for the whole community and were well attended.

A large proportion of children in mining camps either had odd jobs or worked part-time. Children tended the cows and pigs, chopped wood and carried it into the house, and kept the kerosene lamps full. Boys were not allowed underground in the mines, but there was plenty of work to be had on the surface, in the boardinghouses especially. Plenty of boys apprenticed at such things as blacksmithing. One boy of eight in Lake City, Colorado, collected some of the burros that had been abandoned by prospectors who had moved on and started packing the mail and a few supplies up to the camp of Carson. The men there loved it, and he made good money. But he quit when school started.

One of the few fruits available at high altitudes in the Rockies are wild raspberries. They are smaller than garden raspberries but more flavorful. Picking berries was a great pastime for mining-camp kids. Most of the time the results of their labor were used by the family in jams or pies. But these berries were quite marketable, too. Every family had their favorite patch and would be sure to be there when the berries ripened.

Children were about as rare as women in mining camps, and the miners doted upon them. Harriet Fish Backus, when living in Elk City, Idaho, had to put her foot down with the miners about giving her little girl hard candy every time she went to town. She finally had to compromise on gum. Kids could count on being given nickels and dimes by the miners.

Prostitutes

Prostitutes arrived on the heels of the first gold rush to an area. Called soiled doves, sporting women, fallen angels, or fancy women, prostitutes embodied the opposite of the Victorian ideal of perfect womanhood and were treated as such by most respectable women.

Most camps relegated prostitutes to a red-light district. Some went so far as to license and tax them, nearly running the towns on the proceeds from their activities. Early lawmen spent most of their time dealing with the problems in the red-light districts. Many men had a practical attitude about prostitution: It was a necessary evil. Mine management felt that the prostitutes helped keep the men happy. At the Sunnyside Mine in the San Juans, Allan Bird, in *Silverton Gold,* tells of one particularly tough winter. The men in the boardinghouse were especially depressed and unruly. Afraid that fights would break out, the manager contacted a Silverton madam and invited her to bring up some of her girls. They struggled through the snow to the aerial tram and rode up to the boardinghouse. Then they set up shop in one of the rooms in the boardinghouse. When they left a few weeks later, one woman had earned six hundred dollars.

There were different aspects to prostitution. One type of prostitute was a lone woman working out of a "crib." Rows of cribs lined certain streets in the larger camps. These were drab one- or two-room structures with a door and a window opening onto the street. The woman lounged in front of the door or window of her crib, and a man walking down the street could choose between cribs. When her door was closed, she was busy with a customer. Inside, she sold beer and gave her customer what he wanted. Then he was hustled out and she started vying for her next customer. The cribs were considered to be the bottom of the line for a prostitute. Usually the women who found themselves there were no longer young and were addicted to drugs or alcohol.

Most saloons also had prostitutes on hand. A man went to the saloon, had a few drinks, and if he saw a woman he liked, the two of them went upstairs. The bartender (usually the proprietor) managed the women— he was in charge of all the transactions, accepting the money and hiring the women.

There were also fancy parlor houses. These are the places with ornate furniture, champagne, gilded mirrors, and pretty clothes seen in many movies. A madam usually kept the house, and she was usually the one who made the money. The prostitutes themselves rarely made much, but they received room and board.

Drug addiction, alcoholism, suicide, and venereal disease were occupational hazards for prostitutes. *Rocky Mountain Medicine,* by Robert H. Shikes, M.D., states that perhaps as many as fifty percent of the mining-camp prostitutes had syphilis.

Respectable women in town were usually more scandalized than the men about the prostitutes. Nearly every journal we read had at least one example of a man marrying a prostitute who then made the transition to a respectable way of life. Apparently it occurred often enough to appear in journals, but seldom enough to be mentioned in the first place.

Loneliness

One word echoes through the journals of women in mining camps again and again: loneliness. Especially as a camp was becoming established, and particularly in remote places. It was true whether a woman found herself in a raw new mining camp or homesteading on the plains. The loneliness was a formidable presence that had to be addressed. The women who lived in or near a settlement reserved their afternoons, after their work was mostly done, after the noon meal (the big meal of the day) had been cooked and cleaned up after, for visiting with their women friends. They each might bring along sewing to do as they chatted. They would exchange books and then discuss them.

By marrying a mining man, a woman was taking on a life in the most rugged and forlorn places, where the ores are found. A prospecting husband could be gone for weeks at a time checking out new areas, staking claims, and looking for gold. A hard-rock miner might have to leave to find work in another camp when the mine he worked for closed, as it often did.

Most women reported that they didn't feel afraid for themselves when left alone in the wilderness for varying lengths of time, even though a log cabin with a wooden latch for a door lock was not a formidable defense. Travelers stopped in, neighbors came by, and the women awaited anxiously for word from their husbands. The one exception to this confidence was the Native American. Many women were afraid of Indians, probably inordinately so. Some of the women who were most afraid of Indians had never met one.

Men who lived in the earliest days of a boomtown complained that there was actually very little to do for entertainment. After you visited the various saloons and drank, gambled, and played a little pool, then made the rounds of the women in the cribs, you had experienced all the entertainments an early camp had to offer. Anything resembling culture came with the respectable women. These lonely women busied themselves with planning dances, sewing bees, and school and church programs. In an age before television or movies, before record players or radios, these activities were well attended by the community.

Although many a young bride was horrified by her new home in the West when she first alighted from the wagon, most learned to love their adopted home. Dame Shirley said: "I *like* this wild and barbarous life . . . Here, at least, I have been content."

And so the wildflowers spread — peppering the deserts, blanketing the plains, festooning mountainsides — and forever changed the face of the West.

10

THE TOWNS

You may see such . . . places, where only meadows and
forests are visible — and will find it hard to believe that
there stood at one time a fiercely-flourishing little city, of
two thousand souls . . . and now nothing is left of it all but
a lifeless, homeless solitude . . . . In no other land, in
modern times, have towns absolutely died and disappeared,
as in the old mining regions of California.

— Mark Twain, *Roughing It*

Only the winds whisper down the main street of the ghost towns now.
The people are gone, the mining era ended — even their dreams have
been forgotten. Today the mining camps are places of solitude and
quiet. If any buildings remain, they stand quaint and weathered
against a craggy backdrop and kneedeep in Indian paintbrush. The heavy scent of pine
shrouds the place.

But it wasn't always like this. A booming mining camp was not a place of solitude. It
bustled with activity day and night. As a commercial, industrial center for a mining district
it boasted a population much larger than the number of buildings in town might suggest.
Men came into town from nearby regions to buy supplies, get their mail, and have a few
days of fun. Sometimes they spent the winters in towns like this and worked their claims
only in the summer. In their heyday, the streets of mining camps were choked with freight
wagons and strings of burros and mules loaded with supplies for the mines or ore from the
mines. People, mostly men, thronged the streets day and night. Sunday was no exception,
and business continued full pace right on through the Sabbath without so much as a pause
for church services. Strangers would approach people with a mine or real estate to sell. This
was all very exciting for someone who had been working a claim alone or with a buddy out
in the wilderness.

Nor was a booming mining camp a quiet place. The thud of stamp mills could be heard for
miles long before you got into town. Mules wore bells. Burros brayed. Dogs barked. Cats
yowled all night. Planing mills struggled to keep up with the demand for boards, and the
steady drone of the planes could be heard day and night. Steam saws also worked feverishly
to supply board for buildings and rasped all night. Many mining camps had aerial trams
that added a rhythmic clickety-clack to the general din.

Even late at night the streets of a booming mining camp teemed with activity. From Scribner's Monthly Magazine, *Sagstetter collection.*

The smells were different, too. Acrid smoke billowing from the smokestacks of mills and smelters was noxious enough to kill surrounding vegetation. The dust in the streets in the dry season was enough to choke man or beast. Mixed in with these smells was that of animal dung from the horses and mules and oxen. And human refuse was tossed into the streets. Yet journalist Ernest Ingersoll claimed the camps were sweet-smelling because all the buildings were freshly constructed of new pine boards.

But you would hear few complaints. Such noise was music to the ears of a prospector who had heard no human sounds for weeks. To the people of the town the thud of the stamp mill was the heartbeat of the mountain. As long as the mill was operating, everything was all right. The mill only stopped in emergencies or if the mine closed down.

The Birth of a Mining Camp

A mining camp had a life cycle. It was repeated throughout the West hundreds, perhaps thousands of times: Gold was discovered, and a teeming, pulsating town soon flashed to life on the spot. Nineteenth-century diarists were very consistent in their descriptions of the conception of a town in their journals. These towns "sprang magic-like into being," "as if by enchantment," or "like mushrooms in the night."

If you were a prospector working a claim in a remote valley, you might witness the birth of a mining camp yourself if you discovered gold. Suddenly your deserted valley would explode to life. People and freight arrived daily. At first tents blanketed the valley. These were quickly replaced with crude log cabins that straggled along a stream or other natural feature. Other towns were platted in a neat gridwork of streets, and the lots were sold by speculators. Because there was a consuming need for wood for cooking, for heat, for mine timbers, for buildings, for charcoal, the sawmills quickly arrived. The mountainsides soon were denuded of trees. In a matter of weeks, your once quiet valley would be filled with a rickety wooden town. Life coursed through the veins of this new camp. It buzzed day and night with activity and noise. Gold fever gripped everyone.

As you walked down the street, you would see a mining town like most others. The main street was lined with false-fronted commercial buildings. This building style

A new mining town began its life as a ragtag collection of buildings. Here a false-fronted bunkhouse is under construction next to an older log building. The sign on the store reads "German Sox, best made, $1.25 - 1.50," which represented a half day's pay for a hard-rock miner. Sagstetter collection.

Here is a mining camp like most others: The false-fronted buildings, the muddy streets, a few tents. This illustration is from Alaska and the Klondike Gold Fields by A. C. Harris. Sagstetter collection.

was well suited to transient mining camps. The back of the building could be thrown together as haphazardly as conditions warranted. Sometimes a false front was slapped on the front of a log cabin. If so, the front would be the nicest, most finished part of the building. The wide blank space above the door provided a large flat surface perfect for a signboard. Under this sign-board would be a center door flanked by two large windows perfect for displaying merchandise. A false-fronted building was versatile. It proved just as ideal for a saloon as for a dry goods store, or for a pharmacy or a newspaper office. A main street lined with false-fronted buildings made a substantial impression and gave a neater, tidier air to the town than a cluster of shacks. No wonder this architectural style became synonymous with the western frontier.

158

Walking along Main Street, you'd walk on a boardwalk to avoid the mud and dust. The streets of western boomtowns were much wider than in eastern towns, making them easier to turn horse-drawn wagons in. But still, the street was a place to avoid. Punctuating it were a few tree stumps. In the dry season it might be ankle-deep in dust, and in the wet season the mud could be so deep as to swallow a mule. People flung trash out the doors of their cabins into the street — baling wire, tin cans, broken bottles, animal dung. Pigs and burros rooted around in the garbage. Raw sewage sometimes ran in ditches beside the street.

Clumping down the boardwalk in your hobnailed boots, you would be surprised at how cosmopolitan this little burg was: All around you would be voices speaking excitedly in many different languages. At some point you would pass the town well or water pump. This was a reminder that no houses had water piped to them; everyone came to the town well or pump and carried the water home. There were no interior bathrooms; each house had an outhouse behind it. In company towns some of the homes might have electric lights, but only if the mine generated electricity for its own power needs.

One of the first buildings you would undoubtedly encounter would be a saloon.

Saloons and Other Entertainments

> I naturally strolled around the city. There were a number of good stores, meat shops, bakeries, blacksmith shops, etc., but the gambling saloons were the terror of the town. The rooms were spacious, supplied with music, and adorned with mirrors, pictures, and every device to attract the young, and induce them to gamble and drink. (Steele 1901).

A mining camp might not have a church, but it would always have a saloon, even if that were the only building in town. In fact, it would probably have several. Saloons were such mining-camp institutions that they were the most reliable means to determine the number of people in a camp. Mining-camp populations were so transient that it was nearly impossible to count them. It was much more accurate to determine how many saloons a town's population could support.

In saloons young men could also actually see women, who were rare on the mining frontier. Often they could even dance with one of the women, for a price. You might play a few hands of cards or buy a round of drinks for your buddies.

Some of these saloons were hellholes where a man's life and money were at stake. Most were actually quite tame, more like a men's club or meeting place. This was

159

A wild saloon scene as pictured in Alaska and the Klondike Goldfield. *Most saloons were actually quite tame.* Sagstetter collection.

especially true in the early days of a mining camp, before the wives arrived. Until respectable women got there, going to the saloon or to the cribs was about the only choices a young man had for entertainment.

Once wives arrived in town, they organized "civilized" entertainments. Probably the most popular was the weekly dance. No one missed this. Women baked food to be served and decorated the building where the dance was to be held. Men outnumbered women in mining camps, and no female over kindergarten age was allowed to sit out any dances. Usually no drinking was allowed at these affairs. Costume parties were popular, and everyone vied to outdo one another with elaborate costumes.

On holidays the towns went all out. Besides Thanksgiving and Christmas, the Fourth of July and Labor Day were the holidays most celebrated by miners. Even the mines and mills shut down on these days. While the women were busy decorating and baking cakes, pies, and cookies, the men planned games. Horse races and boxing matches were standbys. But the games most looked forward to in a mining town were the drilling contests.

Drilling contests involved one- and two-man teams of single- and double-jackers. These teams would vie for who could hand-drill the deepest hole in a granite block in a certain amount of time. Betting would take place and served to heighten the excitement. In anticipation of the event men would practice for days and use their own special drill steels.

And there would be music. Today all we have to do is push a button to have music. But in those days, if there was music, someone had to make it. You were a very popular person indeed if you knew how to play a fiddle or a piano. For people having to go for weeks without music, it was a powerful lure. Clergymen learned that the miners would listen politely to their sermons and be generous with their offerings, but what they really came to church for was the singing of hymns. The minister would start to call an end to the service and someone would break into yet another old favorite hymn and the service would stretch on and on.

Music was so important that most memoirs we have read recount when the first piano came to town. One story demonstrates just how important music was. A forest fire was sweeping toward an early mining camp. There wasn't enough time to place the only piano in town on a wagon and transport it to safety. So the men, in desperation, decided to bury it! They dug a hole big enough in no time, lowered the piano into it, covered it with dirt, then lit out for safety themselves. When the smoke cleared the piano was exhumed, and in perfect condition. There wasn't a building left standing in the town, but they had a piano, by god!

Most towns began life orderly enough, with the vast majority of men working hard on their claims. The honest miners just minded their own business. But the life also attracted an undesirable element. Sooner or later the town would get out of hand; criminals would have moved into the vacuum created by the absence of formal law. Men would be murdered in their sleep for their gold. Travelers were relieved of their valuables by footpads. Eventually the problems would escalate to such a degree that the honest miners would have to lay down their tools and deal with the problems. Usually a vigilance committee would be the first step. The vigilantes would hang the worst elements or drive them out of town, sending a clear message to the others to behave themselves. Then they would vote a reliable member of the community into office as sheriff or constable. Official law would then have arrived at this little town.

The Death of a Mining Camp

One day the mines start to play out, one by one. Fewer people are arriving, some people move on — empty buildings appear. And then one day the death knell of the camp is sounded: Gold has been discovered in another area. And suddenly the valley is very nearly emptied. The entire cycle might have transpired in a couple or three years, maybe less. The Reverend John Steele described the deserted village of Washington, California, in December of 1850, *six months* after it had been founded: "With a large number of vacant cabins it contained several empty store buildings and quite a large hotel, closed and silent. A few miles further up, where the rocks rose perpendicularly on both sides of the river, leaving but a narrow margin, was the hamlet of Canonville, entirely deserted" (Steele 1901).

But the one incident that created more ghost towns than any other happened in Washington, D.C. — the repeal of the Sherman Silver Act in 1893. With that one stroke, any camp that mined silver was given a death blow. The resulting economic depression not only ravaged the West but was worldwide in its magnitude. Most of the mining camps we visit today became ghost towns on that date. The towns that survived mined gold.

Frank Crampton, in *Deep Enough,* Anne Ellis, in *The Life of an Ordinary Woman,* Mabel Barbee Lee in *Cripple Creek Days,* even Mark Twain all describe returning to mining camps after twenty years to find nothing left. Not a single building, not even stone ones, not a single stick of wood sometimes. Gone in the span of a lifetime. All these writers describe finding grassy foundations.

The fact is that there have always been ghost towns in the American West since the California gold rush. And many of the people who watched or even participated in the birth of a mining camp also lived to see it die.

How did these towns disappear? One of the greatest dangers to mining towns was fire. It was a constant threat. Very few extant mining towns are original, thanks to fire. Often the fires would start from human causes. Some towns were burned in forest fires. Others were consumed by lightning-caused fires. Most mining camps burned at least once. If it were still in its boom phase, the town would be rebuilt, and usually better than before, with more substantial stylish buildings and with less of the slipshodness that typified the earliest camps.

Other mining camps were literally carried off, sometimes a board at a time. Someone needed a shed or a barn and would scavenge some wood from a deserted town nearby. Sometimes, when a miner packed up and left, he disassembled his log cabin and took it with him. One cabin built by "Father" John Dyer was moved at least three times. Log cabins were especially easy to move.

As you approach an old mining-camp site, you will notice many old weathered tree stumps. They dot the area like tombstones and are a sign you are near an old town. Note the diameter of these stumps; often they are larger around than the surrounding trees. Also note how tall the stumps are. The height of a stump can reflect what time of year the tree was cut. A tree cut in winter, when there were several feet of snow on the ground, might leave a very tall tree stump, like the one above right. Some of the old camps we visited in the old mining districts turned out not to be mining camps, but lumber camps. So much wood was required in mining regions that lumber camps were common. The telltale sign of a lumber camp is a large pile of wood chips, bark, and debris cut from the trees, like the one below. Even today such piles can be five feet high — no telling how high it was a century ago. Lumberjacks lived much the same way as the miners did — you might find the remains of a bunkhouse and a mess hall. The debris remaining at lumber-camp sites may be dated as per the information in Chapter 13.

11

LODGING:
LOG CABINS

In accordance with the custom of the country, our door had always
stood open and our board welcome to tramping miners — they
drifted along nearly everyday, dumped their [paused] shovels by the
threshold and took "potluck" with us.

— Mark Twain, *Roughing It*

 Past the twisted, stunted trees that mark timberline, and in the most
inhospitable place imaginable, some brave soul chose to build a log
cabin a long, long time ago. Today it's not much to look at. Just a few
courses of logs and a smattering of artifacts in a place so windswept that
even the trees refuse to go there. Yet at one time someone saw this cabin as home. And
travelers saw it as a place of welcome. In the early days of the West, anyone who showed up
at a cabin door such as this was welcomed. But the traveler was expected to pay something
for this privilege. Even if no one was around, travelers were welcome to make themselves at
home, as long as they replenished the chopped wood they used and left some cash to pay for
the food they ate.

Perhaps because of this early western tradition, the remains of log cabins are actually a
symbol of hardship and self-reliance, of simplicity and a lack of pretense. A log cabin is
almost a synonym for the word "welcome."

Nothing evokes the West and old mining camps more than a log cabin. They are forever
linked with the American wilderness in our imaginations. Former presidents bragged about
having been born in one. But log cabins are not an American invention. They are mentioned in literature as far back as ancient Roman times and probably originated in early
Russia or Scandinavia. According to *Log Construction in the Ohio Country, 1750 – 1850,* by
Donald Hutslar, log cabin construction was brought to this country in the mid-1600s by
Swedish settlers along the Delaware River. But the idea of building a house from logs
quickly spread West with the emigrants.

This sod-roofed cabin had sunflowers growing from it. From New Colorado and the Santa Fe Trail. *Sagstetter collection.*

And it's no wonder the log cabin became a popular building style. A log cabin was ideally suited to frontiers and mining camps. They were fast to throw together — in as little as one day with help and some advanced preparations. One man could build a small cabin by himself, if necessary. They were versatile — logs could be used just as effectively to build a house, a barn, an office, a store. Even a snow fence. In forested areas they were inexpensive: The main material was close at hand and cost only the labor needed to fell and then drag them to the house site. They required few tools and few materials other than logs. A simple log cabin didn't necessarily require special skills to erect. And some lasted for generations.

Most early log cabins were intended to be temporary shelters. If the mine were successful, more substantial buildings would be put up later. If the mine were not successful, the miner could walk away without much regret.

The Evolution of Log Cabins

As early as the 1870s, A. A. Hayes Jr. recognized that there were differences between log cabins when he wrote: "On one side [of Hungry Gulch] stood Nebraska Row, a curious collection of [log] cottages, built in the early days, with sunflowers growing out of their mud roofs."

We, too, noticed differences between the log cabins we were seeing in the backcountry. Some were very rough, even in the old sepia-toned pictures taken when they were new. Others were more like fine log homes, and of these, some are still occupied today.

Terry Jordan, in *American Log Buildings: An Old World Heritage,* identified two overlapping generations of log buildings. A boomtown could go through the two generations in a matter of weeks, or months if a boom held out. Or only first-generation log cabins might be represented if a boom petered out. Transportation was the determining factor in the evolution of log cabins in a region. If goods were readily available — goods like milled wood and iron stoves — the cabins quickly reflected this.

The first-generation log cabins came right after tents and were the first structures built in a boom. The key word was "expediency." It was absolutely necessary to construct shelter, and as quickly as possible. We see the remains of this type of log hut all through the backcountry. These cabins had dirt floors because milled boards probably weren't available. For the same reason, these log cabins also had sod roofs, or sometimes canvas roofs. This cabin generally had one room. A fireplace served for cooking, heating, and lighting. The corner notching on this type of cabin was simple, perhaps just a simple lap. Saddle notching or steeple notching was common,

A classic first-generation log cabin: Sod roof, dirt floor. Only one small window. Simple lapped notching on the corners. Logs fill in the gable ends. Even on the underside of the roof the wood had been split, not sawed. This implies that milled wood was hard to come by. Even remnants of leather hinges still remained on the door frame.

167

CORNER NOTCHING

Simple lap. *These snubnosed notches were simply stacked over one another. Very little shaping of the log end was done. This style was used most often on outbuildings and barns, although we do see them occasionally on surviving first-generation cabins. Sometimes we see different types of notching on the same cabin. Other types of notching exist besides just those mentioned here, but we have never seen these other types in our travels in the backcountry.*

Saddle notching. *The underside of a log was roughly shaped to the log beneath it. By rounding the bottom of a log, it thereby repelled water. Since only one side of each log was shaped, this style is simple and quick to execute. It is seen mostly on first-generation log cabins and is very common in the backcountry.*

Steeple notching. The top of a log was shaped to a sharp ridge, the bottom of the log with a sharp groove. The grooved bottom of each log was fitted into the sharp ridge of the log beneath it when the builders erected the cabin. This system makes it a particularly stable one, not prone to twisting out of shape. It is fast and easy to do, making it a very popular type of notch and seen often in the backcountry. Sometimes it is also called the inverted **V** notch.

Full dovetail notching. This is the strongest and the most elegant of all the types of corner notches. It is complex and required a skilled worker to execute. It was meant to be faced with planed boards and is only seen on second-generation log cabins. It is rare to encounter it in the backcountry.

169

A barrel used as a chimney pot, as pictured in New Colorado and the Santa Fe Trail. *Sagstetter collection.*

and sometimes a combination of the two. We have noticed that logs of this kind of cabin sometimes still have bark in place. How comfortable the cabin was depended upon how well it was chinked and daubed between the logs.

This first generation of log cabins was built with few resources available, so there is occasionally some highly creative recycling of whatever was at hand. One writer in early California stated: "Each of these [houses] had a large fireplace and chimney, built of mud and stones, and surmounted by an empty barrel for a chimney-pot, and after the popular architecture of the mines."

What were these early cabins like inside? The furniture was primitive and hand-made from whatever resources were available. Sometimes poles with the bark still on them were sharpened and driven into the ground to serve as table legs. Anne Ellis describes a bachelor's log cabin:

> Dore's was just the usual miner's cabin — a bunk built in one corner, a
> mattress of straw or pine boughs and over this blankets, with a top cover

of canvas, and a pillow with a dark calico slip (quite shiny in the middle). At the head of the bed is a shelf, either nailed or on pegs set in the logs; on this shelf are matches, a candle, pipes and tobacco, shaving mug and razor, and a small box holding thread, needles, and buttons. Against the wall is a home-made table, on which are cans containing sugar and salt; also a can of condensed milk, a few tin plates and cups, these being turned upside down when not in use, to keep mice and dirt out. . . . Near the door, on a box turned on end, would be a water bucket and wash pan.

Grass grows from this sod roof today. And in it is another version of the barrel as a chimney pot — a powder or a carbide can as a chimney.

Living in a cabin such as this could not have been easy. Isabella Bird described having to shovel mud out of the parlor of her log cabin in Estes Park, Colorado, in 1873, after a heavy storm washed off much of the sod roof. Another woman told a harrowing tale of being pinned in a log cabin for two days when the dirt roof caved in on her. Many early travelers describe waking up in the morning in cabins such as these covered with drifted snow that had sifted in through all the cracks during the night. In wet weather the dirt floor could become a muddy mire. With few if any windows, log cabins were dark and dreary inside. Early writers mention having to open the door in order to read or write. Of these first-generation cabins, most today are badly decayed. It is unlikely for such a structure to have remained inhabited in

171

Although this is a board cabin, not a log cabin, it shows the interior of a typical bachelors' cabin. We assume these men are miners because they have candle drippings on their clothes and the reclining man has on hob-nailed boots. Note how it resembles Anne Ellis' description: The newspaper-lined shelves and on the shelves are shaving mugs and a cigar box, among other items. They smoke pipes. Next to the stove is an upended packing crate with a wash basin on top, next to it a (dirty) hand towel hangs from a nail. This is probably a transition cabin because it has a board floor and iron stove. Because we can see the simple ladder leading to it, it probably had a loft. The photograph is attributed to L. C. McClure, from the Denver Public Library, Western History Department.

its original state without improvements. A man might conceivably build several cabins such as this as he moved from boom site to boom site.

The Transition Log Cabin

Along the trail to Swandyke, Colorado, is an unassuming outline of logs that once was a log cabin. This was a two-room cabin with a root cellar. Pieces of an iron stove indicate that there was a stove here. A rudimentary stone foundation was evident. The roof is long gone, and so is the floor, but notches cut in the "sill" log indicate that the cabin did have a board floor at one time. The log corners were notched in a combination of saddle and steeple notching. Cabins like this one we classify as the transition between the first- and second-generation log cabins.

The transition cabin had a lot of improvements over the first-generation log cabin. More resources were available, and this is reflected in these log cabins. They had shingled roofs or roofs of corrugated metal to replace the sod roof. These cabins would also sport a much-prized wood-plank floor. They might have a second room or a sleeping loft. An iron stove would be one of the first improvements made to a log cabin to replace the inefficient fireplace. There was frequently a root cellar and more windows. Still, many of these cabins were notched in the saddle or steeple style. The log walls would have had the bark removed, and some would have been hand-hewn more or less smooth to achieve a flat interior wall.

Another pioneer recalled a new log cabin his family erected in 1875:

> The new log home was a luxurious one according to pioneer standards. It had a board floor instead of dirt; windows with panes of glass instead of white cotton cloth dipped in tallow, or covered with a gunny sack; and luxury of luxuries, a cookstove at the time when a fireplace usually did triple duty, as a heater, cooking equipment, and evening illumination. . .

In two-room cabins such as these, one room was typically a kitchen and the other a combination living room and bedroom. This two-room house became a popular structure that we often see in the backcountry.

A few pieces of furniture that might have made their way across the plains replaced some of the handmade pieces. In company towns in remote areas, new residents would simply buy the furnishings from the former occupants along with the cabin. Freighting furniture was an expensive proposition. Decades ago, when we first started exploring ghost towns in the backcountry, some of this primitive furniture would still be in place, where the former occupants had simply walked away from it.

The Second Generation

Some log structures were not built for expediency. They are beautifully wrought, like a fine piece of furniture. They were built by experienced craftsmen. Some were never chinked, their hand-hewn logs fitting so tightly together that it would be difficult to insert a knife blade between them. The second-generation log cabins are more like fine log homes than log cabins. They were more carefully built with attention paid to a style of architecture. They might well be two stories, or at least a

The Caledonia sports intricate full dovetail notching. The owner told us it was faced with boards at one time.

story and a half. A fine example of a second-generation structure would be the Caledonia Boardinghouse, near Silverton, Colorado. The building is so strong that even though the mountain is crushing the building, it still stands proudly. The structure is bowed but not broken.

Log cabins were easy to disassemble and move to a new address. This was the type of structure that would typically be moved. A first-generation or transition cabin might be easier to build anew than to go to the trouble of moving. But second-generation cabins were definitely worth the trouble, and many were moved.

Most often this type of log home was built in settlements that had passed the camp stage and had become towns. Tin Cup and St. Elmo, in Colorado, are examples of this type of town. Although they had near-death experiences, they never quite became actual ghost towns. But examples of second-generation log cabins do exist in the backcountry. However, if it is in a town like Tin Cup or St. Elmo, the building is undoubtedly still privately owned and you will not be able to tour it. And although it is tempting to press your nose to the window and look in, you'll scare the daylights out of the residents if you do.

Among the log cabins that are still standing, look for architectural details and styling. Is the front door on the side or on the gable end of the building? Are there low wood triangles over doors or windows reminiscent of classical pediments? What type of corner notching does the building have? Are the gable ends enclosed with vertical boards, or do the horizontal logs taper up to the point in the gable? If you wish to take this study further, there are books that discuss log cabin architecture.

Foundations

Today frequently what we see in the backcountry are just the remains of log cabins. The roofs are long gone and only a few courses of logs are left to suggest a building. In some places all that is left is a vague foundation.

In fact, many log cabins, particularly first-generation cabins, were hastily constructed without much thought of a foundation. Just simply clearing the vicinity of rocks and leveling it was deemed enough. But with transitional cabins we begin to see attempts at making foundations. This usually involves a single line of unmortared stones laid out in the shape of the building, but slightly larger. This rock outline would be filled

This charming second-generation log cabin's gable end is enclosed with milled wood. Note the generously sized window in front. Also, this window and the door are topped with a shallow wooden triangle — an architectural detail reminiscent of a classical pediment. This house is in a near-death-experience town and is privately owned and still occupied. Appropriate town ettiquette applies.

Above is a simple foundation of dry-stacked stone that creates a slightly raised area for the building.

with dirt, creating a slightly raised area. We often see these rough foundations in the backcountry under buildings. Sometimes at burned or otherwise destroyed sites, this rock square or rectangle is all that is left of a former building. Second-generation buildings might have more sophisticated foundations made from unmortared stone.

Root cellars were also common. These can sometimes still be seen as a scooped-out hole in the middle of a foundation. Occasionally these were rock-lined. In a root cellar a family might keep potatoes, onions, cabbages, and carrots. In the best root cellars food would last for months. But if the cabin were at too high an altitude or the root cellar ill-planned, the vegetables would freeze during the winter. The Reverend J. J. Gibbons mentioned a man near Ouray, Colorado, who slept with his potatoes at night because he feared they would freeze in his root cellar.

Above, a foundation and root cellar that were lined originally with dry-stacked stones.

176

Whether it was a large boardinghouse or a tiny log cabin, whether the buildings are standing or collapsed, the telltale signs of human habitation are the same, only the size or volume differs:

BEDSPRINGS

Old rusted bedsprings seem to survive the ravages of time quite well. Even at sites known to have burned, the bedsprings are rusted and twisted but still recognizable. There are two different types of bedsprings: the coil type, like we see on beds today, and a mesh type, pictured on the right. This advertisement is from the Montgomery Ward Catalogue #57 of 1895, reprinted with permission from Dover Publications.

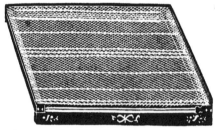

Wire Mattresses.

74740 The Regular Standard Corded Steel Wire Woven Mattresses, perfectly tight joint between end rail and bottom. No putty used. A good clean mattress. Weight, 40 pounds. Each....$1.15

177

COOKSTOVES

An old iron cookstove in a building or near it, or pieces of an old stove, could imply that someone lived here at some time. As was mentioned in the preceding chapter, installing an iron stove was one of the first improvements to be made to a cabin. Therefore, rusting iron stoves are quite common. Boardinghouses usually had large cookstoves; a tiny stove was sufficient for a small cabin. Below, there is embossing on the front edge of this old stove. It reads: Majestic Mfg Co, St Louis. On the right is an advertisement for Majestic cookstoves.

Majestic

You can cook and heat water for the entire house, with either coal or gas, or both at the same time, with the MAJESTIC Combination Coal and Gas Range.

The Highest Economy

of fuel using of either kind. Economy of kitchen space, compared to two separate stoves. One plumbing connection.

Our book, "Cost Saving," tells what you save over buying a coal and gas range separately, what you save over using them separately, what you save over buying or using any other combination range, and gives full description and prices. Address St. Louis office for it.

We make a full line of Majestic Family Coal or Wood Ranges, also Majestic Family Gas Ranges, and are the largest makers of Hotel Ranges in the world. Descriptive circular, showing style and price of any of these Majestic Ranges together with name of nearest dealer handling them, sent on application.

MAJESTIC MFG. CO., 2016 Morgan St., St. Louis, Mo.

WRITING ON THE WALLS

Always look for writing on the walls of any standing structure. This is particularly true of lodging. Below is a name written on the wall of a first generation log cabin. It reads: Jas C. Colvin, Oct 13th 1885. We suspect it is authentic and not the work of vandals because the date coincides with the gold rush to that area, and we found his name in cemetery records for that place. He died in 1889.

In both the examples shown here, the actual writing on the wall is much smaller than it appears in these photographs. We photographed them with a special lens. Above it reads: Larry L. Ewing. Uniontown, Penna. April 2 - 1905.

Besides these things, it is written in pencil. Authentic writing on the walls is never written in ink. Also, authentic writing is faded and small, not huge scrawls meant to be seen, like what vandals do. And it frequently has an old fashioned look about it as this example does: The lettering is almost like calligraphy with carefully executed scrolling letters.

ROOT CELLARS AND FOUNDATIONS

Foundations of dry-stacked stone can often be seen, such as that on the right. Walls from unmortared stone are also common. Many have stood for a century and remain in remarkably good shape. Arthur C. Todd, in his book *The Cornish Miner in America,* attributed many of these walls and foundations to the Cornish miners who were also talented masons.

A stone-lined root cellar was the nineteenth-century equivalent of a refrigerator. At sites where only the foundation is left, the root cellar might appear to be a scooped-out hole in the middle of the foundation like the one below. At large boardinghouses there might be a full foundation or basement.

DEBRIS

Antique household artifacts around a structure or near the foundation of a former structure is a dead giveaway that someone lived there at some time. Typically, the debris spills down the mountain away from a structure as in the picture below.

It is here, among the debris, that you will discover fragments of a bygone era like the shadowgee, left, that was discussed in more detail in Chapter 1.

There is nothing that tells you so much about people as what they left behind. Chapter 13 explores this subject in depth.

12

LODGING:
COMPANY BOARDINGHOUSES

People of today do not realize how hardy men had to be to live in a steamy,
smelly bunkhouse with 200 or more grimy men in damp clothes coming
and going continuously with hob-nailed boots and with no place to go
other than down that wet shaft, to the bunkhouse and boardinghouse or
outdoors into 10 or 12 feet of snow slides and work for 10 hours with
heavy hand tools.

— J. T. Pearson, from a plaque in a Ouray Museum

 Few places are left on earth as high and remote as the Old Hundred boardinghouse near Silverton, Colorado. It clings tenuously to a talus slope so high
above timberline that even eagles have to look up at it. The Old Hundred is
the type of mining camp building we had always dreamed of finding. First of
all, this rambling old building is still standing, which is unusual. And since it is so difficult
and even dangerous to get to, we held high hopes that it would be virtually untouched.
Would it be a time capsule inside — everything exactly as the miners had left it when they
closed the door behind them and left so many years before?

It took several summers to obtain permission to visit the site and gather our courage for the
difficult trek to the structure. The trip there was the most dangerous we have attempted.

When we finally slipped and stumbled down the last of the talus slope, the Old Hundred
boardinghouse loomed before us in all its Victorian glory: a seemingly misplaced structure
defying gravity in an unlikely place. The three-story building (including the basement) faced
a spectacular alpine view. Dormer windows punctuated the gabled roof. Sweeping the front
of the building was that Victorian necessity, a spindly front porch. The corrugated iron
siding was the only concession to practicality. The Old Hundred boardinghouse gave new
meaning to the words "High Victorian."

But it was in worse shape than we had hoped. The roof had been smashed by snow a couple
of years before, dropping the second floor down onto the first. All the exterior wood was
spongy and soft, and the porch was mossy and laced with holes. Animals had chewed nearly
through the basement support beams, leaving the structure in danger of losing its toehold
and plunging down the mountain at any moment.

The Old Hundred upper boarding-house today.

The Old Hundred was laid out just as many of these old boardinghouses were: Downstairs were offices, the dining hall, and the kitchen. Upstairs were the sleeping quarters. The surprise was the old-fashioned (even by the Old Hundred's standards) built-in wooden bunks. There were twenty-five of these bunks in all. In such arrangements, two men usually shared a bunk per shift, and a mine's crew slept in shifts. The sleeping arrangements were nearly primitive, yet the edges of these bunks at the Old Hundred were painstakingly scalloped — a charming but typically Victorian attention to beauty and pride of workmanship rather than to comfort.

Because of this, the Old Hundred is an example of an old-style company boardinghouse, but on a grand scale. It could be called Early Mining Camp Renaissance. Those built-in bunks in a large,

The wooden bunks had shelves inside for personal items. One bed had a horseshoe no longer than an inch hung on the inside wall. Another had written in pencil a tiny name and date which coincided with the dates the mine operated.

184

open, barnlike room were direct descendants of the first lodging houses to be erected during a boom.

The Old Hundred when new. Denver Public Library, Western History Department.

The Evolution of the Company Boardinghouse

When the cry of "Gold!" first rang out in a region, hundreds and sometimes thousands of hopefuls immediately poured into the area. Each of these men needed a place to eat and sleep. At first, travelers would pay for the privilege of throwing a blanket on the floor of a saloon or a general store. Soon an enterprising business-man would erect a huge tent and convert it into an instant hotel. Such was the case at Leadville in 1878. A tent that had served time at the Centennial Exhibition in the East was hastily pressed into service as sleeping quarters.

The tent phase didn't last long. If the gold held out and the boom continued, simple wooden structures replaced the tents. Ernest Ingersoll described one of these structures, the Mammoth Sleeping Palace, in the October 1879 issue of *Scribner's Monthly:* "Among the first in Leadville there happened to be a merchant who . . .

The Mammoth Sleeping Palace could sleep 500 men a night, as pictured in Scribner's Monthly. *Sagstetter collection.*

built a vast shed of slabs and filled it with rows of [wooden] bunks, two tiers high, capable of accommodating 500 sleepers nightly. . . . He furnished a bed for fifty cents, and posted his rules: No talking or laughing, or singing, or drinking."

Wherever mining camps were short of lumber during a boom, they simply used stretched canvas instead. Sometimes a building's roof would be canvas, sometimes a few private rooms would be partitioned off from dormitory bunks by stretching canvas walls. Whole towns would end up constructed partly of wood, partly of canvas. Dame Shirley described them as "rag cities" as early as the California Gold Rush in her letters.

But sleeping conditions were less than ideal in these early lodging houses. Travelers' accounts at the time describe some of these as being infested with bedbugs and the noise of several hundred men snoring at the same time as being thunderous.

If several larger mines developed in the same area and a town grew up to service them, the miners had their choice of private boardinghouses in town. But if a mining operation was in a remote location, the company had no choice but to provide lodging for the men it employed. Such was the case at the Old Hundred. It is these lonely outposts that fascinate us. These are the boardinghouses that are remote even today.

The first company boardinghouses were log versions of the Mammoth Sleeping Palace — simple bunkhouses with tiers of wooden bunks lining the sides. Just as in early private establishments, a man would provide his own bedding, and the establishment would provide the mattress. Sometimes the mess hall would be in the same building, but at other times the mess hall was a separate but still primitive log structure nearby.

Comfort wasn't really a consideration. Duane Smith in his book *Song of the Hammer and Drill,* quoted a mining engineer's description of the North Star Mine's bunkhouse near Silverton, Colorado, circa 1880. Eben Olcott described one large open room in which hams and bags of coffee and sugar jostled picks and shovels for space along with a stove, dining table and double wooden bunks three tiers high. Twenty men lived out of this single room. It must have seemed as though the men were merely being stored here between shifts, along with the equipment. And the corrugated iron buildings were "an oven in summer and an ice box in the winter," even if the corrugated siding did help to fireproof the building.

A stove in the middle of the room struggled to provide heat. "I am alternately freezing one half or other for the stove has no effect upon that side turned away from it," Olcott wrote home. And worse, after a shift the miners would pile their

Many early structures were built from a combination of canvas and logs. Harper's Weekly, *Sagstetter collection.*

187

wet boots around the stove to dry and then light up "a vile pipe." The smell must have been daunting.

Cleanliness wasn't really a consideration, either. Tobacco juice mixed with the mud on the floors. Flies were a real problem. And there was no hiding place safe from the pack rats. The men even had to build screened cages for food storage to keep rodents out of the food.

The larger mining companies quickly figured out that the better the accommodations, the more stable their work crew. Better living conditions also attracted the best miners. Most important of all, a well-run company boardinghouse could actually turn a profit. Hence, good accommodations became good business.

Some writers claim that the Camp Bird Mine boardinghouse near Ouray, Colorado, was the turning point in the evolution of company boardinghouses. And because the owner of the Camp Bird had at one time been an innkeeper, this might well be true.

Thomas Walsh, owner of the Camp Bird Mine, believed that if he treated his miners right, later, when talk of strikes came up, his men would treat him right. Therefore, he spared no expense when he built what is thought to be the first "miner's hotel," instead of a typical primitive company boardinghouse. Walsh insisted on individual bedrooms upstairs, two men to a room. No double wooden bunks for these men: Each man slept on his own iron bedstead with springs. Indoor bathrooms offered hot water for showers. A library was kept stocked with books, magazines, and newspapers. There were no tin plates and cups — the nearly two hundred men ate from hotel china. The cook plied his trade on a giant cast-iron cookstove stretching sixteen feet that was so big it had three fireboxes in a row. The Camp Bird boardinghouse was as well appointed as any fine hotel in its day.

Walsh's daughter, Evalyn Walsh McLean, described the boardinghouse in her book, *Father Struck it Rich:*

> Now I saw it: A great barracks three stories high and more than two hundred feet long, designed to keep its numerous, restless tenants comfortable in all the extremes of mountain cold and heat. Its walls and ceilings were tongued and grooved woodwork, glossy with varnish. The floors were hardwood, kept waxed and polished. . . There was marble in the lavatories, and the bathrooms were of porcelain, as fine as any I had ever seen. . . Against the walls were platoons of brackets supporting the shining reflectors of oil lamps, but over every table there dangled an electric light bulb — ugly but impressive in 1899.

The "miners' hotel" type of lodging was an idea whose time had come. Other remote large mines quickly built their own miners' hotels. By the turn of the century game rooms with pool tables appeared at the larger, most successful mines, such as the Union-Smuggler Mine above Telluride, Colorado. And the nearby Tomboy Mine boardinghouse boasted of a first-aid room staffed by a doctor and a nurse. But these amenities were still the exception rather than the rule. Smaller mines could not afford such luxuries, and their accommodations remained spartan. In fact, we see far more examples of these small, primitive company boardinghouses in our backcountry travels than we do of the large miners' hotels. And although even the small mines abandoned the concept of built-in wooden bunks in favor of individual beds, the sleeping quarters at some of the smaller mines were still large open rooms.

When travelers found themselves in the vicinity of one of these remote mining operations, they were welcomed at the company boardinghouse and paid the same price as a miner, usually a dollar a day for food and lodging.

The inhabitants of the company boardinghouses were men, most of them single. A few married men, whose wives were far away, also stayed there — including recent immigrants whose families were back in the old country. These men worked ten-hour shifts seven days a week. In the large company boardinghouses, no guns or alcohol were allowed on the premises. The management sometimes went to great lengths to enforce the rules.

In most of the American West the boardinghouses operated on the American Plan. Both food and lodging were included in the price of the American Plan. But on the West Coast, particularly in California and Nevada mining towns, a miner slept in one place and dined somewhere else in town, paying for each service separately. This was called the European Plan.

The Most Important Person in Camp

Not the superintendent. Not the assayer. Not even the mine owner. The most important man in camp was the cook. When the miners themselves were not yet unionized, the cooks and their helpers were. And at the larger mines, these cooks were no slouches. The head cook at the remote Sunnyside Mine boardinghouse once worked at a fancy New York hotel.

The miners accepted the dangerousness of their work and its difficulties. And if accommodations seem overly primitive to us today, they might have been consid-

Note the prominent position of the cooks, front and center. Of the hundreds of archival pictures we studied in the libraries and historical societies, camp cooks were often placed in a place of honor. Denver Public Library, Western History Department.

ered merely average then. But there was one thing miners would not compromise on — food. Miners were passionate about good food. Even gourmet food. And they demanded huge quantities of it.

Boardinghouse food has been much maligned. And in the earliest days of a boom, when supplies were iffy and no fresh vegetables could be had at any price, perhaps that reputation was well earned. Many gold rushers despaired of the inevitable dried-apple pies that were commonly served as dessert in early boomtowns.

Apparently, boardinghouse food was pretty darn good. T. A. Rickard, a respected mine engineer from Europe, had been involved in mine operations all over the world by the turn of the century. He had this to say about mine boardinghouse food in the American West:

> It will not be out of place to refer to the food that miners get in localities like these; it is surprisingly good, as a rule, even at mines which are a couple of miles above sea-level and a corresponding distance from the main distributing points for provisions. The companies usually charge one dollar per day for board and lodging, where the standard wages are $3 per shift. The fare which the miner gets three times a day is superior to that

of the second-class hotel of the neighboring mining towns and far better
than that which is the daily portion of workmen in other countries. There
is always one weak spot — the coffee; . . . it is a concoction out of
keeping with the excellence of the remainder of the miner's fare and
much better adapted for staining floors or removing boiler-scale.

Miners were always a transient group. It took very little to irritate a man enough to
pack up and leave. Otis Young, in his *Western Mining,* said that something as
earthshaking as his pancakes being "a little out-of-round" could set a miner off and
packing to another mine. Smart mine superintendents made sure their men were
well fed.

Perhaps what is more telling is what happened when the food *wasn't* good. One
miner applied for work at a mine, but there weren't any mining jobs available. The
only job unfilled was that of cook, so he took that job just until something opened
up underground. Unfortunately for all the miner's, he didn't know anything about
cooking. His new job only lasted a few days. At first the miners grumbled vocifer-
ously. But the day he burned the bread and forgot to cook the roast, open warfare
erupted. The new cook quit before he was run out of the camp by the angry miners.

At another camp, when the men complained about the food, the cook grabbed a
butcher knife and flourished it in the face of each one of the one hundred miners
until every one of them had admitted that he was indeed a good cook.

Few boardinghouse menus survive. Those that do are generally for a celebration or
special occasion. The best examples of everyday menus are in two books by Anne
Ellis, *The Life of an Ordinary Woman* and *Plain Anne Ellis.* She was a miner's widow
who worked as a camp cook shortly after the turn of the century. This was unusual;
most camp cooks were men. One of her jobs was cooking for seventy-five sheep-
herders and shearers in a boardinghouse in southwestern Colorado. She says the
"food was carefully selected, cooked and decorated as though we were in an expensive hotel." She had two assistants, both young girls, and their preparations for
breakfast started at 4:00 A.M. Rarely did they get to bed before 10:00 P.M. On the
following page are menus culled from her two books. Every day, three times a day,
they faced preparing these meals on two old-fashioned wood- or coal-burning
ranges.

These menus are a testimony to how hard these working men toiled. It took an
enormous number of calories to maintain the energy level of men who were single-
and double-jacking for ten hours a day. And in remote locations, there weren't
many other physical comforts available. The men might face hardships daily, but
they would eat well, by damn!

Breakfast

    Oatmeal or some other hot grain cereal

    Two slabs of bacon or ham

    Huge pans of fried potatoes

    Large pans of biscuits, refilled again and again

    Condensed milk in cans on the tables, some diluted in pitchers

    Stewed fruit (stewed dried fruit when fresh was unavailable)

    Syrup

    Preserves

    Cookies

    Coffee cake or doughnuts

    Dozens and dozens of eggs, fried and boiled

    Huge pots of coffee

    Sugar and butter on each table

Lunch (or "dinner," as it was then called) was the biggest meal of the day. Preparation for it started immediately after Anne and her two assistants had finished washing all the white enameled plates the men ate from at breakfast.

    Soup

    Meat and gravy

    Potatoes

    Vegetables

    Hot homemade rolls

    Twenty pies (more than a quarter-pie per person!)

    Butter and preserves

    Coffee

Supper was much the same as lunch, but without soup. It was not usually as big a meal as dinner.

    Meat and gravy

    Potatoes

    Vegetables

    Pan after pan of cornbread

    Cakes, carefully iced, decorated on special occasions

    Butter and preserves

    Coffee

On Sundays they made lemon meringue pies and plates of candy as a special treat.

Unbelievably, at one point the shearers complained they were not getting hearty enough food! They wanted more "strengthening" meals, and demanded steaks twice a day.

MEALTIME IN A TYPICAL COMPANY BOARDINGHOUSE

So what was mealtime like in a typical company boardinghouse? What follows is a composite of several descriptions of mealtime.

The tables are laden with heaping serving bowls of food before the meal is called. These will be passed around once the meal is underway. Then, at the proper time, the doors to the dining room are flung open and a hundred hobnail-booted feet thunder to benches beside the long tables. The seats of all the work pants barely touch the bench before a hundred calloused hands reach for those serving bowls. Food is piled high on the plates.

Amid loud slurping and chomping noises, helpers frantically run to and from the kitchen in a futile attempt to keep these serving bowls full. These men waste no time in chitchat or etiquette; they approach mealtime as serious business, and mountains of food are dispatched forthwith.

Before most people would have finished sipping their soup, these men are already starting on dessert. And then it is over as quickly as it started. The room empties as though someone had pulled a stopper and drained it. The entire process, from the time the doors are flung open until the hobnail boots pound their way out those doors again, might take only five minutes.

Harper's Weekly *captioned this engraving "Dinner in a Logging Camp in the Northwest by John Durkin." Lumber camps and mining camps had much in common. Sagstetter collection.*

The dining rooms of the old company boardinghouses we have visited all have many similarities. The only difference is in the scope. Even small dining rooms had a long plank table. On each side of the table would be a bench with notched legs. Larger boardinghouses would have many tables and benches. The furniture was simple, sturdy, and usually unfinished.

The Writing on the Walls

We see the remains of their work. We see the places where they lived. But are there no clues left about the miners themselves? *Adventures at Timberline,* by Jack Foster, describes a trip to the Old Hundred upper boardinghouse in the early nineteen-fifties. Jack and his wife arrived to find "rat-chewed" magazines and catalogs still lying on tabletops. Thumbing through them they noticed certain items had been checked. One of those checkmarked items was a wedding dress. Every now and then we find references to the inner workings of the minds of the miners — possibly a window to their dreams — and get a sense for why they were in the camps. The Fosters found other markings as well, but these were penciled on the wall. One miner had written "This is Hell. We started to heaven and landed square in Hell."

Nearly forty years later, when we arrived at the Old Hundred boardinghouse, we explored the tabletops to find that the magazines and catalogs were gone. The rats must have finished them off entirely. We also searched for the writing on the wall the Fosters had reported but couldn't find it. We suspect the marking was somewhere on the collapsed second floor that we were unable to study.

But we did find other writing inside the bunks, in the closest thing to privacy these men knew. Some of the men had personalized the insides of the wooden bunks. A few of the bunks had shelves to hold personal items. One man had hung a tiny horseshoe, not more than one inch in length, on the wall of his wooden bunk. Beside it was a penciled name. The horseshoe is a symbol of good luck, and we frequently find them at mining-camp sites.

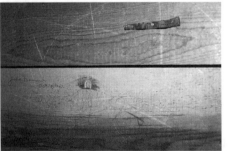

The inside of one bunk had been personalized with a strip of leather and a tiny horseshoe, presumably for luck. A nearby name reads John Bernard, Oct. 14, 1907.

Because of that experience, we now are very careful to look for writing on the walls whenever we explore boardinghouses. The miners must have made notes on the walls quite often, because we frequently find them. Sometimes these are notations: "Joe owes Fred $2." Perhaps a loan or gambling debt. Sometimes the writings are names and dates, thereby helping us to approximately date an unknown site. Once, we found an etching

The boarding-house at Alta, Colorado.

of a woman's head on the wall of an old boardinghouse. In California these can sometimes be found carved on trees. They were called "Miner's Nellies."

Although there might also be modern graffiti nearby, it's easy to tell the difference between recent graffiti from vandalism and the original, authentic writings of miners. Modern vandalism is always hugely lettered in paint or carved. The old miners' writing is always tiny, written in pencil, and is never scrawled in large letters. In order to see the miner's markings on the wall you have to work hard — it will not catch your eye at a casual glance like modern graffiti will.

The most intriguing miner's writing we ever found was at the boardinghouse at the deserted mining camp of Alta, Colorado. This is a fine example of a miners' hotel, with individual bedrooms upstairs. Today those individual bedrooms are bare — no beds remain. The walls are raw unfinished wood. But there are smudges on the walls that suggest where the beds might originally have been.

All through these individual rooms on the second floor modern vandals had scrawled the usual graffiti. But against one unfinished wall, right at what would have been bunk level, were some markings that were distinctly different from the rest. A pencil had been used, and the letters were tiny, as though they were not

Long columns of numbers on the wall of the Alta boardinghouse.

meant to draw attention to themselves. It consisted of columns of numbers carefully executed in small scrolled figures. The handwriting had an old-fashioned look about it — ornate, with a period after nearly every word, similar to the handwriting of our grandfathers' era. Each double column of numbers was headed by a month, one of which was spelled "Oktober," and was dated 1919. At the bottom the writer identified himself as from Finland but did not record his name. We checked our research and found the mine was indeed operating in 1919. But we were stumped as to what the long columns of numbers meant.

It wasn't until several years later that we had the opportunity to show the writing on the wall to a retired miner friend of ours. Ed Van Westenberg took one look at the columns of numbers and exclaimed, "Why, he was a contract miner! He was keeping his own records here — to make sure the company was honest!" A contract miner didn't work for a daily wage. He bid a job and worked for himself. Ed told us he had liked contract mining work, for an industrious man could make good money at it. The list of numbers on the wall increased daily by about eight. Ed surmised that this man was actually timbering the mine and that he timbered eight feet of tunnel per shift.

The rows of numbers continued only four months — during the last month the numbers stopped partway through. Did our timbering Finn pick up and leave for another mine? Or did he decide the company was fair and simply stop keeping his own records? Were there a wife and children waiting for him back in Finland? Since he didn't record his name for us, we will never know any more about him than this. But this faceless man, a long way from Finland, symbolizes all those who worked the mines so long ago. They came from all points of the globe, searching and striving for a better way of life for themselves and their families.

Now we always check buildings for writings on the walls. The writings can take several forms. Sometimes the walls were papered with newsprint. Looking over what remains of these newspapers, we sometimes can find a date, thereby helping to pinpoint when the building was occupied.

At the Old Hundred boardinghouse we found yet another example of writing on the walls. Each timber, each board that was used in the construction of the building was numbered. Apparently the building materials were cut and numbered at the bottom of the mountain. Then the pieces were sent up on the aerial tram to be erected at the site, by the numbers.

In the Basement

Very few old boardinghouses actually had basements. Many barely had what could pass as a foundation. Most sat right on the dirt, particularly the smaller boarding-houses. Ed Van Westenberg had told us that in some boardinghouses a Chinese man was employed to keep the place clean. He would live in a room in the base-ment. We did in fact find a room in a boardinghouse basement once — it was in one of the larger miner's hotels. The basement was dirty and spider-infested, as we had expected. In the corner of the basement was a room with a closed door. When we pushed the door open, we were surprised to find a room that was still neat even today, whitewashed and clean. A single bed took up most of this room, and there were nails around the perimeter of the room to hang clothes on, and shelves, for closets were unheard of. Had a Chinese man occupied this small, neat room? We felt quite confident *someone* had lived in this tiny room, but we could find no indication of who it might have been.

The beams at the Old Hundred had numbers painted on them. These were probably remnants of when the building had been created in the valley below, and then sent up the tram to be as-sembled at the site.

197

13

LODGING:
THE TELLTALE CLUES

To see a World in a Grain of Sand

And a Heaven in a Wild Flower

Hold infinity in the palm of your hand

And Eternity in an hour

— William Blake, "Auguries of Innocence"

 The trail ascended a narrow and heavily wooded valley. Up we kept going, never seeing a campsite. Darkness wasn't far away, and we were getting worried. Imagine our delight when we spotted a surprisingly level grassy area complete with a fire ring overlooking the tumbling mountain stream. We reveled in our good fortune of finding such an ideal place as we hurried to set up camp. Later, as we headed down the slope at the edge of the meadow to get water from the creek, we stumbled across antique household debris. Hundreds of rusted, crumpled tin cans spilled down the slope to the creek. Among them were bits of gnarled leather hobnailed boots, a few battered pots and pans, shards of china, and a bleached animal bone or two.

The water forgotten, we headed back up to our camp in the meadow for a closer look. Had we missed something? Upon closer scrutiny, we realized that the moss-covered stones that had looked perfectly natural a few minutes before now looked as though they had actually been laid out in a large, neat rectangle. We had often seen crude foundations such as this under cabins.

The volume of debris and the huge size of the rough foundation led us to believe we might have stumbled across the site of a former boardinghouse. We knew from the history books that this area had been a thriving mining district in the 1880s. All around us were the weathered remains of forgotten mining operations. The Mary Murphy Mine, the largest of them, was about a mile below us on the trail.

But did this old place burn or was it dismantled and moved? As was discussed earlier, the old log buildings were very easy to dismantle and move when mining activity shifted to a new area. It happened all the time.

199

All that remained of the former building was a stone outline of its foundation.

Just at that point we spotted a smooth stone that was nearly translucent on one side. When we picked it up we realized this was no stone. It was a fist-sized glob of melted glass. Our impression was that it had been a bottle. Even the color was right — it was the pale aqua of old glass left out in the sun. But it would take an awfully hot fire to melt a bottle down to this size and shape. We looked even more closely around the site. Scattered around and near the old foundation and hidden beneath the grass we found rusted nails, some square, others round. And metal fittings for roof beams. And the round metal holders for window shades. These were bits of a building that probably would have gone with it if it had been moved but would have been just as we found them if it had burned.

We suspect this old structure had probably burned. And even though all that remains is a "footprint" of a foundation, the antique debris told us there had indeed been a building here at one time and that people had lived in it.

Through devastating fires, through a century of crushing snows, through avalanches, even through intense visitation, there is one thing that survives: rubbish. Whether it was a huge company boardinghouse or a rude log cabin, if people lived

200

there, more than likely there will be a trash heap. In fact, if the site is one of the many that burned to the ground, the trash pile might be the only thing to survive.

Today you have to look closely to even find the household debris. The tin cans have rusted to the color of the mountain. Indian paintbrush sprout among the shards of broken china. But once you find what people left behind, it speaks volumes about who lived here.

Granted, finding antique household debris is not as thrilling a prospect as discovering a three-story boardinghouse clinging to the face of a cliff. But an extensive rubbish pile can actually have more to say about the former inhabitants than an empty building. And the information is more personal than the information offered by a building. Where else could you learn that smoking a pipe was a favorite pastime for a miner?

In remote areas, household debris was generally heaved down the mountainside from the door of the structure. This was particularly true of the kitchen refuse. Rusted tin cans, old pots and pans, and shards of dishes frequently mark the

Antique household debris around a former building is a sign that someone lived here at one time.

location of the mess hall at a company boardinghouse. The more debris, the more people who came to supper each night or the longer the place was inhabited.

Some of the larger mining camps had a specific place for the community to discard items. Caribou and Alta, in Colorado, are like that. But we have found the community site to be the exception rather than the rule.

Once the discard site has been located, a stroll through it reveals individual artifacts that are clues to what went on here and when. There is no need to dig; there will be plenty of clues left lying where they were last tossed, waiting to tell their story.

Certain articles show up consistently in most mining-camp discard sites. These artifacts give us a certain picture of nineteenth-century mining-camp life: what was eaten and smoked, what was worn, what tools were used, how certain objects were recycled. Classic mining-camp debris typically includes rusted tin cans, gnarled black scraps of hobnailed boots, old pots and pans and household gadgets, glass and china shards, and animal bones.

Tin Cans

Of all the debris to be found at a site, the most common artifact by far is the tin can. Yet when understood, this humble object is a potential gold mine of information.

The idea of canning food came about in the struggle to feed the armies of the world. Napoleon nearly lost a battle because some of his men were plundering the surrounding countryside for whatever food they could find. These men returned just in time to reinforce their comrades and win the battle, but it was a little too close for comfort. Napoleon offered a prize of twelve thousand francs to anyone who could invent a process for keeping food fresh.

A French chef, Nicholas Appert, won that prize in 1809. Appert successfully processed food in champagne bottles. (No wide-mouthed glass jars would be available until 1858, when they were first patented. Appert later resorted to making his own wide-mouthed jars for canning purposes.) Even though Napoleon tried to keep canning a military secret, it was an idea whose time had come. Within a decade, similar techniques had been patented in England and then in the United States. For commercial applications, bottles or jars did not work out well, and most food processors quickly turned to tin-plated canisters, or tin cans.

In the United States, the growth in the use of canned food was, in fact, closely aligned with the gold rushes. At the time of the California gold rush, canning in tin cans was a fledgling industry. Its growth had been slow, held back by consumers' concern for wholesomeness. This was long before the Food and Drug Administration existed, and most people feared the contents of tin cans might be tainted.

Also dampening growth was the idea that processed foods were a luxury item. Tin cans were expensive because they were handmade by skilled tinsmiths. And the first food to be processed was fish, allowing landlocked diners to enjoy something they might not have otherwise — herring, lobster, and oysters. Later, inhabitants of northern climes could enjoy pineapple and grapefruit at any time of the year. Processed food was a small, almost inconsequential luxury market.

That all changed when gold was discovered in California in 1848. Suddenly the need for nonperishable food exploded. Armies of hungry prospectors made processed food a necessity, not a luxury, and they were willing and able to pay high prices for it.

Now food that was grown in the Midwest could be processed and canned in, say, Cincinnati, taken to the coast, and placed on a clipper ship bound for the gold-fields. After spending months on board ship rounding South America, the food would arrive in the bay of San Francisco in perfectly edible condition. In fact, as early as 1850 California newspapers complained of being buried under tons of rusting tin cans. By 1859 the Colorado Pikes Peak gold rush provided additional impetus to food processors. Thus the canned food industry helped keep the miners alive, and the miners kept the food-processing industry alive until the Civil War took over the role the miners had filled.

The earliest tin cans were completely handmade at the food-processing factory. First an iron sheet was plated in tin and cut into strips as wide as the height of the can and the length of its circumference. This strip made up the sides of the can. Then a top and bottom were laboriously snipped out of another tin-plated sheet. A skilled tinsmith then hand-soldered the side seam using lead solder. Next he soldered the top and bottom to the can body. The top of the can consisted of two pieces — the lid, which had a hole in it to admit the contents of the can, and a cap to fit over that hole once the can was filled. These

A hole-and-cap tin can. The solder looks whitish against the dark rust of the can. Note how it looks handmade — The solder is uneven and there are drips.

An early factory scene where workers construct hole-and-cap tin cans from metal sheets. This is thought to be Empson's in Longmont, Colorado, possibly before World War One. Sagstetter collection.

pieces — the completed can body and its cap — were then sent to the food-processing part of the plant to be filled.

After the tin-plated canister was filled with food, the cap was soldered over the hole. In the center of this cap there was a tiny pinhole. When the can and its contents were heated as part of the canning process, the steam escaped through the hole. At the proper time, a dab of solder was applied over the pinhole and the processing was complete. After the can was labeled, it was ready for market. This type of can was called a "hole-and-cap" tin can. The hole-and-cap tin cans remained the norm until after the turn of the century.

On the left pieces of tops of hole-and-cap cans showing the holes in the lid and the cap that fit over it. On the right, a complete can except for its missing cap.

204

When the Civil War began in 1861, an army again became the impetus behind a new explosion in the need for large quantities of processed food. This time it was the Union Army. And one of the products to benefit most was condensed milk.

Gail Borden patented a way to can sweetened milk. Below is an advertisement for his product, dated 1911. The bottom picture is of the man who developed a way to can milk without sugar.

BORDEN'S EAGLE BRAND CONDENSED MILK

Gail Borden had struggled for several years to find a way to process milk and can it. After several failures, in 1856 he was finally issued a patent for a method where the milk was heated with sugar as a preservative. This product did well in the goldfields. Well enough that Borden had just enlarged his factory when the Civil War began. Like Napoleon, the Union Army saw the value of canned food — especially milk — in feeding its men and bought Borden's newly remodeled factory. Borden promptly set about building a new factory. And it was a good thing he did. The sweet canned milk became a favorite with the soldiers. When these men later returned home, they were able to vouch for the wholesomeness of the product. Gail Borden's Eagle Brand condensed milk quickly became a best-seller.

A way to can milk without sugar as a preservative was not patented until 1884. Swiss-born John B. Meyenberg invented the process, and unsweetened canned milk was first introduced by the Helvetia Milk Condensing Company that same year. But the technology was inconsistent and the customers hesitant. It was not until shortly after the turn of the century that sales of unsweetened condensed milk overtook that of the sweetened version.

The "open-top" tin can was introduced in 1904, and can-making would never be the same again. The open-top can is the modern tin can as we know it. The lids of these tin cans

JOHN B. MEYENBERG
INVENTOR
EVAPORATED
MILK

MEYENBERG
MM
BRAND
EVAPORATED
UNSWEETENED
MILK

The first open-top can, introduced by the Sanitary Can Company in 1904.

are one piece and have no solder on them at all. Open-top cans were produced entirely by machine. The end pieces of the can were interfolded with the sides of the can and then flattened. A sealing compound (not solder) between the folds made it water-tight. In the field, this tin can appears to have no solder on it whatsoever.

The open-top cans were first produced by the Sanitary Can Company, a name that was probably chosen to ease any lingering fears consumers had about canned food. These tin cans have the word "Sanitary" embossed on the bottom. American Can Company bought the Sanitary Can Company in 1908, and the name "Sanitary" lapsed into a generic term for "open-top" tin can.

So was all this early canned food tasty? Apparently not. Although the early canned foods tasted darn good when compared to the alternatives available in that day and age, by today's standards they wouldn't be considered very good. Food-processing techniques have come a long way.

The Language of Tin Cans in the Field

Have you ever *really* looked at a tin can before? Studied it? We hadn't. At a cursory glance, the old tin cans don't look a lot different from those of today. A vegetable can from a hundred years ago is roughly the same size and shape as a vegetable can of today that holds approximately fifteen ounces. But close scrutiny reveals many differences between them — enough to easily determine whether we are looking at antique trash or modern trash.

The most obvious difference is between hole-and-cap cans and open-top cans. Solder ages differently from the rest of the can — it appears whitish against the rusted can body. Thus, the cap and its pinhole in hole-and-cap cans are clearly outlined in solder, making them easy to spot in the field. Open-top cans do not appear to have solder on them and look exactly like tin cans of today. Hole-and-cap cans in a trash pile date its last occupation to before 1904. Sites comprised solely of open-top cans are dated sometime after 1904.

But hole-and-cap cans were made from about the 1830s until after the turn of the twentieth century. Are cans that were made during the Civil War different from cans made in 1890? Yes they are. And it is possible to roughly date a site to within a decade or so by studying the tin cans that were in use at the time. However, keep in mind that there were always a few technological holdouts who preferred to do things "the old way."

The earliest cans were heavy, because they were made of tin-plated iron. Steel began being used in the 1880s, and the cans became lighter in weight. On the earliest of cans, the individual pieces did not fit tightly together because they were hand-cut. Solder filled in all the gaps between the parts, also contributing to the surprising weight of the piece. All seams were thick and lumpy. It's not unusual to see a raw edge of metal sticking out slightly above a seam. In short, these cans have a hand-made look about them.

Later, as the parts on the tin cans were stamped out of tin-plated-steel sheets, the pieces were more uniform and fit together better, requiring less and less solder. By the mid-1890s, only the solder on the hole and cap is obvious.

The cans on the ends are hole-and-cap cans. Note how they differ from the center can, which is an early open-top can.

It was the forgotten little mining camp of Rexford, Colorado, that would establish a baseline for us in the technology of nineteenth century tin cans. Scattered across the

American West are the remains of many company towns like Rexford. The outlines of a half a dozen buildings remain as either a heap of boards or a few courses of logs. In Rexford, the only frame building was supposed to have been a general store, but today it's impossible to tell from the pile of boards what its original purpose was. To the untrained eye Rexford looks uninteresting, and perhaps because of that it has remained surprisingly untouched.

But an eagle eye quickly spots the trash pile, and it is this that makes Rexford and all the camps like it so interesting. Rexford was only inhabited from 1880 to about 1884, and the trash heap is full of excellent examples of the hole-and-cap tin cans that were made in those years.

The early 1880s are important because technological advances in tin-can making during that decade were so far-reaching that it became a separate industry. Most food processors switched during the eighties from making their own tin cans to buying the completed can bodies and their caps from an increasingly automated tin-can maker. But the cans still had to be capped in the food processor's plant after being filled. In the field today, this translates into a can body and a can cap that display different types of soldering techniques.

Visiting a site like Rexford — one that's seen only limited visitation, that was inhabited for a specific and short period of time and was never reinhabited at a later date — teaches us how the fruit and vegetable tin cans appeared in the early 1880s, when the industry was poised for massive changes.

How did an early 1880s fruit or vegetable tin can differ from later tin cans? From Rexford we learned that the key is in the side-seam seal. The side-seam edges of the can bodies in the late 1870s and early 1880s were overlapped, and then a neat, thick ribbon of solder covering the overlap sealed it. The technique is consistent enough from can to can to have been

Above, the sides of the tin cans of the 1870s and early 1880s were simply lapped over one another and then sealed with a wide swath of solder.

Below, Norton's 1887 side seam created a side seam that had no visible solder.

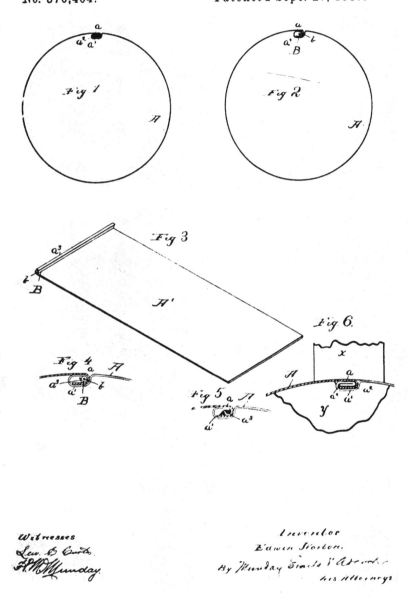

E. NORTON.

SHEET METAL CAN AND THE ART OF MANUFACTURING THE SAME.

No. 370,404.   Patented Sept. 27, 1887.

done at least partially by machine. But the caps and the pin holes were a different matter entirely. The solder job around the caps looks almost crude to our machine-age eyes: It is uneven, smeared, lumpy, and there are drips of solder on other parts of the can. The caps were being applied by a different technology at the food-processing plant. This was a state-of-the-art tin can from the late 1870s to just before 1890.

Hole-and-Cap, Simple Lap Side Seam. The earliest tin cans look handmade. They have a hole-and-cap top and a side seam that is simply overlapped and heavily soldered.

Hole-and-Cap, Norton's 1887 Side Seam. In 1887, Norton's new side seam changed the seam to a neat crease with no visible solder. But the hole-and-cap top remained unchanged.

Open-Top with a side seam that looks like Norton's 1887 Side Seam. In 1904, the open-top can was introduced by the Sanitary Can Company. The top was one piece. The side seam looked the same as Norton's 1887 side seam. No solder is visible anywhere on the can.

Timeline

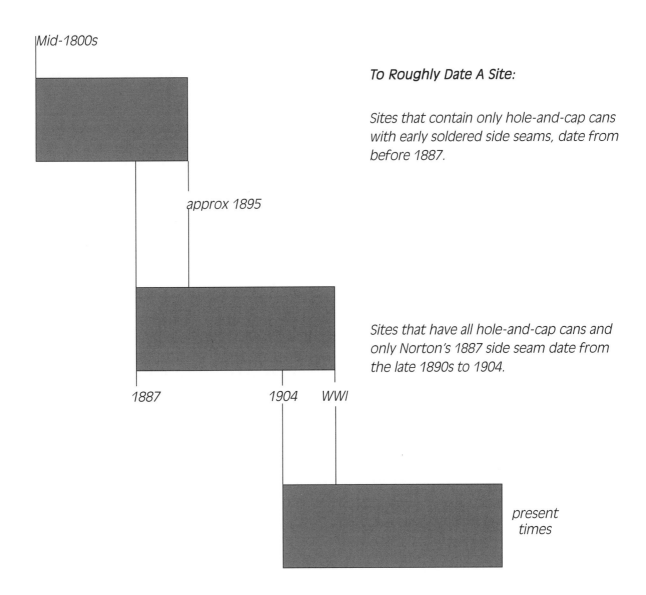

Mid-1800s

approx 1895

1887

1904   WWI

present
times

To Roughly Date A Site:

*Sites that contain only hole-and-cap cans
with early soldered side seams, date from
before 1887.*

*Sites that have all hole-and-cap cans and
only Norton's 1887 side seam date from
the late 1890s to 1904.*

*Sites that contain only open-top cans
date after about WWI.*

In 1887 technology took a leap forward. Edwin Norton, owner of one of the largest can-making companies of the time, was issued patent #370,404 for an interlocked sideseam where a strip of solder was tucked inside the interlocking metal folds. Then the can was heated to melt the solder and seal the joint. This resulted in a side seam in which no solder is visible on either the inside of the can or the outside. Since the Norton Brothers company was such a major player in the tin-can industry at the time, this invention became pivotal in making tin cans.

By 1889, cans of this type were widespread. A large proportion of the cans in the mining camp of Chihuahua, Colorado, which burned in 1889 and was never reinhabited, were of this type. Not a single can of this type was found at nearby Rexford, which was abandoned about 1884. But since the caps were applied by the food processor, not the can maker, they remained essentially the same as before. This style was state of the art from the late 1880s until the introduction of the open-top tin can in 1904.

The Contents of Those Tin Cans

Today the cans are rusted hulks — the colorful lithographed labels are long gone, and any trace of the former contents has been erased with time. In many cases the cans are in pieces, perforated with rust, and only a few short years away from being completely reclaimed by nature. We will never know for sure what originally was contained in the vast majority of these cans. But with some close scrutiny we can allow ourselves a few educated guesses.

It was a lonely miner's cabin along what could have been a busy mountain road a hundred years ago. We had not yet learned the language of the mining camps, and this example was in such a sorry state that we almost didn't stop to look at it. The roof was gone, and only three courses of logs remained to outline what had once been a home in a rugged wilderness. We shook our heads sadly and said, "If only this old place could talk."

When we accidentally stumbled upon the old trash heap at the back of the cabin, we looked at the rusted jumble with perplexity. But one rusted lid stood out as different from the others. We studied it and eventually a pattern emerged from the rust: words! This lid had been embossed. We were able to decipher: "Dr. Price's Cream Baking Powder." Until this point we had despaired of ever knowing what had been in all those rusted tin cans. Now we felt that at least sometimes we would be able to know. These old mining camps could talk after all!

Dr. Price's Cream Baking Powder can we discovered. Many baking powder cans seem to have been embossed.

The only time we will ever feel certain about what a can originally held is when that can is embossed. Only a few cans were ever embossed, so finding them is doubly exciting, not only because they are uncommon but also because of the facts they convey.

Embossing sometimes gives information other than the contents of the can, such as a date or a patent number. Both numbers can help to approximately date a site. More than once, armed with the number, we looked up the patent and it told us not only when the patent was issued (thus roughly dating the site) but also who the patent had originally been assigned to. This gave us the name of the company that produced the product that was in the can and answered the question, What was in this can?

Knowing a can contained baking powder allows us to ask questions of it. Questions like, What does a baking powder can lid tell us about the miners? It tells us that they ate a lot of foods requiring baking powder. Foods like biscuits and pancakes would have been as flat and as hard as a dinner plate without baking powder. Accounts from the past about their daily lives verify that the miners did indeed eat a lot of biscuits and pancakes.

Some of the most numerous tin cans to be found in a mining-camp site are the size and type of can fruits and vegetables come in today. Food historians tell us that the most common items to be canned a hundred years ago were beans, tomatoes, and corn. So it would not be surprising that the most common type of tin can we are seeing at the mining camps is the type that beans, tomatoes, and corn would have come in.

Above, three different-sized holes and caps, outlined in solder. The dab of solder in the center is the vent hole.

Below, possible milk cans. How they were opened suggests that the contents could be poured out through a tiny opening.

Still, that information is a little too general and left us feeling frustrated. But by studying a tin can very carefully, some clues emerge that narrow the search down just a bit more. One clue is the size of the hole in the original hole-and-cap can. A can that held a liquid would usually be a hole-and-cap can that contained a very small hole, because the can could be filled through a tiny opening. A medium-sized opening was plenty large enough to pack small pieces or chopped contents, such as corn or beans. But a large opening was necessary for contents such as tomatoes or peaches. There are exceptions to this, but the size of the hole in a hole-and-cap can will suggest the *possible* size of the original contents.

A way to double-check the size of the original contents is by determining how the can was opened. Some cans were punctured with a tool much like an ice pick, leaving two small round openings opposite each other, suitable for pouring. At other times the cook simply jabbed the top of the can with a sharp knife, leaving two slashes opposite each other and also suitable for pouring. If this can also has a tiny hole-and-cap opening, it probably contained a liquid. If this same

These cans were opened in such a way that suggests the contents couldn't be poured out. Perhaps they held something like tomatoes or peaches.

can is about the same diameter as a fruit or vegetable can but shorter, it might have contained condensed milk. This type of can, opened in this way, is extremely common at old mining-camp trash heaps.

Some cans were opened with a can opener, leaving a wide mouth from which to extract the contents. Other cooks didn't bother with a can opener and just attacked the top of the can with a large knife, jabbing an X in the top and then prying the four points open to get at the contents (You sure wouldn't want to complain about *this* cook's food!). The original contents in either case probably couldn't be poured out. If this can also has a medium- or large-sized hole and cap, we can speculate that its original contents were probably somewhere between morsel-sized and large-sized.

A lonely cabin below Rexford had a different lesson to teach us. Sometimes individual cans reveal only limited information, but the relationship between all the cans can give important clues. This cabin had an extensive trash heap, perhaps even larger than Rexford's. Because the side seams on the cans were all soldered on the outside and we found a four-pound can of Dr. Price's Cream Baking Powder, we assumed that the site was occupied about the same time as Rexford, and that quite a few hungry men came to supper here every day. The unique aspect of this site is that there are many cans but only a few *different types* of cans among them. We will never know for certain what these men ate, but we're willing to wager it was pretty much the same fare every day — a very monotonous diet.

We don't know what this reworked item was intended to be. Perhaps a sieve or collander.

A shadowgee made from a Towle's Log Cabin Syrup can.

Reuse of Artifacts

Nothing is a greater testimony to American ingenuity than the miner's creative reuse of resources. In remote mines such as those we love to visit, every article needed to run the mine — all the food, the supplies for the animals, sometimes even the coal for power — all had to be transported great distances over treacherous terrain on the backs of burros. The freighting charges made material goods very expensive. And waiting times for necessary items were long. Sometimes this must have been very frustrating.

This was driven home to us at the high, windswept site of the Esmerelda Mine in the San Juan Mountains of Colorado. Among the boardinghouse refuse we spotted the familiar shape of a large tin-can lid, but to our surprise, it had been punched full of holes. Since the holes appeared as rusted as the rest of the lid, it seemed to have been "operated upon" very long ago. The lid made a very passable sieve or colander. As discussed earlier, we have found old lard buckets re-used as candle lanterns.

One of the most creative reuses we ever spotted involved a Towle's Log Cabin Syrup container, in the shape of a house. This had been set up as a lantern or shadowgee. The entire container had been punched with holes, and a candle placed in a hole punched in the floor of the tin house. The pour-spout chimney was the vent. We have seen variations of this charming house lantern rarely. Often makeshift lanterns are found at mines that had electricity. This gives us yet another bit of information about miners' lives. Mines in southwestern Colorado were the first to use electricity on a large scale. But because we also find parts of kerosene lamps and makeshift lanterns there, it must not have been dependable.

216

We have also frequently found tin cans of various sizes and types that have been opened and flattened. These "new" tin-plated sheets were used for everything from patching holes in walls and roofs to lining walls behind an iron stove as insulation against the heat.

Sometimes the reuses were simple and impossible to detect a century later. For example, oyster tin-cans and pickle jars were in great demand for carrying gold dust in the 1860s. This type of reuse was probably very common, but we will never know for sure.

And the reuses continued after the mine closed, too. We have seen old boilers with the ends cut out and insides removed, that have been reused as culverts on the back roads in mining areas. Since our discovery of the makeshift colander at the Esmerelda we have become fascinated with the reuse of artifacts and look specifically for such items at every site. Rarely do we leave disappointed.

Hobnailed Boots

In nearly every site we can count on finding the gnarled remains of a hobnailed boot or two. These must have been standard gear for a hard-rock miner a century ago. But hobnailed boots are one of those items that very little is known about. Consider this. When you save something, you save "special" things — wedding dresses, ceremonial objects, rare or unusual, hard-to-replace items. But most of us don't go to the trouble of saving everyday things. Neither did our ancestors. Consequently, more is known about weddings a hundred years ago than is known about

Below, a hobnailed boot today.

the workman's blouse and the hobnailed boots a man wore to work every day. Because of this, libraries and archives have very little information about hobnailed boots.

The most information we located was in the Sears, Roebuck Catalogue reprint from 1902, and the Montgomery Ward and Company Catalogue no. 57 reprint from 1895. Sears, Roebuck and Company advertised their "Men's Mining Shoe" as "made from a good selection of stock, with full double soles and thoroughly nailed heel and toe. At an additional cost we have fitted this shoe with a heavy iron plate, thereby making it practically indestructible. $1.50." The Sears boots and the Montgomery Ward boots weighed as much as eighty-five ounces, over five pounds! The price seems a real bargain until we realize that a miner's wages ran about three dollars a day in those days, so a pair of new hobnailed boots cost him a half a day's pay.

Occasionally we have found long slender screws with the boots, and we wondered what role these screws played. Did some boot makers use screws on the bottoms of the boots instead of hobnails? But a blurb in the old Sears catalogue answered our questions: "The soles are cut from the best leather fastened on with standard screws. . . ."

Hobnailed boots may have been nearly indestructible, but they couldn't have been comfortable. Besides their extraordinary weight, those nails in the soles may have conducted the ground temperature, making them cold in the winter and hot in the summer.

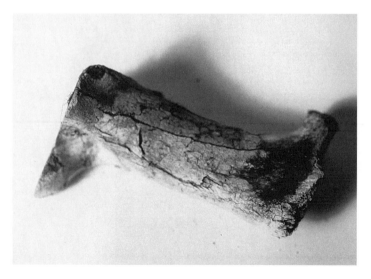

Animal Bones

Having been picked bare a hundred years ago and bleached by a century of sun and wind, the bones gleam white among otherwise rust-colored debris. They also have a story to tell us.

By far the most common animal bones appear to be from beef. This agrees with what English novelist Anthony Trollope noticed about American suppers in 1861 (and remember, supper was not the main meal of the day): "Beefsteaks, and tea, and apple jam and hot cakes, and light fixings, to all of which luxuries an American deems himself entitled." Our ancestors ate well!

Studying the bones closely reveals saw marks where the meat was butchered and dressed. In many places the easiest way to transport meat to the mine was on the hoof. Then it was butchered at the site. Today it is the whitened remains we see, the bones of those animals that made a last journey up a narrow trail to the mine.

Pots and Pans

Most antique household debris will include a pot or pan or wash basin that no longer fulfilled its purpose and was discarded. Sometimes it's as simple as a crumpled pie pan or tin plate. At other times it will be something more elaborate, like a rusted coffee pot.

Of all the pots and pans to be found at a site, the most exciting for us to find are the old coffee pots. Because miners appeared to have drunk a lot of coffee, pots are fairly common. However, we have found relatively few teapots. This leaves us with a mystery. We know that the Cornish were important to the development of mining in the American West, and being good Britons, they loved their tea. We have found square, embossed Lipton tea tins in the rubbish heaps, and we have found references to tea in the literature of the mining camps. But we have found teapots only rarely. So how did the Cornish miners prepare their tea?

Coffee percolators were apparently not in use until after the turn of the century. Prior to that, ground coffee was dumped directly in water and boiled for a while. Fresh grounds were dumped on top of the old ones each day, and more water was added. Talk about strong and bitter! This explains all the condensed milk cans we see in the trash heaps. T. A. Rickart wasn't exaggerating when he said the coffee was better suited for "staining floors or removing boiler scale."

Another story illustrates how strong the coffee must have been. In *Silverton Gold,* Allan Bird tells of the coffee at the Sunnyside Mine boardinghouse above Silverton, Colorado. Unbeknownst to anyone, a patch of ceiling plaster fell into the coffee urn below. But no one noticed any difference in the taste when they drank the coffee at dinner! Later, all the men were stricken with diarrhea. The outhouse didn't have enough holes to accommodate all the men at the same time, so through the long night the carbide lights of the miners' helmets flickered over the mountainside like fireflies. The next morning they discovered the plaster in the coffee urn.

Many old coffee-pots in the rubbish heap are found without a spout. This was a common problem with coffee pots of that time. This coffeepot was gray graniteware.

On early coffeepots the handles, spouts, and knobs were soldered to the bodies. This did not work out well. Soldered spouts often leaked. And if a soldered pot got hot enough on the stove, the solder would melt and the parts would fall off. We have found the remains of soldered coffeepots in dumps with the spout missing and wondered if this pot got too hot and self-destructed. By the mid-1870s welding or riveting replaced solder on stove-top coffeepots. Sometimes a mining-camp coffeepot will have a concave bottom to fit exactly the hole in a wood burning or coal stove.

Graniteware

The pots and pans are all rusted now. But sometimes, if you look carefully, you can find a flake of enamel still clinging to the pan. More than likely what you'll see is light and dark gray mottled enamel. "Graniteware" is a generic term and refers to the enameled ironware of several manufacturers. Gray graniteware enjoyed the most widespread use and was manufactured for the longest time.

Because gray graniteware could be made in one step, it was cheaper and quicker to make than the white or brightly colored ware that required at least two coats of enamel. It was about the time of World War I that colored graniteware became wildly popular. White was also a favorite about this time. Gray graniteware was still available through those years and up until World War II. It has not been manufactured since then, however.

Miners could order gray graniteware from both the Montgomery Wards and Sears, Roebuck catalogues. Today we can see drawings of those sets in these catalogue reprints. But in the old days graniteware was available from a great many sources.

Miscellany

Only the glass shards remain today. Gone with the whole bottles are the engraved messages on their sides, so we will never know how much liniment or shoe blacking or lemon extract was used in the mining camps. An occasional embossed shard can be found, however, and just like the tin cans, it can give us information about what happened in a camp. But since all that remain are the pieces, we get only a partial message.

Such was the case in Mayflower Gulch. Glittering in the sun on a trash heap, a shard of fancy glass with "Des Pat 9290_" written on the bottom caught our attention. We photographed the artifact and recorded what we could read of the number. Later we looked up the number in the patent books, design section, and there it was: Designed by William Guyer of New York, and dated July 31, 1934, the patented design was assigned to the Joseph E. Seagram and Sons Company. And there with the design patent was a picture of the whole bottle. The shard had come from a fancy whiskey bottle.

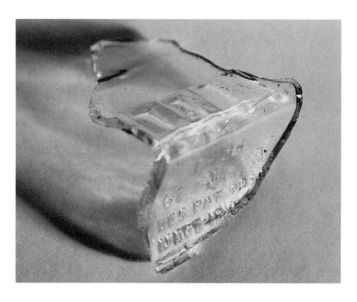

The bottle shard we found that day.

Other information can also be inferred from shards. At the site of Chihuahua, Colorado, which burned while it was still occupied, we found scraps of beautiful cut glass or crystal and etched glass. We found these in the building foundations, not the trash heaps. This was the type of glass one might see on a lampshade or a decorative serving bowl — the kinds of items that would have been removed if the residents had left the site in an orderly fashion because of economic conditions. The fact that these items remained in the houses and were destroyed implies a mad dash to safety, the people leaving their valuables behind.

The bottle as pictured in the patent.

Among the most common shards to be found at mining camp sites are those of dishes. At old boardinghouse sites the most common type of dish is from Homer Laughlin hotel china. Homer Laughlin began in the china business as early as 1869 in East Liverpool, Ohio. Later he joined with his brother, Shakespeare, and made china under the name Laughlin Brothers. In 1877 Homer bought out his brother but continued to make white granite porcelain. Homer Laughlin China Company became

Homer Laughlin hotel china is the most common type of china we see at old board-inghouses.

the official company name in 1897, and it remains so to this day. Through the years the company has used many symbols on the bottom of its china. The most common Homer Laughlin emblem we find at mining camps is a circle with "Homer Laughlin" printed along the inner perimeter and "hotel" blazed across the center. This mark was in use after 1897 (because of the company name) but before 1904. The Homer Laughlin China Company still makes china today.

There are many other artifacts one will occasionally encounter in the trash heap: metal barrel hoops, pieces of potbellied stoves, and broken bits of furniture, to name just a few.

The old buildings, mining equipment, and mills are inspiring. We see what a man could accomplish with only a few hand tools, a vision, and a lot of energy. They stand as monuments to human ingenuity in the face of hardship. But their scale is larger than life. They are impersonal. They are empty. Who were the men who hammered these square nails? We see the buildings, we see the square nails, we see the results of their hard work. But what about the hand that held the hammer?

It is when we touch a tiny clay tobacco pipe, or a comb with missing teeth discarded a century before, that we feel the handprint of humanity. Generations have come and gone, and yet this smallest of debris still has a story to tell us. Whether it is a bone button or those ubiquitous tin cans from the food they ate, the debris of human habitation tells us that real people lived and worked here. Real people like you and me. And those hands that hammered these square nails were reaching for their dreams and for a better way of life, just like you and me.

A COFFEE CAN SPEAKS

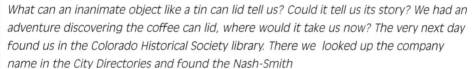

Tucked in the corner of a ruined cabin in Mayflower Gulch, we found an elaborately decorated lid. Through the rust we could read "Wedding Breakfast Coffee," but the name of the company that had produced it was mostly rusted through and we couldn't quite make it out. Someone had carefully placed it there many years ago. Perhaps after the coffee was gone, it held something special at one time. But now only the lid remained. It appeared to be an intriguing dead end, so we photographed our find and filed the pictures away.

Then, a couple of years later, while in an antique store, we spotted a like-new Wedding Breakfast Coffee can. The company name was legible this time. It said, "Nash Coffee and Spice Company, Denver, Colorado." We bought the can and took it home to compare with the pictures of the other can, and Bingo! It was a near match.

What can an inanimate object like a tin can lid tell us? Could it tell us its story? We had an adventure discovering the coffee can lid, where would it take us now? The very next day found us in the Colorado Historical Society library. There we looked up the company name in the City Directories and found the Nash-Smith Coffee and Spice Company. One George Nash was listed as the president of the company in 1902. The secretary was listed as George A. Nash. They were father and son residing in the family home at 1440 Detroit. We wondered if the house was still standing. Would the house help to put a human face on our story? We drove by that address on our way home, and discovered a house we would describe as a gracious mansion in the Italianate style. The Nashes appeared to be a well-to-do family with a thriving family business in the early part of the century.

On the bottom of the can was embossed "Hardesty Mfg Co. Denver, Colorado," and we checked that out, too. Rudd Hardesty was born in 1870 in Mumfordsville, Kentucky, and moved to Denver in 1888. He organized R. Hardesty Manufacturing Company in 1899. He started the company at first to produce tin cans, flavoring extracts and baking powder. Hardesty's Gold Label Baking Powder sold throughout the West. Through each succeeding City Directory

The Nash family home at 1440 Detroit in Denver.

we followed the rise of the company, and the man. His company grew and eventually opened up branches in Utah, Idaho, and Montana.

The company got out of the food business early and stuck to metal products and moved to larger and larger digs. So did the man. He married in 1908 and eventually had seven children. He and his family lived in several elegant homes until they finally settled in a four-square mansion at 1585 Monaco Boulevard, accomplishing all this within eighteen years. It was like seeing a Horatio Alger story unfold before our eyes.

It all might have ended there with the products of two thriving businesses having an impact in the remote parts of the state, but destiny had other plans. In 1910 George Nash, Sr. was no longer listed as president of the company and no longer listed at the family home. A Miss Virginia J. Nash was the sole resident of 1440 Detroit. Had George Sr. died?

George Jr. had married about this time and lived in a stately home at 1620 Oneida. In 1919 he was listed as president and dropped "Smith" from the company name, making it the Nash Coffee and Spice Company.

Since the lid we found in Mayflower Gulch said "Nash-Smith Coffee and Spice Company," and the trade mark had been applied for in 1902, this coffee can lid was probably stashed in Mayflower Gulch sometime between 1902 and 1919.

Our adventure took us deeper into the City Directories and what had been a charming story took a dramatic turn. In the pivotal year of 1929 Rudd Hardesty was no longer *president of Hardesty Manufacturing, and an unfamiliar name held that that position. Hardesty Manufacturing no longer listed tin cans as part of their products and the Continental Can Company was sharing the Hardesty Manufacturing address. Furthermore, Rudd Hardesty's son, Roy Hardesty, was listed as general manager of Continental Can Company. Had Rudd Hardesty sold out the tin can making part of the business to Continental Can Company? Rudd Hardesty listed no profession after 1929, but continued to live on Monaco Boulevard. Had he retired? He would have been about sixty then.*

But the noble Nash Company was no longer listed after 1929. Had the company succumbed to the Great Depression as so many others had? George A. Nash was still listed at his house on Oneida, but listed no profession. But by 1932 he was no longer listed at the house on Oneida, but in "rooms" in a seedy part of 20th Street. He was probably in his late fifties or early sixties. He died a dozen years later in Hollywood, California.

This book is about stories, adventure stories. First, the adventure of discovering fragments like a coffee can lid in the backcountry. Pieces of the past like this await discovery in the gulches and among the mountaintops of the American West. But since they are fragments — like jigsaw puzzles — the stories are as of yet unassembled. For the most part, they do not appear in the history books. This discovery is thrilling enough, but the adventure does not end in the backcountry. A second adventure comes in the archives and historical societies. Exploring the archives and then fitting the fragments together with archival research glues all the pieces into a more or less whole story. This is a new way to explore the American West, and it is open to everyone.

The Hardesty family home at 1585 Monaco Boulevard in Denver.

Tin Cans

HOLE-AND-CAP TIN CANS

Finding antique household debris around a building or the foundation of one is an indication that someone lived in this structure at one time. The debris was usually tossed downhill from the structure. Through the years it has probably gravitated downhill even more. The most common objects to be found among the debris are tin cans, old pots and pans, hobnailed boots, and bottle and china shards.

At a site, study a few cans. Ask questions of them: Is it a hole-and-cap can (solder on it)? These are the oldest of the tin cans. The can above right is a hole-and-cap can, the solder outlines the cap and plugs the venthole in the center. These cans began being phased out in 1904.

Does it have a simple lapped and soldered side seam like the lower left can? This type of side seam started being phased out in 1887. If the side seam is interfolded and no solder is apparent on it, like the can on the lower right, then this would date the can after 1887.

Tin Cans

HOLE-AND-CAP CANS

What size is the cap of the hole-and-cap tin can? A large cap suggests large-sized contents, like tomatoes. A medium-sized cap could indicate something like corn or beans. A tiny cap might indicate liquid contents, like condensed milk. On the right are two different cans from the field with two different hole sizes. The small can not only has a small hole-and-cap but also was opened in a way that suggests the contents had to be poured out. Below, these cans illustrate a medium-sized hole and cap. The can on the right is from a museum and the label identifies what the contents were. Comparing the can on the left from the field with the one on the right shows us the relationship that could exist between the size of the cap and the contents.

Tin Cans

OPEN-TOP CANS

If the can has no visible solder, it might be an open-top can. These cans look like modern cans and date from after 1904. If so, is the word "Sanitary" embossed on the bottom? This would date the can from between 1904 and 1908. The can pictured here is an open-top can. It probably dates before 1927, because the Kuner company bought the Empson Packing company at that time and the name of the company changed to Kuner-Empson.

Tin Cans

CAN OPENER TYPE

How was the can opened? Was it opened in such a way that the contents could be poured out, or was it opened in such a way as to suggest the size of the contents? The can on the right was opened with a can opener that punched a hole in the middle first. Pictured below it is an example of the type of opener that opened it. We often see cans opened in this fashion in the backcountry. There were actually many can openers that opened cans in this way. On the bottom right, the three cans were opened in three different ways with a knife.

What might be indicated by the way the containers on the below left were opened? On the bottom left, the cook didn't bother to remove the lid on this tall rectanglar tin, just punched a hole in it and poured through the lid.

Star Can Openers, Steel Bar and Blade, Wood Handle, Sardine Scissors, Full Polished Steel,

229

Tin Cans

DISTINCTIVE-SHAPED CANS

Scattered among the many fruit/vegetable type tin cans are always a few with distinctive shapes that sometimes suggest their original contents. Unless they are embossed, distinctive cans only give us possibilities regarding the original contents — they do not give us hard and fast information. Once the food processors bought their cans instead of making them, tin-can types changed frequently. A certain brand of ground coffee might be packed in a tall can for a couple of years, then in a short, squat tin for a while, then in a bucket-type container. One look in a tin-can collector's book will give you an idea of all the different types of cans a single product used. Yet there are a few certain products that maintained a modicum of consistency through the years.

Baking powder cans are easy to spot in the field today for several reasons. They are about the same size and shape as baking powder cans are today. The can body has a raised bead just below the opening for the lid to rest against. This is an identifying mark to look for in the field. Baking powder cans were almost always embossed, so we can feel sure of the can's original contents. On the right is a museum example of a Dr. Price's Cream Baking Powder can. Above is an example of how they look today in the field.

Tin Cans

DISTINCTIVE-SHAPED CANS

There were many different types of baking powder, and we see examples of them often in the backcountry. Above left is an embossed lid that reads: Royal Baking Powder. On the right is how it must have looked originally with its cheerful red lithographed label, from a magazine advertisement in 1921. Below left, is an example of Schilling's Baking Powder from a museum, and the lid to a can of K C Baking Powder from the field on the right.

DISTINCTIVE-SHAPED CANS

Of all the rusted tin cans at a site, the condensed milk cans are probably the most numerous. They are also fairly easy to identify. The old condensed milk cans are similar in size and shape to today: roughly the same diameter as an approximately fifteen ounce fruit/vegetable can, but a little shorter. The picture on the right illustrates the difference between a probable fruit or vegetable can on the left and and a likely condensed milk can on the right. Milk cans also usually had a small hole-and-cap and were opened in such a way as to pour out the contents. Condensed milk cans were some of the last cans to make the switch to open-top cans because of the difficulty in filling the open-top cans. The liquid had a tendency to splash, creating a sticky mess. Later, condensed milk was sold in a "vent-top" can that had a tiny opening in the top that was used to fill the can, which was then sealed with a neat dab of solder. The picture below is a vent-top can from Hunziker's book.

Condensed milk cans like the one on the lower left, were shorter than the evaporated milk cans like the one on the lower right. Both were shorter than a fifteen ounce fruit/vegetable can, but the same diameter.

NET WEIGHT ONE POUND

COLUMBINE

EVAPORATED
STERILIZED, UNSWEETENED

MILK

DISTINCTIVE-SHAPED CANS

We know what was in the can on the right from a mining camp because it is embossed. It contained Borden's Condensed Milk. The can in the advertisement matches the one on the right. Note how the can was opened with a can opener; this illustrates why the information in this book will always be just rule-of-thumb or ballpark information.

DISTINCTIVE-SHAPED CANS

One of the most recognizable cans to be found at a site is the Towle's Log Cabin Syrup can. Because it is shaped like a little house with the chimney as a spout, it is fun to find. Towle's Log Cabin Syrup was first manufactured in 1887, although the patent for the distinctive container is dated in the early 1890s. The rusted can on the left is the oldest of the three tins and has solder on it. It is an example from the field today. The advertisement below appeared in 1928.

The Most Famous Syrup Flavor in the World

MUSEUM EXAMPLE

DISTINCTIVE-SHAPED CANS

Even Towles Log Cabin Syrup was sometimes packaged in tall rectangular tins like these. So too, were many other brands. The older tins have solder on them. These tin cans were frequently reused by opening the can up and flattening the sides out to form tin sheets. We often see the remains of tins like these reused to protect the log walls from the stove heat or to cover holes in the roof. The lid of the tin on the left appeared never to have been opened; instead the cook opened it in his own unique way. Below right is a museum example.

DISTINCTIVE-SHAPED CANS

Smoking a pipe must have been a popular pastime for miners, because one of the most common tins to be found in a mining-camp site is the tobacco tin. Tobacco cans are so many and so varied that it's impossible to narrow them down to the most typical type. Probably most we don't recognize. But one that we do recognize has the same distinctive shape today — the "hipflask" pocket-sized tins pictured here. Keep in mind that Prince Albert wasn't the only brand to be packaged in this type of tin. The one on the right is from the field. Below is an advertisement from the 1920s era. Snuff and chewing tobacco came in the same flat, round type of tin that chewing tobacco comes in today.

PRINCE ALBERT
—no other tobacco is like it!

Tin Cans

DISTINCTIVE-SHAPED CANS

Tobacco makers frequently went to extraordinary lengths to make tobacco tins attractive, some specifically to be reused. The lunch-box type of tobacco tin pictured here is another example of a very common tobacco can that we find often. Many a child and many a husband carried his or her lunch in a tin such as this.

The example on the left is how it often appears in the field, today. Below is an example from a museum.

Tin Cans

SEAFOOD CANS

Is the sardine can above very old? Or was it made later using old techniques? We really don't know. The can is a hole-and-cap type that is very nearly held together with solder. The solder is lumpy and has dripped onto other parts of the can. The raw edges of the roughly cut sides jut through the solder in several places. On one end the can reads: Mustard Sardines, Royal Brand. On the other side it is written in French. Another side has a bay scene with masted ships. It was all hand-painted over the solder. On the left is an embossed oyster can. Oysters must have been a favorite treat because we frequently find oyster cans at mining camp sites and in remote places as far from the ocean as you can possibly get. Sometimes a family in mining towns would split a case of mail-order oysters or some other luxury food with another family.

SEAFOOD CANS

Above, fish are being canned in an 1888 Astoria, Oregon, cannery. Sagstetter collection.

DISTINCTIVE-SHAPED CANS

The lard bucket is one of the most numerous tin cans found at old sites. It came in several different sizes, but except for the size, the buckets all have the same distinctive shape: sloping sides, a wire bail handle, and a fitted lid. The handle fit into the center of a circle of raised-metal holders that were soldered to the body. Sometimes these old buckets are embossed with the manufacturer's name, thus confirming its contents. The buckets below both read _ K Fairbank & Co. The rusted one on the left has a patent date of 1876 embossed under the logo. It was discovered at a site that was abandoned in 1883. The lard bucket was one of the most reworked and reused of all the old tin cans.

Above right is an advertisement showing a lard bucket. Below, both these lard buckets are embossed with _ K Fairbank and Company and the logo. The lard bucket on the right is from a museum and reads Chicago. The one on the left is in the field and reads both St. Louis and Chicago. But other than that, both the buckets are the same.

Solid Lip Coffee Pots.

TIN, WITH BAIL.

For lumbermen and miners' use. The body and lip being in one piece, the latter will not drop off when heated

		Each.
44663	2 quarts	$0.20
	3 quarts	.25
	4 quarts	.28
	6 quarts	.35

This battered coffee pot undoubtedly presided over many meals. Since it is rather small — not more than two quarts at the most — we can assume it did not belong to a boardinghouse or a large family.

The coffee pot advertised above is from the Montgomery Ward Catalogue of 1895. The ad was specifically aimed at lumberjacks and miners, and we discovered the old coffee pot on the right at an old mining camp site. Note how the spout is not a separate piece, but is formed from the body. The ad promised the spout would not fall off and, indeed, the old, rusted coffee pot we discovered is one of the few that still has its spout.

Pots and Pans

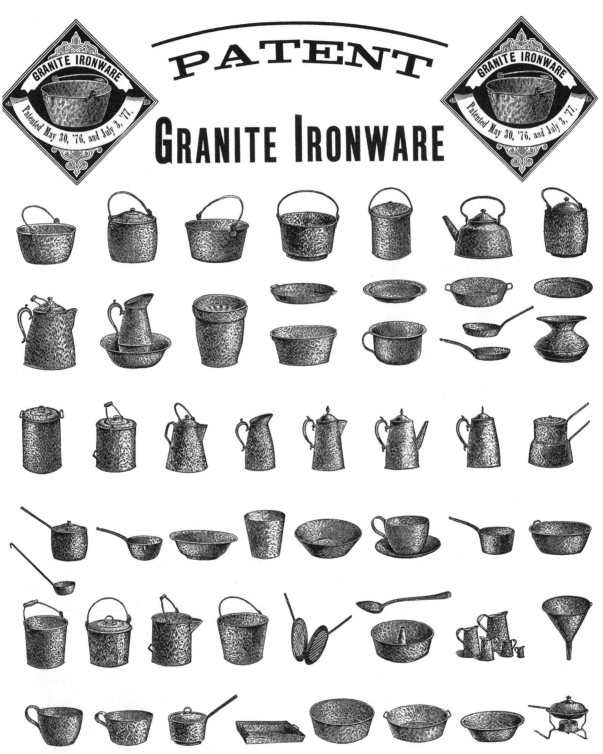

PATENT

GRANITE IRONWARE

ST. LOUIS STAMPING CO., St. Louis

GRANITEWARE

Enameled graniteware must have been a favorite of the miners because we often find old pots or pans at sites that have a flake or two of enamel still clinging to them. On the facing page is an advertisement for gray graniteware. This was the first enamelware to be produced, and has not been manufactured since World War II. On the right are examples of gray graniteware. The gray graniteware is the most common type we see at sites. Below is an example of white enamelware. This became wildly popular about World War I. We see examples of the white graniteware and and other colors less often.

Bottle and China Shards

Much has been written regarding bottles and china, and there are any number of good books on the subject. Therefore, we did not go into much detail on them, but there are a few things one can look for that will give ballpark information. On the right, this bottle neck still holds its cork, indicating it predates bottle caps. Check the color on the old bottle shards like this. If it has turned an amethyst color, it predates World War I. A chemical was sometimes used in bottle glass that turns it purple when it's exposed to sunlight over a long period of time. The chemical was not available during the war and stopped being used at that time.

Always check for writing on bottles and china. Like the tin cans, they sometimes have useful information embossed on them like patent numbers or dates or the manufacturer. China marks are also telling. The Homer Laughlin symbol on the right was in use before 1900, according to *Lehner's Encyclopedia of U.S. Marks on Pattery, Porcelain and Clay,* by Lois Lehner. The mark on the china shard on the lower left was in use from 1897 to 1904 and is very common at old mining camp sites. The mark on the lower right reads "Dresden."

244

Hobnailed Boots

Miners' Boots

Weight, 85 ounces.

52537 Men s Miner's Boots. whole stock light kip, long leg, tap sole, hob nailed. best quality: sizes, 6 to 11.
Per pair $4.00
52539 Men's, Miners' Boots, heavy S kip, double sole, hob nailed, all solid; sizes, 6 to 11. Per pair.....$2.25
Weight, 74 ounces.

The old hobnailed boot on the above left probably walked the underground tunnels and clumped through the boardinghouse. The boots were undoubtedly very familiar with the saloon floor and spent some time dancing at the town's Saturday night dances.

They are very common at the old sites. Above right is an early ad in the Montgomery Wards Catalogue of 1895, reprinted with permission from Dover Publications. As you can see, the boots were very heavy and almost indestructible. In the archival photo on the left the reclining miner wears a pair of these boots, the reflection of the light off the hobnails making them more visible to us. This picture is from the Denver Public Library, Western History Department.

245

14

CEMETERIES:
THE LAST CHAPTER

 Perhaps you've heard this legend, too. Off by itself near Central City, Colorado, there is said to exist a single lonesome grave. The inscription on the stone indicates it is the grave of a woman. But what is surprising is that the dates given are several years *before* the Pikes Peak gold rush began. We have never seen this grave. But still it haunts us. Who was this woman? What was she doing in such a wild place before the gold rush?

At some mining-camp sites, the only thing that remains is the graveyard. Some of the weathered gray tombstones are quite elaborately carved and are made from marble. They inspire in us questions. Not only about the people who came here before us, but also about the tombstones themselves. Who carved these stones? How did they get to remote, wind-swept places? Surprisingly, the Sears, Roebuck Catalogue of 1902 offered marble tombstones for sale. These were inscribed with the purchaser's message and then shipped by railway from Vermont. The smallest stone weighed 125 pounds, the largest weighed 800 pounds. Prices ranged from $5.10 to $26.70, plus inscription and shipping. We have often wondered how many of the tombstones we see in the old ghost-town cemeteries came from a mail-order catalogue like Sears.

A stroll through an old cemetery is like a roll call of the names of those who came to this place, dreaming of returning home rich someday, and never made it back. At a cursory glance, names and dates don't offer anything much more fascinating than skimming the pages of a phone book. But with a careful reading, much can be gleaned just by studying the inscriptions. Think beyond the confines of a name and date. For example, clusters of dates can indicate times when epidemics swept through the camp. For instance, influenza raged in

A grim reminder to the gold rushers was the mining-camp cemetery. Many never made it home. This one is pictured in New Colorado and the Santa Fe Trail *by A. A. Hayes, Jr.*

1918. Many graves will undoubtedly belong to children, for the life expectancy of children in the nineteenth and early twentieth centuries was tragically brief.

Besides the name and dates of birth and death, some inscriptions will share country of origin. But occasionally we are lucky and find an intriguing poem. A popular one that we often see went something like this:

> As you are now,
> So once was I.
> As I am now,
> So you shall be.
> Prepare for death and follow me.

Inscriptions on gravestones rarely tell how the person died. Finding one that does relate that information makes it doubly special. For example, one unusual gravestone in the Fairplay, Colorado, cemetery states that it is the resting place of a little boy who drowned in a flume in the 1870s.

Most inscriptions merely hint at a tragedy. One of the most intriguing clusters of graves we ever saw was of a mother and her three children. They all died on the same exact day. We are left to wonder, Could they all have succumbed to illness on the same day? Was there an accident of some kind? A fire? An avalanche? Murder, even? Cemeteries brim with such mysteries.

In the graveyard of Georgetown, Colorado, a cluster of three graves hint at another mystery. They all record the same day of death: May 31, 1877. The three stones were identical in design. Two of the three men were identified on the stones as from Cornwall, England. Since Cornishmen were considered some of the best hard-rock miners in the world at that time, we suspected these men might have died in a

mine accident. Just how much can one surmise from tombstone inscriptions?

Other mysteries about these three graves also emerged. The graves were well tended; someone had placed a sprig of flowers at the base of one. Who would still care for the graves of strangers after a hundred and twenty-five years?

We were left with many intriguing questions. Could a stroll through an old cemetery suggest fascinating stories from bygone times? Surely the old newspapers of that era would have mentioned a mine accident. We decided to find out.

In the *Rocky Mountain News* of June 6, 1877, we found this headline: "Fatal Explosion in Georgetown." The article that followed read:

> The *Miner Extra* of today, has the following: This morning when the day
> hands went to work in the Silver Ore tunnel, near the Terrible Mine,
> Brownville, they found the mangled corpses of the night miners, John
> Gregory, Harry Walters and a man named Pope. There had been an
> explosion of Giant Powder and the bodies were dreadfully mutilated and
> disfigured. How the explosion occurred will never be known, as all who
> were in the tunnel were killed.

The three stones matched, even to a carving of three links of a chain with the letters F and L and T inside each link. This is a symbol used by the Oddfellows. Organiza-

John Pope, Henry Walters and John Gregory were from Britain and died in an 1877 mine accident in the American West. Yet there were flowers on their graves.

249

tions like the Oddfellows, Masons, and Elks were very active in the mining camps. We contacted our friend Erik Swanson — historian, museum curator, and Oddfellow. He confirmed that the Oddfellows promise to educate the orphan, assist the widow, and bury the dead. The local Oddfellows more than likely buried these three men who were so far from home and bought the stones which still mark their graves today. They would also care for the graves indefinitely. The F and L and T stand for Friendship, Love and Truth. Just a little bit of research and asking questions confirmed the story we had pieced together that day in the cemetery. It also explained why the graves appeared well kept. Stories do indeed exist among the headstones.

The old graveyards are disappearing today. Places like Caribou, Colorado, had a charming cemetery when we first went there in the 1960s. But now it is gone. The headstones have all been broken and removed by vandals. Because of vandalism such as this, some cemeteries are closed to visitors. However, we have found that even at closed cemeteries, there is one date that one can usually visit: Memorial Day. It is on Memorial Day that even casual visitors are welcomed. We usually begin our ghost town season each year with a visit to a mining camp cemetery that is accessible on Memorial Day.

The people have gone from the old ghost towns. The mines are closed up and in ruin. Even the old towns are mostly gone. Today the mining camps speak only in a whisper.

But there is a message to be heard, murmuring among the pines, rasping above the windblown sand, echoing down canyons. Not everyone will hear it. Not everyone will understand it. But *you* will . . . now that you are fluent in the language of the mining camps, now that you can hear the mining camps speak.

APPENDIXES

Appendix A: Glossary

Adit: Horizontal tunnellike opening to the underground workings at a mine. Technically, a tunnel is open at both ends, and an adit is only an entrance.

Aerial Tram: Ore buckets hung from a moving cable to transport ore.

Amalgamation: Gold has a natural attraction to mercury. Amalgamation is a process using mercury to remove gold and silver from ground rock.

Assay: A test that determines the valuable metal content of ore or rock.

Blick: A flash of light that occurs as a dore gives up its heat during assaying.

Chink: A substance filling the spaces between the logs in a log cabin. Horsehair was one popular type of chinking in the nineteenth century, as was moss or mud. This substance had to be replaced when necessary.

Concentration: The act of grinding ore and then removing as much worthless material from it as possible, thereby incurring less freighting expense.

Corduroy Road: Logs laid side by side across a road in bogs and areas of loose sand. Vehicles traveled on top of these logs to avoid sinking.

Crosscut: A passageway that crosses a vein, usually to connect with another tunnel or as an air vent. The opposite of a drift.

Crucible: A fired clay container used in the assaying process.

Cupel: A walnut-shell-sized container made of bone ash, used as part of the assay process.

Double-Jack: A form of hand drilling where two hard-rock miners take turns striking a drill steel with an eight-pound hammer and turning the drill steel.

Drift: A horizontal passage following the course of a vein.

Fool's Gold: Iron pyrite; glittery, showy rock that is sometimes mistaken for gold by amateurs.

Grass-level: Surface mine workings.

Grubstake: To provide a prospector with foodstuffs, supplies, and equipment to work his claim in exchange for a percentage of the valuable ore he discovers.

Hard boil: A felt hat that has been repeatedly boiled in a resin until it is stiff. An early version of a hard hat.

Head Frame: The tall wooden or steel structure above a shaft with a grooved sheave wheel that supports the hoist cable. Sometimes called the "gallows frame".

Highgrade: Rich ore, or to filch a rich piece of ore.

Lode: A vein of rich ore in solid rock.

Mill: A plant for concentrating or reducing ore into a smaller bulk or for treating it to capture the valuable minerals. Mills were differentiated by their method of fine-grinding ore. A stamp mill crushed the ore with heavy iron stamps that were lifted by cams and then dropped. A ball mill used cannonball-like weights in an enclosed revolving unit to pulverize the ore. A rod mill used heavy rods in a revolving tube-shaped unit to accomplish the same thing.

Muck: Blasted, broken rock, or to shovel broken rock.

Muller: A rocking hammer used to grind ore by an assayer on a bucking-board base.

Ore: Metal-bearing rock. "Refractory" ore resists common treatments and requires roasting or other additional processing to retrieve its metal content.

Salt: To make a mine or ore sample test richer than it actually is by adding gold to it from another source.

Shaft: A vertical hole in the ground used for access to the underground workings at a mine.

Silicosis: A disease of the lungs common to hard-rock miners at one time and caused by rock dust created by an old type of machine drill.

Single Jack: A type of hand drilling done by one man with a four-pound hammer.

Slag: In smelting, the glassy waste material of molten ore.

Sluice: A long wooden trough used to capture gold from streambeds in placering.

Tailings: The pulverized remains of rock and the metals extracted from it at a mill.

Tommyknockers: Gnomes said to inhabit mines; originated with immigrant Cornish miners.

Tuyere or Tuy iron: (Pronounced *twee air, twee iron*) An air pipe to the heart of a fire in blacksmithing.

Vein: A crack in the rock filled with minerals from a deeper source.

Waste rock: Worthless rock removed from underground mine workings.

APPENDIX B:
APPROXIMATE PATENT TIMETABLE

If you should find an object with a patent number on it, locate the nearest number in the patent number reference point list, and the corresponding year across from it will give you a rough date for the object.

Patent Number Reference Point	Approximate Date
7,000	1850
13,000	1855
27,000	1860
48,000	1865
98,000	1870
165,000	1875
223,000	1880
320,000	1885
420,000	1890
542,000	1895
640,000	1900
792,000	1905
945,000	1910
1,143,000	1915
1,327,000	1920
1,542,000	1925
1,743,000	1930
2,005,000	1935
2,185,000	1940
2,378,000	1945
2,500,000	1950

MUSEUMS AND MINE TOURS

APPENDIX C

Just as Richardson wrote of mining towns having a "mysterious family resemblance," conversely each was also unique. Every mining district has its own tale of discovery, its own legends, its own villains, its own heroes. The place to go for these wonderful stories is to the historical society, museum, or mine tours in an old mining district. The museums and historical societies are the repositories for the stories and legends as well as the facts of a region. Most have photos and archives, sell books on the subject, and can answer your questions.

We also love to go to these places because we have a chance to see the old mining equipment whole — and sometimes even operating — that we have glimpsed in the nearby backcountry rusted and in pieces.

The following list is by no means complete. It is merely a sampling of possible places to visit when you are in a particular area. These places will complement what the book is about.

Listings are alphabetically by state, then within the state, alphabetically by town. The mailing address is shown in parentheses, the actual physical address is shown without them. Keep in mind these museums and mine tours are usually open only during the travel season.

ALASKA

Wrangell - St. Elias National Park
(P.O. Box 439)
Copper Center, AK 99573
Phone: (907) 822-5234
Kennicott is said to be the world's largest ghost town; visiting the mill there is popular. Throughout the rest of the park a network of trails leads to ghost town sites, for experts only!

Copper Valley Historical Society Museum
Mile 101 Old Richardson Hwy
(P.O. Box 84)
Copper Center, AK 99573
(907) 822-5285

Cordova Historical Museum
622 First St.
(P.O. Box 391)
Cordova, AK 99574
(907) 424-6665

Denali National Park
(Box 9)
Denali Park, AK 99755

(907) 683-2294 (park headquarters)
Trails in the park were originally old mining trails and there are sites such as old miners' cabins scattered along the trails. Since this was mostly a placer mining region, little mining equipment remains.

Eagle Historical Society and Museum
1st and Berry at Courthouse for tours
(P.O. Box 23)
Eagle City, AK 99738
On the border of Alaska and Canada. Six restored buildings display early mining techniques done by hand.

Alaskaland
Fairbanks North Star Borough
(P.O. Box 71267)
Fairbanks, AK 99701
(907) 456-8579

University of Alaska Museum
Campus at University of Alaska
907 Yukon Drive
(P.O. Box 756960)

Fairbanks, AK 99775-6960
(907) 474-7505 (general information)
Houses the largest public collection of gold nuggets in the state. Extensive Fairbanks history exhibit.

Sheldon Museum and Cultural Center, Inc.
11 Main St.
(P.O. Box 269)
Haines, AK 99827
(907) 766-2366

Juneau Douglas City Museum
114 - 4th St.
(155 South Seward)
Juneau, AK 99801
(907) 586-3572
A third of the exhibits are devoted to mining.

Last Chance Mining Museum
1001 Basin Road
Juneau, AK 99801
Located in the historic compressor building of the Alaska Juneau Gold Mining Company.

City of Skagway Historical Museum and Archives
Trail of '98
Second and Broadway
(P.O. Box 521)
Skagway, AK 99840
FAX: (907) 983-3420
Email: skgmus@ptialaska.net
As a port town, Skagway provisioned the prospectors who passed through on their way to the goldfields.

Klondike Gold Rush National Historic Park
Second and Broadway
(P.0. Box 517)
Skagway, AK 99840
Gateway to the Klondike Gold Rush

Valdez Museum and Historical Archive
217 Egan Avenue

(P.O. Box 307)
Valdez, AK 99686
Was called the "All American Route to the Goldfields". Little Giant pneumatic drill and other mining equipment on display. An unrestored stamp mill 6 miles up Mineral Creek.

Dorothy G. Page Museum and Visitors Center
323 Main St.
Wasilla, AK 99654
(907) 373-9071
FAX: (907) 373-9072
Simulated mine tour, hand drills and an ore crusher on display.

Independence Mine State Historical Park
HC 32, Box 6706
Wasilla, AK 99654
(907) 745-2827
(907) 745-3975 Headquarters
This ghost town is intact and accessible to the public. Tour about six original mine buildings, hardrock mining equipment on display. There are 38 mining camps in the Willow Creek, Hatcher Pass Management Area.

Museum of Alaska Transportation & Industry
3800 W. Neuser Dr. [Park Hwy mi.47, next to Wasilla Airport]
(P.O. Box 870646)
Wasilla, AK 99687
(907) 376-1211
FAX (907) 376-3082
home page: http://www.alaska.net/~rmorris/mati1.htm
Major exhibit on the Alaska Gold Rush Centennial on display until December 2004.

Wrangell Museum
318 Church St. (lower level)
(P.O.Box 1050)
Wrangell, AK 99929
(907) 874-3770

MUSEUMS AND MINE TOURS

ARIZONA

Bisbee Mining and Historical Museum
No. R Copper Queen Plaza
(P.O.Box 14)
Bisbee, AZ 85603
(520)432-7071

Gold King Mine and Ghost Town
(P.O. Box 125)
Jerome, AZ 86331
Most equipment on display is operational, including an old saw mill. A short mine tour.

Jerome Historical Society
Main St. and Jerome Ave.
Jerome, AZ 86331
(520)634-5477

Jerome State Historic Park
Douglas Road
(P.O. Box D)
Jerome, AZ
(520) 634-5381
FAX (520) 639-3132

Mohave Museum of History and Arts
400 W. Beale
Kingman, AZ 86401
(520) 753-3195

Pimeria Alto Historical Society
136 N. Grand Ave. (in original City Hall)
(P.O. Box 2281)
Nogales, AZ 85621

Arizona Mining and Mineral Museum
1502 W. Washington
Phoenix, AZ 85007
(602)255-3795
FAX: (602) 255-3777

Phoenix Museum of History
105 N. Fifth St.
(P.O. Box 926)
Phoenix, AZ 85001
(602) 253-2734
FAX (602) 253-2348

The Sharlot Hall
415 W. Gurley
Prescott, AZ 86301
(520) 455-3122
Exhibits on gold discovery and the territorial period. Stamp mill and steam engine that powered it on display. Some of the equipment is operational.

Discovery Park
1651 - 32nd St.
Stafford, AZ 85546
(520) 428-6260
Opening in 1998 will be a mining exhibit and simulated mine ride. Also has a Tunnel of Time train, observatory and hiking trails.

Tombstone Courthouse State Historic Park
219 Toughnut St.
(P.O.Box 216)
Tombstone, AZ 85638
(520)457-3311
An extensive mining display includes a reconstructed assay office, lighting devices, drills, hoists, and ore buckets.

Arizona Historical Society State Headquarters
949 East 2nd St.
Tucson, AZ 85719
(520) 628-5774
FAX (520) 628-5695
The Arizona Mining Hall contains a full-scale recreation of an underground tunnel, an assay office, miner's tent, blacksmith shop and a stamp mill. Also contains the American Mining Hall of Fame.

CALIFORNIA

Gold Country Museum
1273 High St. in Gold Country Fairgrounds
Auburn, CA 95603
(916) 889-6500
FAX: 889-6510
Email:jerryr@placer.ca.go
Exhibits on gold rush, mining technology and miners' lifestyle. Walk-through mine tunnel, operational stamp mill replica and saloon tent. Gold panning.

Plumas - Eureka State Park
310 Johnsville Rd.
Blairsden, CA 96103
(916) 836-2380
A high sierra mining town with working blacksmith shop. Ruins of historic buildings.

Bodie State Historic Park
Hwy 395 to Hwy 270
(P.O. Box 515)
Bridgeport, CA 93517
(619) 647-6445
FAX: 647-6485
A genuine California gold-mining ghost town, now maintained in a state of "arrested decay." Walking tours of the town. Unless otherwise noted, all buildings are closed to the public.

Marshall Gold Discovery State Historic Park
310 Back St.
(Box 265)
Coloma, CA 95613
(916) 622-3470
This is where western mining started. 14 museum buildings including an operational replica of Sutters saw mill, stamp mill, blacksmith shop, tin smith, and gun smith.

Columbia State Historic Park
4 mi no. of Sonora off Hwy. 49 on Parotts Ferry Rd.
258(P.O. Box 151)

Columbia, CA 95310
(202) 532-4301 and 532-0150
FAX: (209)532-5604
An example of a near-death-experience town. Many small shops are in the restored business district.

Downieville Museum
330 Main St.
(P.O. Box 484)
Downieville, CA 95936
(916)289-3423
Operational replica of 5-stamp gold mill, gold nugget collection.

Gold Drift Museum
32820 Main St.
Dutch Flat, CA 95714
(916) 889-6500
History of the Alta, Baxter, Dutch Flat, and Gold Run region.

Folsom History Museum
823 Sutter St.
Folsom, CA 95630
(916)985-2707
FAX: 985-7288
Replica of working dredge, Wells Fargo assay office.

North Star Powerhouse
Allison Ranch Rd. at Empire St.
Grass Valley, CA
(mailing: P.O. Box 1300, Nevada City, CA 95959)
(916) 273-4255
Tools from the early years of mining in the Northern Mines, 30-ft. Pelton Wheel.

Eastern California Museum
155 Grant St.
(P.O. Box 206)
Independence, CA 93526
(760) 878-0364 and 878-0258
FAX: (760) 872-2712
Artifacts from the mining town of Cerro Gordo in the Inyo Mountains on display.

Amador County Museum
225 Church St.
Jackson, CA 95642
(209)223-6368

Wells Fargo History Museum
333 So. Grand Ave.
Los Angeles, CA 90071
(mailing address: History Dept.
420 Montgomery St.
San Francisco, CA 94163)
(213)253-7166
This company history museum has mining displays
and gold nugget display as well as a Concord stagecoach.

Madera County Museum
210 W. Yosemite Ave.
(P.O. Box 478)
Madera, CA 93639
(209) 673-0291

California State Mining and Mineral Museum
Mariposa County Fairgrounds
(P.O. Box 1192)
Mariposa, CA 95338
(209)742-7625
The official state of California gem and mineral
collection, over 20,000 specimens, including the
Fricot Nugget found in 1865. Walk-in 200-foot rep-
lica of mine tunnel with turn-of-the-century tools.
Replica of assay office. Working model of gold stamp
mill.

Alpine Museum and Historical Complex
#1 School St.
(P.O.Box 24)
Markleeville, CA 96120
(916) 694-2317
Email: nthornburg@telis.org
Blacksmith shop, rocks and gems, mining tools.

Malakoff Diggins' State Historic Park
23579 No. Bloomfield Rd.

Nevada City, CA 95959
(916) 265-2740
Largest hydraulic mining operation in California.
Walk through sluice tunnel 556 feet long.

El Dorado County Historical Museum
104 Placerville Dr.
Placerville, CA 95667
(916) 621-5865
FAX: 621-6644
Operating stamp mill, small train, minerals, a very
extensive collection.

Gold Bug Mine Park
549 Main St.
Placerville, CA 95667
(916)642-5207 or 642-5232
Underground mine tour, model of a stamp mill.

Calaveras County Museum
30 N. Main
(P.O. Box 1281)
San Andreas, CA 95249
(209) 754-6579
Gold rush artifacts include a small Pelton wheel and
a replica of an arrastra.

Shasta State Historic Park
Hwy 299, 4 miles west of Redding
(P.O.Box 2430)
Shasta, CA 96087
(916) 243-8194
Several gold rush era ruins in park. Courthouse
Museum emphasizes lifestyles and transportation,
including a freight wagon and stage coach.

J. J. Jackson Memorial Museum
508 Main St.
(P.O.Box 333)
Weaverville, CA 96093
(916)623-5211
Main Street in Weaverville is an historic district. At
the museum is an operable steam-powered two- 259

stamp mill, demonstrations periodically in the black-smith shop and tin shop. Much on the Chinese history of the area. The History Center has Trinity County records going back for 140 years.

Whiskeytown/Shasta/Trinity National Recreation Area
Kennedy Memorial Drive
(P.O. Box 188)
Whiskeytown, CA 96095
(916) 246-1225
FAX (916) 246-5154
A walking tour winds around the El Dorado Mine, includes a stamp mill and ore crusher.

Siskiyou County Museum
910 S. Main St.
Yreka, CA 96097
(916) 842-3836

COLORADO

Aspen Historical Society
620 Bleeker St.
Aspen, CO 81611
(907) 925-3721
Guided tours of the ghost towns of Independence and Ashcroft by "ghosts" (actually students of historical preservation).

Country Boy Mine Gold Mine Tour
0542 French Gulch Rd.
(P.O. Box 8569)
Breckenridge, CO 80424
(970)453-4405

Gilpin History Museum
228 E. High St.
(P.O. Box 247)
Central City, CO 80427
(303) 582-5283
Mining display in the Schoolhouse Museum building. Also has an award-winning shaft building. Even-
260 tually plans to offer tours of the Coeur d'Alene Mine.

Western Museum of Mining and Industry
(125 N. Gate Rd.)
Colorado Springs, CO 80921
(719) 488-0880
FAX (719) 488-9261
www.wmmi.org.
The history of Western mining and related industries. Guided tours, operating machinery, gold panning, mining exhibits, and a working stamp mill. Research library, gift shop, picnic area, classes, special events.

Creede Historical Society
Main Street, in old Denver and Rio Grande RR depot
P.O. Box 608
Creede, Co 81130
Specializes in the miners' way of life. Complements the Underground Museum. Many photos of early miners.

Creede Underground Mining Museum
Forest Service Road 503
(P.O. Box 432)
Creede, CO 81130
(719) 658-0811
Museum was blasted out of a cliff face by hardrock miners. 22 displays on the different methods of mining.

Cripple Creek District Museum
500 E. Bennett Ave.
(P.O. Box 1210)
Cripple Creek, CO 80813
(719) 689-2634
Three museum buildings house a gold ore display and a working assay office among other things. Hardrock Park is a self-guided tour of an outdoor display of mining artifacts.

Mollie Kathleen Gold Mine
(P.O. Box 339)
Cripple Creek, CO 80813
(719) 689-2466

One of the first mines in Cripple Creek. The workings 1000 feet underground are toured. Gold display.

Colorado History Museum
1300 Broadway
Denver, Colorado 80203
(303) 866-3682
A permanent mining exhibit is downstairs. Often have temporary exhibits.

Denver Museum of Natural History
2001 Colorado Blvd.
Denver, CO
(303) 322-7009 or (800) 925-2205
Mining and mineral display.

Animas Museum
31st and W. 2nd Ave.
(P.O. Box 3384)
Durango, CO 81302
(970) 259-2402
Changing mining exhibits. Smelting exhibit currently on display.

Center of Southwest Studies
Top floor of Reed Library Bldg.
(1000 Rim Drive)
Durango, CO 81301
(970) 247-7456
http://www.ftlewis.edu/acad-aff/swcenter
Soon to have a new building to exhibit more of their holdings.

South Park City Museum
100 - 4th
(P.O. Box 634)
Fairplay, CO 80440
(719) 836-2387
A cluster of authentic ghost town buildings has been moved to the site to form the charming town of South Park City. Buildings include a furnished assay office and blacksmith shop, as well as many others.

Frisco Historical Society
120 Main St.
(P.O. Box 820)
Frisco, CO 80443
(970) 668-3428
Mining tools are on display in the Jail Building. Photographs of different types of mining in the area, including photographs of the nearby ghost town site of Masontown.

Clear Creek County Mining Museum
Powder Cache Antiques
612 Sixth St. (second floor)
(P.O. Box 984)
Georgetown, CO 80444
(303) 569-2848
Probably the largest miners' candlestick collection in the U.S.

Lebanon Mine Tour and Georgetown Loop Railroad
P.O. Box 217
Georgetown, CO 80444
(303) 670-1686
www.gtownloop.com
The Lebanon Mine is accessible only by the Georgetown Loop narrow gauge railroad. Tour includes a brief train ride to the mine site, a short walking tour of the mine tunnel, and looking over several reconstructed mine buildings.

Kauffman House Museum
Pitkin Street
(P.O. Box 656)
Grand Lake, CO 80447
A few artifacts of a brief gold boom are on display in an interesting solid log building originally used as a hotel.

Pioneer Museum
South Adams and Hwy. 50
(696 County Rd. 16)
Gunnison, CO 81230
(970) 641-4530

Large mineral collection from across the U.S. and around the world, as well as Colorado.

Edgar Experimental Mine
(Colorado School of Mines)
365 - 8th Avenue
(P.O. Box 1184)
Idaho Springs, CO 80452
The Edgar Mine is an underground laboratory for the Colorado School of Mines. Here research is carried out and mining students gain experience. Yes, the general public is welcome. Both the past and the present are covered.

Heritage Museum and Visitors Center
2660 Miner St.
(P.O. Box 1318)
Idaho Springs, CO 80452
(303) 567-4709 or 4100
90% of their collection is mining artifacts, including an assay office, ore cart, and other equipment.

Phoenix Mine
1 mile west of Idaho Springs on Stanley, 1/2 mile south on Trail Creek Road.
(P.O. Box 3236)
Idaho Springs, CO 80452
(303) 567-0422
This is an underground tour of an actual working mine which produces gold, silver, and copper. Gold panning on the creek.

Lafayette Miners' Museum
108 E. Simpson St.
Lafayette, CO 80026-2322
(303) 665-7030
Coal mining artifacts housed in a building that was originally a miner's home at the Gladstone Mine.

Hinsdale County Historical Society
2nd and Silver Sts.
(P.O. Box 353)
Lake City, CO 81235
Chamber of Commerce: (800) 569-1874

www.Hindsdale-county.com

Matchless Mine Museum
414 W. 7th St.
Leadville, CO 80461
(719) 486-1899

Bachelor/Syracuse Mine Tour
County Road 14
P.O. Box 380
Ouray, CO 81427
(970) 325-0220
Working blacksmith shop, an underground tour of old mine workings.

Ouray County Museum
420 - 6th Ave.
Ouray, CO 81427
(970) 325-4576

Salida Museum
406 1/2 W. Rainbow Blvd.
Salida, CO 81021
(719) 539-2311 and 4602

Old Hundred Gold Mine Tour
(P.O. Box 430)
Silverton, CO 81433
(800) 872-3009
Underground tour of old gold mine. Air compressor, mucking machine, machine drills are sometimes demonstrated. Gold panning at no extra charge.

San Juan County Historical Society Museum
1557 Greene
(P.O. Box 154)
Silverton, CO 81433
Besides the Museum on Greene St. which has bellows, hoist, and drill steels on display, also operates the Mayflower Mill, a huge flotation mill that closed down in 1991 and is now a museum.

Tread of the Pioneers Museum
800 Oak St.

(P.O. Box 772372)
Steamboat Springs, CO 80477
Major mining exhibit from April to Nov. 1998 on the history of mining in Routt County, featuring the Twenty Mile Mine.

Telluride Historical Museum
317 N. Fir St.
(P.O. Box 1597)
Telluride, CO 81435
Part of the original Ames generator on display, which was the first long-distance transmission of alternating current. 40% of the museum is devoted to mining and alternating current.

IDAHO

Idaho Museum of Mining and Geology
2455 Old Penitentiary Rd.
Boise, ID 83712
(208) 368-9876
Extensive information on Idaho's old mining camps, mineral collection, gold panning demonstrations.

Idaho State Historical Museum
610 N. Julia Davis Dr.
Boise, ID 83702
(208) 334-2120
Mock-up of mine shaft, placer exhibit of tools.

The Land of the Yankee Fork Historic District
Custer Museum
Intersection of Hwys 75 and 93
Clayton, ID 83227
(P.O. Box 1086, **Challis,** ID 83226)
(208) 879-5244
Gold panning, 988-ton Yankee Fork gold dredge, 15 buildings of the old town of Custer, ID.

Museum of North Idaho
115 N.W. Blvd.
(P.O.Box 812, Coeur d'Alene, ID 83816-0812)
Coeur d'Alene, ID 83814

(208) 664-3448
Blaine County Historical Museum
N. Main St.
(P.O. Box 124)
Hailey, ID 83333
(208) 788-4185

Owyhee County Historical Museum
P.O. Box 67
Murphy, ID 83650
(208) 495-2319
Operating 2-stamp mill complete with steam engine. The closest museum to the near-ghost town of Silver City.

Clearwater Historical Museum
315 College Ave.
(P. O. Box 1454)
Orofino, ID 83544
(208) 476-5033

Sierra Silver Mine Tour
420 - 5th St.
(P.O. Box 712)
Wallace, ID 83873
Hard-rock miner guides take visitors on a tour of this old mine.

Wallace District Mining Museum
509 Bank St.
(P.O. Box 469)
Wallace, ID 83873
(208) 556-1592

MONTANA

Anaconda/Deer Lodge County Historical Society
401 E. Commercial
Anaconda, MT 59711
(406) 563-2422
Includes a section on smelting, on the location of the largest smelter in the world. Railroad and working turntable.

World Museum of Mining
West Park and Granite Sts.
(P.O. Box 33)
Butte, MT 59703
(406) 723-7211
On the site of the Orphan Girl Mine, extensive equipment includes a 100-foot steel headframe. Also, Hell Roarin' Gulch, a small town of 33 buildings filled with antiques. Tunnel exhibit.

Mineral Museum
Montana Bureau of Mines and Geology
1300 West Park St.
Butte, MT 59701
An extensive mineral collection 1/2 block from the World Museum complements the World Museum nicely.

Bannack State Park
25 mi. SW off hwy. 278
(4200 Bannack Rd.)
Dillon, MT 59725
(406) 834-3413
Guided tour of an old cyanide mill, remnants of hydraulicking, parts of an old dredge.

Beaverhead County Museum
15 So. Montana
Dillon, MT 59725
(406) 683-5027
History of the early mining camps and ghost towns in the area.

Cascade County Historical Society and Museum
1400 First Avenue N
Great Falls, MT 59401
(406) 452-3462
Coal mining exhibits on occasion.

Montana Historical Society
225 N. Roberts St.
(P.O. Box 201201)
Helena, MT 59620-1201

(406) 444-2694
FAX (406) 444-2696
Montana Homeland exhibit includes mining equipment.

Park County Museum
House of Memories
118 W. Chinook
Livingston, MT 59047
(406) 222-4184
http://www.avicom.net/parkmuseum/
Information of the ghost town of Castle, MT, and others, as well as a small mining exhibit.

Musselshell Valley Historical Museum
524 First West
Roundup, MT 59072
(406) 323-1403
Replica of a coal mine, blacksmith shop.

Mineral County Museum and Historical Society
302 E. 2nd Ave.
(P.O. Box 533)
Superior, MT 59872
(406) 822-4626 or 822-4891
History of the area gold rush, railroads, and a mineral collection, but the main focus of the museum is the Mullan Military Road, built in 1859-1862. Parts of this road are popular with hikers and mountain bikers.

NEVADA

White Pine Public Museum
2000 Altman St.
Ely, NV 89301
(702) 289-4710
Within fifty miles of Ely there are examples of every type of mining that has ever been done. The central theme of the museum is mining and equipment ranges from a headframe to an air compressor and drills.

Clark County Heritage Museum
1830 S. Boulder Hwy.
Henderson, NV 89015
(702) 455-7955
FAX: (702) 455-7948
Five miles outside Las Vegas. Museum includes a resurrected ghost town, railroad depot, and steam engine, and the entrance to a gold and silver mine.

Central Nevada Museum
Logan Field Road
(P.O. Box 326)
Tonopah, NV 89049
(702) 482-9676
FAX: (702) 482-5423
Along with old miners' cabins, museum also has a railroad depot, assay office, and blacksmith shop on display.

Tonopah Historic Mining Park
(P.O. Box 326)
Tonopah, NV 89049
(702)482-9676
Located at an old mine, several buildings are filled with equipment that is operational. Tours are not underground at this time.

NEW MEXICO

Raton Museum
216 South First St.
Raton, NM 87740
(505) 445-8979
Lots of different camps in the area, museum focus is coal mining.

Silver City Museum
312 W. Broadway
Silver City, NM 88061
(505) 538-5921
FAX: (505) 388-1096 call first
Two rooms of the museum are devoted to mining. One room is an example of the office of a mine, the other has equipment such as assaying tools. Also

has local ore samples.

Deming Luna Mimbres Museum
301 S. Silver St.
Deming, NM 88030
(505) 546-2382
A gem and mineral room; coming soon is a collection of geodes and thunder eggs, most from this area.

OREGON

National Historic Oregon Trail Interpretive Center
Oregon Hwy 86, on Flagstaff Hill
(P.O. Box 987)
Baker City, OR 97814
(514) 523-1843
FAX: (541)523-1834
Demonstrations of gold hard-rock mining, old shaft building, millhouse, and stamp mill.

Cottage Grove Museum
H St. and Birch Ave.
(P.O. Box 142)
Cottage Grove, OR 97424
(541) 942-3963
Equipment from the old Bohemia Mines. Miniature operating stamp mill in annex.

Coquille River Museum
270 Fillmore St.
(P.O. Box 737)
Bandon, OR 97411
(541) 347-2164

Eastern Oregon Museum
3rd and Wilcox
Haines, OR 97833
(541) 856-3233

Sumpter Valley Dredge State Park
(P.O. Box 97)
Sumpter, OR 97877
(541) 894-2486 or (541) 523-2499

At this day use park, the old remains of a dredge are currently being repaired.

Josephine County Kerbyville Museum
24195 Redwood Hwy 199
(P.O. Box 34)
Kerby, OR 97531
(541) 592-2076
Offer a sluice box for gold panning by visitors. An old miner's cabin has been reassembled on site.

SOUTH DAKOTA

Big Thunder Gold Mine
604 Blair
(P.O. Box 459)
Keystone, SD 57751
(605) 666-4847
FAX: (605) 348-9637
An underground tour through this 1880s mine, gold panning offered.

Keystone Historical Museum
3rd St.
(P.O. Box 177)
Keystone, SD 57751
(605) 666-4494

Black Hills Mining Museum
323 W. Main
(P.O. Box 694)
Lead, SD 57754
(605) 584-1605
Equipment from the Homestake Mine. In the lower level of the museum there is a simulated underground tour. Gold panning.

Museum of South Dakota State Historical Society
Cultural Heritage Center Building
900 Governors Dr.
Pierre, SD 57501
(605) 773-33458
FAX (605) 773-6041

Visitors walk through hard-rock mine and sluice with rocker and pan.

Minnilusa Pioneer Museum
222 New York St.
Rapid City, SD 57701
(605) 394-6923
FAX: (605) 394-6940
Interactive displays.

UTAH

Tintic Mining Museum
241 W. Main
(P.O. Box 218)
Eureka, UT 84628
(801) 433-6842

Western Mining and Railroad Museum
296 S. Main
Helper, Utah 84526
(801) 472-3009
Emphasis is on coal mining.

Park City Museum
528 Main St.
(P.O. Box 555)
Park City, Utah 84060
(801) 645-5135 or (801) 649-6104
Walk-in simulated mine tunnel and shaft.

Park City Silver Mine Adventure
1 1/2 mi. so. of Park City on Utah 224.
Park City, Utah 84060
(801) 655-7444
(801) 649-8011
Visitors descend in mine to 1500-foot level, then take a train 3/4 miles to the compressor room.

WASHINGTON

Black Diamond Historical Society
Railroad Avenue and Baker Street

(P.O. Box 232)
Black Diamond, WA 98010
(360) 886-2142
Replica of a mine under the museum building.

Chelan County Historical Museum
600 Cottage
(P.O. Box 22)
Cashmere, WA 98815
(509) 782-3230
Contains a Pioneer Village of 21 log structures, including the assay office from the Blewett Mine and a blacksmith shop.

Chewelah Museum
N. 501 3rd St.
(P.O. Box 913)
Chewelah, WA 99109
(509) 905-6091
Mining equipment from the NW Magnasite Co.

Cle Elum Telephone Museum
221 E. 1st
(P.O. Box 11)
Cle Elum, WA 98922
(509) 674-5702
Focus is on coal mining; includes a display on miners' lunch pails.

Stevens County Historical Society
700 N. Wynne St.
(P.O. Box 25)
Colville, WA 99114
(509) 684-5968
Tour of a short mine tunnel.

Pickett Museum
510 Avenue A
(P.O. Box 107)
Index, WA 98256
(360) 793-1534
Superb photo collection of the area.

Renton Historical Society and Museum
235 Mill Ave. South
Renton, WA 98055
(206) 255-2330
FAX: (same)
Coal mining artifacts, such as lamps and lighting.

Klondike Gold Rush National Historical Park
117 S. Main St.
Seattle, WA 98104
(206) 553-7220
FAX: (206) 553-0614
Museum stresses the importance of the role of outfitting gold rushers. Seattle was the jumping-off point for the Klondike Gold Rushers of 1897-1898. Gold panning demonstrations.

WYOMING

Grand Encampment Museum
817 Barnette Ave.
(P.O. Box 96)
Encampment, WY 82325
(307) 327-5329 or 327-5308
Equipment, 14 bldgs, and part of the aerial tramway from the Ferris Hagerty Copper Mine. Currently are developing the tram trail up the old aerial tram course for hikers.

Pioneer Museum
630 Lincoln St.
Lander, WY 82520
(307) 332-4137
One gallery of the museum is devoted to mining. Display includes horse-drawn equipment such as a dump wagon, as well as hand tools. Information on the Oregon Trail.

South Pass City State Historic Park
125 South Pass Main
South Pass City, WY 82520
(307) 332-3684

MUSEUMS AND MINE TOURS

FAX: (307) 332-3688
Gold mining ghost town of 30 buildings, mostly
log construction. Walk-in blacksmith shop. Major
mining exhibit.

---

*If you would like your museum or mine tour included in the next edition of the book, please contact the publisher.
We would be delighted to hear from you.*

BIBLIOGRAPHY

Bachman, David, and Tod Bacigalupi. *The Way it Was: Historical Narrative of Ouray County.* Ouray, Colo.: Wayfinder Press, 1990.

Backus, Harriet Fish. *Tomboy Bride.* Boulder, Colo.: Pruett Publishing Co., 1969.

Barlow, Ronald S. *A Price Guide to Victorian Houseware, Hardware and Kitchenware.* El Cajon, Calif.: Windmill Publishing Co., 1992.

Barney, Libeus. *Letters of the Pike's Peak Gold Rush, or, Early Day Letters from Auraria.* 1859. Reprint, San Jose, Calif.: Talisman Press, 1959.

Bealer, Alex W. *The Art of Blacksmithing.* New York: Funk and Wagnalls, 1969.

Bergevin, Al. *Tobacco Tins and Their Prices.* Greensboro, N.C.: Wallace-Homestead Book Co., 1986.

— . *Food and Drink Containers and Their Prices.* Greensboro, N.C.: Wallace-Homestead Book Co., 1988.

Beringer, C., and J. J. Beringer. *A Text-Book of Assaying for the Use of Those Connected with Mines.* London: N.P. 1890.

Bird, Allan G. *Silverton Gold: The Story of Colorado's Largest Gold Mine.* N.P., Lakewood, Colo.: 1986.

Bird, Isabella L. *A Lady's Life in the Rocky Mountains.* 1879. Reprint, Norman: University of Oklahoma Press: 1960.

Blandford, Percy W. *Practical Blacksmithing and Metalworking.* Blue Ridge Summit, Pa.: Tab Books, Inc., 1988.

Bleakley, Geoffrey T. *A History of the Chisana Mining District, Alaska, 1890–1990.* Resources Report NPS/AFARCR/CRR-96/29. Anchorage: National Park Service, 1996.

Bronikowski, Lynn. "Soiled Doves and Fallen Angels," *Rocky Mountain News,* April 2, 1993.

Browne, Jeanne, ed. *The Restless Longing: A Prospector's Story.* Vermillion: Dakota Books, University of South Dakota Press, 1992.

Brown, Robert L. *An Empire of Silver.* Denver: Sundance Publications Ltd., 1984.

Brown, Ronald, C. *Hard-Rock Miners: The Intermountain West 1860-1920.* College Station: Texas A & M University Press, 1979.

Canty, J. Michael, and Michael N. Greeley, eds. *History of Mining in Arizona.* Tucson: Mining Club of the Southwest Foundation, 1987.

Clark, Hyla M. *The Tin Can Book.* Bergenfield, N.J.: New American Library, 1977.

Clemmer, Gregg S. *American Miners' Carbide Lamps: A Collector's Guide to American Carbide Mine Lighting.* Tucson: Westernlore Press, 1987.

Cobb, Harrison S. *Prospecting Our Past: Gold, Silver and Tungsten Mills of Boulder County.* Boulder,

Colo.: The Book Lode, 1988.

Colorado Iron Works Company. *Cyanide Plants, Machinery, Tanks and Appliances,* catalogue No. 10-B, 1908.

Compressed Air Institute. *Compressed Air Handbook: Applications, Equipment, Engineering Data and Test Procedure.* New York: Compressed Air Institute, 1947.

Conlin, Joseph R. *Bacon, Beans, and Galantines: Food and Foodways on the Western Mining Frontier.* Reno: University of Nevada Press, 1986.

Council for Small Industries in Rural Areas. *The Blacksmith's Craft.* Salisbury, England: Council for Small Industries in Rural Areas, 1955.

Cox, Terry. *Inside the Mountains: A History of Mining Around Central City, Colorado.* Boulder, Colo.: Pruett Publishing Co., 1989.

Crampton, Frank A. *Deep Enough: A Working Stiff in the Western Mine Camps.* 1956. Reprint, Norman: University of Oklahoma Press, 1982.

Crossen, Forest. *Western Yesterdays.* 9 Vol. Boulder, Colo.: Boulder Publishing Co., 1963.

Crucible Steel Company of America. *Crucible Steel Company of America Catalog,* 1925.

Dallas, Sandra. *Colorado Ghost Towns and Mining Camps.* Norman: University of Oklahoma Press, 1985.

Darley, George M. *Pioneering in the San Juan: Personal Reminiscences of Work Done in Southwestern Colorado During the "Great San Juan Excitement."* 1899. Reprint, Lake City, Colo.: Community Presbyterian Church of Lake City, 1986.

Davis, Richard Harding. "The West from a Car Window." *Harper's Weekly* XXXVI, no. 1842 (April 9, 1892).

Decker, Sarah Platt, Chapter of DAR. *Pioneers of the San Juan Country.* Volumes I, II, III, IV. Durango, CO: 1942, 1946, 1952, 1961.

Delano, A. *Life on the Plains and at the Diggings.* 1854. Reprint, Alexandria, Va: Time-Life Books, 1981.

Dempsey, Stanley and James E. Fell Jr. *Mining the Summit: Colorado's Ten Mile District, 1860 — 1960.* Norman: University of Oklahoma Press, 1986.

Denver and Rio Grande Railroad Timetable. November 1889.

Denver City Directories, 1900 to 1935.

Denver Equipment Company. *Mineral Processing Flowsheets.* 2nd ed. Denver: Denver Equipment Co.

Denver Post. 1900 through 1945.

DeQuille, Dan. *The Big Bonanza: An Authentic Account of the Discovery, History, and Working of the World-Renowned Comstock Lode of Nevada.* 1876. Reprint, New York: Alfred A. Knopf, 1947.

Dickey, Art. *Dickey's Old General Store Notebook.* N.P. 1986.

Dyer, J. L. *Snow-Shoe Itinerant.* 1890. Reprint, Breckenridge, Colo.: Father Dyer United Methodist Church, 1976.

Ellis, Anne. *The Life of an Ordinary Woman.* Lincoln: University of Nebraska Press, 1929.

— . *Plain Anne Ellis: More About the Life of an Ordinary Woman.* Boston: Houghton Mifflin Co., 1931.

— . *Sunshine Preferred: The Philosophy of an Ordinary Woman.* Boston: Houghlin Mifflin Co., 1934.

Elsensohn, Sister M. Alfreda. *Idaho Chinese Lore.* Cottonwood: Idaho Corporation of Benedictine Sisters, 1970.

Farquhar, Francis P. *History of the Sierra Nevada.* Berkeley: University of California Press, 1965.

Fell, James E. Jr. *Ores to Metals: The Rocky Mountain Smelting Industry.* Lincoln: University of Nebraska Press, 1979.

Fiester, Mark. *Blasted, Beloved Breckenridge.* Boulder, Colo.: Pruett Publishing Co., 1973.

Fisher, Vardis, and Opal Laurel Holmes. *Gold Rushes and Mining Camps of the Early American West.* Caldwell, Idaho: Caxton Printers, 1970.

Fosssett, Frank. *Colorado: Its Gold and Silver Mines, Farms and Stock Ranges, and Health and Pleasure Resorts.* 1876. Reprint, Glorieta, N.M.: Rio Grande Press, 1976.

Foster, Jack. *Adventures at Timberline.* Denver: Monitor Publications, Inc., 1963.

Francaviglia, Richard V. *Hard Places: Reading the Landscape of America's Historic Mining Districts.* Iowa City: University Iowa Press, 1991.

Freed, Elaine. *Preserving the Great Plains and Rocky Mountains.* Albuquerque: University of New Mexico Press, 1992.

Friggens, Myriam. *Tales, Trails and Tommyknockers: Stories from Colorado's Past.* Boulder: Johnson Publishing Co., 1979.

Gibbons, Reverend J.J. *In the San Juan: Sketches.* 1898. Reprint, Ouray, Colo.: St. Daniel's Church, 1987.

Gleason, Sarah A. *I'd Do It Again: Teaching in Colorado for over Half a Century 1926 – 1978.* N.P.: Century One Press, 1982.

Green, Harvey. *The Light of the Home: An Intimate View of the Lives of Women in Victorian America.* New York: Pantheon Books, 1983.

Gregory, Marvin, and P. David Smith. *Mountain Mysteries: The Ouray Odyssey.* Ouray, CO: Wayfinder Press, 1984.

Greguire, Helen. *The Collector's Encyclopedia of Granite Ware: Colors, Shapes and Values.* Paducah, Ky.: Collectors Books, 1990.

Groh, George W. *Gold Fever: Being a True Account, Both Horrifying and Hilarious, of the Art of Healing (so-called) During the California Gold Rush.* New York: William Morrow and Co., 1966.

Hambleton, Chalkley J. *A Gold Hunter's Experience.* 1898. Reprint, Fairfield, Wash.: Ye Galleon

Press, 1988.

Harris, A. C. *Alaska and the Klondike Gold Fields.* N.p., 1897.

Hayes, A. A., Jr. *New Colorado and the Santa Fe Trail.* New York: Harper & Brothers, 1880.

Henderson, Charles W. *Mining in Colorado: A History of Discovery, Development, and Production.* United States Geological Survey Professional Paper 138. Washington, D.C., 1926.

Hollister, Ovando. *The Mines of Colorado.* 1876. Reprint, New York: Promontory Press, 1974.

Holmstrom, J. G., and [?] Holford. *American Blacksmithing and Twentieth Century Toolsmith and Steelworker's Manual.* 2 vols. in 1. Chicago: Frederick J. Drake & Co., 1911 - 1916.

Hume, Ivor Noel. *Historical Archaeology.* New York: Alfred A. Knopf, Inc., 1969.

Hunziker, Otto F. *Condensed Milk and Milk Powder.* 4th Ed. La Grange, Ill.: N.P., 1926.

Hutslar, Donald A. *Log Construction in the Ohio Country, 1750 – 1850.* Athens: Ohio University Press, 1992.

Ingersoll, Ernest. "The Camp of the Carbonates: Ups and Downs in Leadville." *Scribner's Monthly,* XVIII (October, 1879).

—.　*The Crest of the Continent: A Summer's Railroad Ramble Through the Rocky Mountains.* 1883. Reprint, Glorieta, N.M.: Rio Grande Press, 1969.

International Correspondence School Reference Library. Vol. 10, 29, 34, 72, 73, 120, 146, 148, 149, 153, 155, 230. Scranton: International Textbook Company, 1897 – 1911.

Johnson, William W. *The Forty-Niners.* The Old West Series. Alexandria, Va.: Time-Life Books, 1974.

Jordan, Terry G. *American Log Buildings: An Old World Heritage.* Chapel Hill: University of North Carolina Press, 1985.

Kahler, D. E. *Secrets of Gold Panning.* N.P.: Geodek, Inc.: 1984.

King, Joseph E. *A Mine to Make a Mine: Financing the Colorado Mining Industry, 1859 – 1902.* College Station: Texas A&M University Press, 1977.

Kresge's Katalog of 5¢ and 10¢ Merchandise. 1913. Reprint, New York: Random House, 1975.

Lakes, Arthur. *Prospecting for Gold and Silver in North America.* 3rd. Ed. Scranton, Pa.: The Colliery Engineer Co., 1899.

Lee, Mabel Barbee. *Cripple Creek Days.* Lincoln: University of Nebraska Press, 1984.

Lehner, Lois. *Lehner's Encyclopedia of U.S. Marks on Pottery, Porcelain and Clay.* Paducah, Ky.: Collector Books, 1988.

Leonard, Stephen J. and Thomas J. Noel. *Denver: Mining Camp to Metropolis.* Niwot, Colo.: University Press of Colorado, 1990.

Lingenfelter, Richard E. *The Hardrock Miners: A History of the Mining Labor Movement in the American West, 1863 – 1893.* Berkeley: University of California Press, 1974.

Luchetti, Cathy and Carol Olwell. *Women of the West.* St . George, Utah: Antelope Island Press, 1982.

Magnuson, Richard G. *Coeur D'Alene Diary: The First Ten Years of Hardrock Mining in North Idaho.* Protland, Ore.: Metropolitan Press, 1968.

Marryat, Frank. *Mountains and Molehills, or, Recollections of a Burnt Journal.* 1855. Reprint, Alexandria, Va: Time-Life Books, 1982.

Martin, Andy. *Blasting Cap Tin Catalog.* Tucson: N.P., 1991.

McLean, Evalyn Walsh. *Father Struck It Rich.* 1936. Reprint, Ouray, Colo.: Bear Creek Publishing, 1981.

Meitus, Marty. "Homestead, Sweet Homestead." *Rocky Mountain News,* November 27, 1992.

Mine and Smelter Supply Company, catalogue, 1912.

The Mining Catalog. Metal and Quarry edition. Pittsburgh: Keystone Consolidated Publishing Company, Inc., 1923.

Mining History Association. P.O. Box 150300, Denver, Colorado 80215.

Montgomery Ward and Company. Catalogue, Number 57. 1895. Reprint, New York: Dover Publications, 1969.

Morrison, Tom. *Hardrock Gold: A Miner's Tale.* Norman: University of Oklahoma Press, 1992.

Moynihan, Betty. *Augusta Tabor: A Pioneering Woman.* Evergreen, Colo.: Cordillera Press, 1988.

Murie, Olaus J. *A Field Guide to Animal Tracks.* Boston: Houghton Mifflin Company, 1974.

Nevin, David. *The Expressmen.* New York: Time-Life Books, 1974.

Niebur, Jay E. *Arthur Redman Wilfley: Miner, Invernter, and Entrepreneur.* Western Business History Research Center, Colorado Historical Society.

Noel, Thomas J. Denver: *Rocky Mountain Gold.* Tulsa, Okla.: Continental Heritage Press, 1980.

Noel, Thomas J., Paul F. Mahoney and Richard E. Stevens. *Historical Atlas of Colorado.* Norman: University of Oklahoma Press, 1993.

Northern Miner Press. *Mining Explained.* Toronto: Northern Miner Press, Ltd., 1968.

Nossaman, Allen. *Many More Mountains.* Vol. I and II. Denver: Sundance Publications, 1989, 1993.

O'Donnell, J. C. "Buck". *The Good Old Days.* Shaft and Development Machines, Inc., 1968.

Parker, Ben H., Jr. *Gold Panning and Placering in Colorado, How and Where.* Information Series 33, Colorado Geological Survey. Denver, Colo. 1992.

Paul, Rodman Wilson. *Mining Frontiers of the Far West, 1848 – 1880.* Albuquerque: University of New Mexico Press, 1974.

Paul, Wolfgang. *Mining Lore: An Illustrated Composition and Documentary Compilation with Emphasis on the Spirit and History of Mining.* Portland, Ore.: Morris, 1970.

Petralia, Joseph F. *Gold! Gold! A Beginners Handbook and Recreational Guide: How to Prospect for Gold.* San Francisco: Sierra Trading Post, 1982.

Pohs, Henry A. *Early Underground Mine Lamps: Mine Lighting from Antiquity to Arizona.* Museum Monograph #6. Tucson: Arizona Historical Society, 1984.

Preble, Glen R., ed. *Impressed in Time: Colorado Beverage Bottles, Jugs and etc. 1859 – 1915.* Littleton, Colo.: Antique Bottle Collectors Club, 1987.

Rathje, William, and Cullen Murphy. *Rubbish! The Archeology of Garbage.* New York: HarperCollins, 1992.

Raymond, Roert. *Out of the Fiery Furnace: The Impact of Metals on the History of Mankind.* University Park: Pennsylvania State University Press, 1986.

Reichelt, Richard. *Heartland Blacksmiths: Conversations at the Forge.* Carbondale and Edwardsville: Southern Illinois University Press, 1988.

Reiter, Joan Swallow. *The Women.* Alexandria, Va.: Time-Life Books, 1978.

Rice, Frank A. *The Mines of Ouray County.* Rev. ed. Ouray, Colo.: Bear Creek Publishing Co., 1980.

Richards, Robert H. and Charles E. Locke. *A Test Book of Ore Dressing.* New York: McGraw-Hill Book Company, Inc., 1925.

Richardson, Albert D. *Beyond the Mississippi: From the Great River to the Great Ocean.* Hartford, Conn.: American Publishing Company, 1869.

Rickard, T. A. *Across the San Juan Mountains.* 1907. Reprint, Ouray, Colo.: Bear Creek Publishing Co., 1980.

Ricketts, Pierre de Peyster. *Notes on Assaying and Assay Schemes.* New York: John Wiley & Sons, 1880.

Riley, Glenda. *The Female Frontier: A Comparative View of Women on the Prairie and the Plains.* Lawrence: University Press of Kansas, 1988.

Rocky Mountain News. 1864 through 1945.

Root, Waverly and Richard de Rochemont. *Eating in America: A History.* New York: William Morrow and Co., 1976.

Schlissel, Lillian. *Women's Diaries of the Westward Journey.* New York: Schocken Books, 1982.

Sears, Roebuck Catalogue, 1897. Reprint, New York: Chelsea House, 1968.

Sears, Roebuck Catalogue, 1902. Reprint, New York: Bounty Books, 1969.

Shikes, Robert H. *Rocky Mountain Medicine: Doctors, Drugs, and Disease in Early Colorado.* Boulder, Colo.: Johnson Books, 1986.

Shirley, Dame. *The Shirley Letters: Being Letters Written in 1851 – 1852 from the California Mines.* Salt Lake City, Utah: Peregrine Smith Books, 1983.

Simonin, Louis L. *The Rocky Mountain West in 1867.* Reprint, Lincoln, Nebraska: University of Nebraska Press, 1966.

Sloan, Robert E., and Carl A. Skowronski. *The Rainbow Route: An Illustrated History.* Denver: Sundance Publications, 1975.

Smith, Duane A. *Rocky Mountain Mining Camps: The Urban Frontier.* Bloomington: Indiana University Press, 1967.

— . *Song of the Hammer and Drill: The Colorado San Juans, 1860 – 1914.* Golden: Colorado School of Mines Press, 1982.

Spude, Robert L. *Historic American Engineering Record of the Sound Democrat Mill.* HAER no. CO-69. Denver: National Park Service, Rocky Mountain Region, 1991.

Steele, Rev. John. *In Camp and Cabin.* 1901. Reprint, New York: Citadel Press, 1962.

Stoehr, S. Eric. *Bonanza Victorian: Architecture and Society in Colorado Mining Camps.* Albuquerque: University of New Mexico Press, 1975.

Strasser, Susan. *Never Done: A History of American Housework.* New York: Pantheon Books, 1982.

Taggert, Arthur F. *Handbook of Ore Dressing.* New York: John Wiley & Sons, Inc, 1927.

Taylor, Bayard. *Eldorado, or, Adventures in the Path of Empire.* Vol. I and II. 1850. Reprint, Alexandria, Va.: Time-Life Books, 1983.

— . *Colorado: A Summer Trip.* 1876. Reprint, Niwot: University Press of Colorado, 1989.

Thayer, William M. *Marvels of the New West: A Vivid Portrayal of the Unparalleled Marvels in the Vast Wonderland West of the Missouri River.* Norwich, Conn.: Henry Bill Publishing Co., 1892.

Tin Type. Newsletter for the Tin Can Collectors Club. Box 440101, Aurora, Colo. 80044.

Todd, Arthur Cecil. *The Cornish Miner in America: The Contribution to the Mining History of the United States by Emigrant Cornish Miners — the Men Called Cousin Jacks.* Glendale, Calif.: Arthur H. Clark Co., 1967.

Twain, Mark. *Roughing It.* 1872. Reprint, Alexandria, Va.: Time-Life Books, 1982.

Varney, Philip. *Arizona Ghost Towns and Mining Camps.* Phoenix: Arizona State Transportation Department and Arizona Highways, 1994.

Voynick, Stephen M. *Leadville: A Miner's Epic.* Missoula, Mont.: Mountain Press Publishing Co., 1984.

Wallace, Robert. *The Miners.* Alexandria, Va.: Time-Life Books, 1976.

Watkins, T. H. *Gold and Silver in the West: The Illustrated History of an American Dream.* Palo Alto, Calif.: American West Publishing Co., 1971.

Weslager, C. A. *The Log Cabin in America.* New Brunswick, N.J.: Rutgers University Press, 1969.

West, Elliott. *The Saloon on the Rocky Mountain Mining Frontier.* Lincoln: University of Nebraska Press, 1979.

Wheeler, Keith. *The Townsmen.* Alexandria, Va.: Time-Life Books, 1975. 1910. Berkeley: University of California Press, 1979.

— . *The Chroniclers.* Alexandria, Va.: Time-Life Books, 1976.

Williams, Richard L. *The Loggers.* Alexamdria, Va.: Time-Life Books, 1976.

Williams, Susan. *Savory Suppers and Fashionable Feasts: Dining in Victorian America.* New York: Pantheon Books, 1985.

Wilson, Rex L. *Bottles on the Western Frontier.* Tucson: University of Arizona Press, 1981.

Wolle, Muriel S. *Stampede to Timberline: The Ghost Towns and Mining Camps of Colorado.* 1949. Reprint, Chicago: Swallow Press, 1974.

Wood, Frances, and Dorothy Wood. *I Hauled These Mountains in Here!* Caldwell, Idaho: Caxton Printers, 1977.

Wyman, Mark. *Hard Rock Epic: Western Miners and the Industrial Revolution, 1860 – 1910.* Berkeley: University of California Press, 1979.

Young, Otis E., Jr. *Western Mining: An Informal Account of Precious-metals Prospecting, Placering, Lode Mining, and Milling on the American Frontier from Spanish Times to 1893.* Norman: University of Oklahoma Press, 1970.

— . *Black Powder and Hand Steel: Miners and Machines on the Old Western Frontier.* Norman: University of Oklahoma Press, 1975.

Adits, 50
Aerial trams, 89–90, 155
Air compressors, 46
Akins classifiers, 73
Alaska, 10, 24, 31,158, 160
Alma, Colorado, 27, 51
Alpine Loop, Colorado, 61
Alta, Colorado, 195–196, 202
Amalgamating pans, 60, 61
    Field Guide, 72
Amalgamating plates, 56
Amalgamation/concentration mills,
    56
American Can Company, 206
Americans, 16, 37
Animal bones, 218–219
Animas Forks, Colorado, 5, 54, 59
Appert, Nicholas, 202
Arizona, 149, 257
Arrastras, 72
Asafetida, 148
Aspirin, 148
Assay furnaces, 115, 128–130,
Assay offices, 5–6, 113–116, 117–
    120
    assay furnaces, 115, 128–130,
    bucking boards, 115–116,
        121, 131
    combination furnaces, 129
    crucibles, 114,122,123,127
    cupels, 115, 124–125, 127
    Field Guide, 127-131
    interior, 117–119
    mullers, 116, 121
    portable furnaces, 128
    scales, 120
    splitters, 121
    stationary furnaces, 130
    worktables, 113, 115
Assay tests
    chemical (wet), 120
    cupellation, 124–125
    dore, 125
    fire (dry), 120–126

    fluxes, 122
    litharge, 123, 125
    smelting, 123
    splits, 121
Assayers, 116–117
    custom, 116
Athearn, Rick, 8–9, 54
Austrians, 37

Baby's shoe, 134
Backcountry traveling, xiv
Backus, Harriet Fish, 138, 150
Baking powder, 212, 213, 215, 223
    tin cans, 213, 230–231
Ball mills, 69
Bedsprings, 177
Belknap, Keurah Pention, 136
Bellows, 100, 108
Beringer, C., 125
Bird, Allan, 150, 219
Bird, Isabella, 19, 133, 137, 171
Blacksmiths, 99–102, 104
Blacksmiths
    bellows, 100, 108,
    Field Guide, 107–111
    forges, 109
    and machine-made hardware,
        101–102
    shops, 99, 102–106
    stumps, 107
    as toolmakers, 99, 100, 101,102
    tuyeres (tuy irons), 102,103
    workbenches, 110
Blake, William, 199
Blake Jaw Crushers, 58, 67
Blasting, 39–40
    powder, 43
Boardinghouses, 142–143, 183, 187
    Alta, Colorado, 195–196
    American Plan, 189
    basements, 197
    Caledonia boardinghouse, 174
    Camp Bird Mine boarding-

        house, 188
    company-owned, 185–189
    cooks, 189–194
    European Plan, 143, 189
    evolution of, 185–189
    food, 190–191, 192, 193
    Mammoth Sleeping Palace,
        185–186
    mealtime, 193
    Old Hundred, 183, 184, 185,
        186, 197
    Sunnyside Mine cook, 189
    tents, 185
    Tomboy Mine boardinghouse,
        189
    Union-Smuggler Mine board-
        ing-house, 189
    writing on walls, 179, 194–197
Boardwalks, 159
Boilers, 2, 52–54, 217
    tubular, 53
Bonanza, Colorado, 143–144
Bones, animal, 202, 218–219
Books, companion,10
Borden, Gail, 205
Borden's Condensed Milk, 205, 233
Breckenridge, Colorado, 32, 33, 142
Bucket-line dredges, 30, 33
Bucking boards, 115–116, 121, 131
Buckskin Joe, Colorado, 72,
Bunkhouses, 157
Bureau of Land Management, 8, 54
Burros, 79, 80–81, 82, 155. *See
    also* Horses, Mules, Stables

Cables, 49
Caledonia boardinghouse, 174
California, 10, 155, 136, 137, 143,
    161, 162, 170, 186, 189,
    195, 202, 203, 225, 258–
    260
    gold rush, 18, 25
    socks, 145

Callow settling and pulp thickening tank, 73
Camp Bird Mine boardinghouse,188
Camphor, 148
Can openers, 229
Canaries, 140
Candle-lanterns, 2–3, *3*
Canonville, California, 162
Canvas, 186
Carbide, 36
    kegs, 45
Caribou, Colorado, 5, 202, 250
Carson, Colorado, 92
Castor oil, 148
Cats, 155
Cautions, vii
Cemeteries, 247, 248, 249, 250
    clusters of dates, 247–250
        tombstones from Sears,Roebuck, 247
Chemical (wet) assay tests, 120
Chicago, 63, 240
Chihuahua, Colorado, 212, 221
Children, 149–150
China (dishes), 135, 221
    shards, 133, 221, 244
Chinese, 16, 20
Clements, Eric, 121
Clinkers, 52
Code of the West, 16, 19, 143
Coffee cans, 223–225
Coffee pots, 219–220, 241
Colorado, 260–263
    gold rush, 27
Colorado Historical Society, 223,261
Colorado Iron Works Company
        catalogue, 69, 70, 74
Columbine milk, 232
Colvin, James C., 179
Combination assay furnaces, 129,
Comstock District, Nevada, 59
Concentration tables, 56, 60–61, 71
    Field Guide, 71
Concord stages, 85
Condensed milk, 205
    cans, 205, 227, 232–233
Cone mills, 69
Consolidated Virginia Mill, 59
Cooking, 143–144
Cooks, 189–194, 190
Cookstoves, *See* Stoves
Cornish, 36–37, 219, 180, 248
278 Crab winches, 65

Crampton, Frank, 15, 40, 162
Crucibles, 114, 122, 123, 127
Crushing rolls, 70
Cupellation, 124–125
Cupels, 5–6, 115, 124–125, 127
Custom assayers, 116
Cyanide process, 61–62

Dances, 160
Darley, George M., 80–81
Delaware, 44
Denver Fire Clay Company, 116,117
Denver Rock Drill Company, 111
Digging, 8
Divorce laws, 135
Dodge crusher, 58, 67
Dogs, 155
Doll's head, 134
Donner Lake, 133
Dore, 125
Double-jacking, 39
Dr. Price's Cream Baking Powder, 212, 213, 215
    tin cans, 230
Dredging, 29–31, 33
    bucket-line, 30, 31
    Field Guide, 32–33
Drill steels, 40, 99, 101
Drilling contests, 160
Drinking, 19
Dry assay tests, 120–126
Dumont, Colorado, *53*
Durango, Colorado, 136
Dyer, John, 162

Elk City, Idaho, 150
Elks, 37, 250
Ellis, Anne, 143–144, 162, 170–171, 191
Embossing,43, 44, 46, 63, 96, 129, 206, 212, 213, 228, 230, 231, 233, 238, 240
Empson's, 204, 228
English, 16
Epsom salts, 148
Esmerelda Mine, 216
Etiquette, 7–9
Ewing, Larry L., 179

False-fronted buildings, 157–158,
Field Guides, 3–4, 11

amalgamating pans, 72
assay offices, 127–131
blacksmiths, 107–111
concentration tables, 71
dredging, 32–33
hard-rock mining, 43–47
hoists, 64–66
household clues, 226–245
jaw crushers, 67
lodging, 177–181
lodging clues, 226–245
mills, 67–75
mining camps, 163
mining equipment, 63–75
placering, 32–33
recovery process, 71–75
roads and trails, 93–96
stables, 97
stamp batteries, 68
towns, 163
transportation, 93–97
Fine grinding equipment, 69–70
Finnish, 16
Fire (dry) assay tests, 120–126
Fires, 200
Floating concentration mills, 29–30
Flotation process, 62, 75
Flowers, 140
Fluxes, 122
Flywheel pumps, 47
Food, 190–191, 192, 193,
    in tin cans, 203, 205, 212–215
Forges, 109
Foundations, 175–176, 180, 199, 200
Fraternal organizations, 37, 249–250
Freemasons, 37
Freight wagons, 78, 79, 82–83
Furniture, 172, 194

Gambling, 19
Georgetown, Colorado, 248–250
Germans, 16
Ghost towns, 9, 161–162. *See also* Mining Camps
    clues to what went on, 1–5
    defined, 4
    exploration etiquette, 7–9
    looking for colors and shapes, 5
    from miner's viewpoint, xiii
    refraining from removing things, xv
    safety precautions, vii

tree stumps, 163
Gibbons, J. J., 77, 88, 176
Gleason, Sara A., 147
Godfrey, Charles, 27, 31
Gold. *See also* Assay tests, Hard-rock
    mining, Placer mining,
    Silver
    prices, 25, 28
    qualities, 21
    searching for, 23–24
    weight of, 21, 23–25
Gold panning, 23–27
    pans, 25
    rockers, 27, 29
    technique, 26
Gold Prince Mill, 59
Goldfield, Nevada, 117
Graniteware, 220, 242–243
Graveyards. *See* Cemeteries
Greeley, Horace, 14
Green, Harvey, 135
Gregory, John, 249–250
Grizzlies, 56, 58, 67
Groh, George, 15–16
Guyer, William, 221

Hard boils, 35
Hard-rock miners, 21, 36
    Bucket-riding, 38
    candles, 36, 38
    clothing, 35
    fraternal organizations, 37, 249–
        250
    hard boils, 35
    highgrading, 40–42, 126
    hoistmen, 51–52
    labor unions, 37
    lunch pails, 36, 37
    national origins, 37
    silicosis, 37
    skills, 35
    superstitions, 38
    teasing, 37
    technique, 35
    and Tommyknockers, 38
Hard-rock mining
    air compressors, 46
    blasting, 39–40
    blasting powder, 43
    carbide kegs, 45
    double-jacking, 39
    drill steels, 40, 99, 101
    drilling, 39, 40, 41

Field Guide, 43–47
    less gold found as mine deep-
        ens, 41–42
    misfires, 39–40
    mucking, 40
    mules, 39
    powder kegs, 43–44
    shift bosses, 37, 39
    single-jacking, 39
    steam engines, 47
Hardesty, Roy, 225
Hardesty, Rudd, 223–225
Hardesty family home, 225
Hardesty's Gold Label Baking
    Powder, 223
Hardware, 101–102
Hartz jigs, 75
Hayes, A. A. Jr., 113, 135, 137, 140,
    166, 170
Head frames, 49–50
Herbal medicines, 148
High-altitude sickness, 148
Highgrading, 40–42, 126
Hispanics, 20
Hobnailed boots, 202, 217–218,
    226, 245
Hoistmen, 51–52
Hoists, 50–51, 52, 64, 65, 66
    crab winch, 65
    Field Guide, 64–66
    horse-powered hoisting whim,
        66
Hole-and-cap tin cans, 203, 204,
    226, 227
Holford, 99
Holidays, 160
Hollister, Ovando, 20
Home life, 137–140
Home medicine chests, 148
Homer Laughlin China Company,
    221–222, 244
Honest Miner, 16–20, 21
Horse-powered hoisting whims, 66
Horses, 80, 82. *See also* Burros,
    Mules, Stables
Horseshoes, 78
Household clues, 5, 6–7, 181,
    199–200, 201, 222. *See
    also* Lodging, Lodging
    clues, Shadowgees, Tin
    cans, Trash
    animal bones, 218–219
    coffee pots, 219–220, 241
    Field Guide, 226–245

glass and china shards, 220–
    222, 244
graniteware, 220, 242–243
hobnailed boots, 217–218,
    245
pots and pans, 219–220,
    241–243
reuse of artifacts, 216–217
See also Shadowgees
tin cans, 202–216
Household supplies, 141
Housework, 140, 141
Hutslar, Donald, 165
Hydraulicking, 29

Idaho, 18, 60, 82, 89, 150, 224, 263
Illinois, 63
Impact screens, 74
Improvised items, 6. *See also*
    Shadowgees
Indiana, South Bend, 78
Ingersoll, Ernest, 86, 117, 156, 185–
    186
Irish, 16, 37
Italians, 16, 37

Jaw crushers, 56, 58, 67
    Field Guide, 67

K C Baking Powder, 231
Kegs
    carbide, 45
    powder, 43–44
Kentucky, 223
Keystone's The Mining Catalog, 43,
    45, 111
Klondike, 10, 158, 160
Kuners, 204, 227, 228

Labor Unions, 37
Lake City, Colorado, 150
Lakes, Arthur, 21
Lard buckets, 240
Laughlin, Homer, 221–222
Laundry, 140–142
Leadville, Colorado, 185–186
Lee, Mabel Barbee, 162
Lehner, Lois, 244
Lingenfelter, Richard E., 35
Litharge, 123, 125

Lodging. *See also* Household clues
  Field Guide, 226–245
Log Cabin Syrup, 234
Log Cabins, 165–166,167, 170
  chimneys, 170, 171
  corner notching, 167–170
  in Europe, 165
  evolution of, 166–172
  first-generation, 167–172
  foundations, 175–176, 180
  full dovetail notching, 169,
    174
  furniture, 172
  interiors, 171
  roofs, 167, 171
  saddle notching, 167–170
  second-generation, 173–175
  simple lap notching, 168
  steeple notching, 167–170
  transition, 172–173
London Butte Gold Mine, 51, 52, 53
Loneliness, 20, 151
Longmont, Colorado, 203
Lunch pails, 36, 37
Lumber camps, 163

Mail, 20, 86, 89
Mail-order catalogues, 10
Majestic Mfg. Co., 178
Malachite, Colorado, 146
Mammoth Sleeping Palace, 185–186
Marryat, Frank, 85, 86
Mary Murphy Mine, 199
Masons, 250
Mattresses, 177
McLean, Evalyn Walsh, 188
Medicines, 148
Meyenberg, John B., 205
Midwifery, 149
Mill-in-a-box, 13–14, 15
Miller, Jim, 104
Mills, 54-62
  Akins classifiers, 73
  amalgamating pans, 72
  amalgamating plates, 56
  amalgamation/concentration,
    56
  callow settling and pulp thicken-
    ing tank, 73
  concentration tables, 56
    60–61, 71
  Diagram, 56
  Field Guide, 67–75

fine grinding equipment, 69,
    70
grinding section, 58–59, 68–70,
grizzlies, 56, 58, 67
Hartz jigs, 75
impact screens, 74
jaw crushers, 56,58, 67
ore feeders, 75
recovery process, 59–62, 71–75
screening devices, 74
stamp, 55
stamp batteries, 56, 57, 58–
    59, 68
tram terminus, 55, 57
trommels, 74
water tanks, 57
Mine and Smelter Supply Company
    catalogue, 53, 54, 59, 66,
    69, 73, 100
Mine tours, 255–267
Miners, 17, 18, 19, 20. *See also*
    Honest Miner, Prospectors
  appearance and clothing, 17–18,
  and bragging, 20
  cheerfulness, 19
  drinking, 19
  entertainment, 19
  hard-rock, 21
  hoistmen, 51–52
  lunch pails, 36, 37
  and mail, 20
  Mark Twain's description, 14-15
  national origins, 16, 37
  optimism, 13–14
  prejudices, 20
  sharing, 19
  tool set, 16, 21
  and top hats, 20
  trading rock specimens, 19
Mines, 21
  buying and selling, 21–22
  cautions, vii, 34
  salting, 21–22
Mining. *See also* Hardrock mining,
    Placer mining
  differences in success between
    placer and hard-rock
    mining 41–42
Mining camps. *See also* Ghost towns
  birth of, 157–159, 161
  boardwalks, 159
  bunkhouses, 157
  crime, 161
  dances, 160

death of, 161–162
defined, 4
drilling contests, 160
entertainment, 159–161
false-fronted buildings, 157–158
Field Guide, 163
heyday, 155-156
holidays, 160
law and order, 161
music, 161
noise of, 155, 156
saloons, 159–160
smells of, 156
stores, 157
vigilance committees, 161
women in, 133–153
Mining equipment
  boilers, 52–54
  cables, 49
  Field Guide, 63–75
  head frames, 49–50
  hoists, 50–51, 52
  mills, 54–62, 67–75
  name plates and embossing, 63
  ore bins, 53–54, 55–57
  sheave wheels, 49–50
  wire ropes, 49
Misfires, 39–40
Missouri, 78, 178
Montana, 10, 224, 263–264
Montgomery Ward Catalogue, 10,
    36, 37, 148, 177, 218, 220,
    245. *See also* Sears,
    Roebuck Catalogue
Morrison, Tom, 35
Mountain fever, 148
Mucking, 40
Mule shoes, 78
Mules, 39, 78, 79, 80, 81–82, 155.
    See also Burros, Horses,
    Stables
Muller, 116, 121
Murie, Olaus, 2
Museums, 255–267
Music, 161

Name plates, 63
Napoleon, 202
Nash, George (father), 223–224
Nash, George A. (son), 223–225
Nash, Virginia J., 224
Nash Coffee and Spice Company,
    223–225

Nash family home, 223,224
Native Americans, 20, 152
Nevada, 18, 59, 117, 143, 189, 264–265
New Jersey, 62
New Mexico, 10, 265
Newspapers, 86
New York, 62, 129
North Star Mine, 187
Norton, Edwin, 209 – 212
Nursing, 147–147,148,149

Oddfellows, 37, 249–250
Ohio, 221
Olcott, Eben, 187
Old Hundred boardinghouse, 183–185, 186, 197
Open-top tin cans 205, 206, 207, 228
Ore bins, 53–54, 55–57
Ore feeders, 75
Oregon, 31, 136, 239, 265–266
Oregon grape root, 148
Ouray, Colorado, 11, 176, 188
Overland Trail, 134
Oxen, 83

Pack trails, 79–82
Paden, Melvin, 15–16
Parker, Ben H. Jr., 26
Pasties, 36
Patents, 44, 209
    timetable, 254
Pearson, J.T., 183
Pennsylvania 63, 104, 179
Petroleum jelly, 148
Pitch plaster, 148
Pittsburgh, 104
Placer mining, 23
    dredging, 29–31
    Field Guide, 32–33
    hydraulicking, 29
    more gold found as one digs
        deeper, 41
    panning, 23–27
    sluicing, 27–29
Pope, John, 249–250
Portable assay furnaces, 128
Pots and pans, 202, 219–220, 226, 241–243
    graniteware, 220
Powder kegs, 43–44

Pregnancy, 149
Prince Albert tobacco, 236
Prospectors, 20–22, 23, 29
Prostitutes, 150–151

Quinine, 148

Railroads, 85
Raspberries, 150
Recovery process, 59–62, 71–75
    amalgamation, 59, 60, 61, 72
    cyanide process, 61–62
    Field Guide, 71–75
    flotation process, 62, 75
    Reuse of artifacts, 216–217,
    See also: Shadowgees
Rexford, Colorado, 4, 5, 91, 207–208, 212, 215
Richardson, Albert D. 1, 11, 23, 25, 88
Rickard, T. A., 89, 190, 219
Roads and trails, 7, 77–79. See also
        Transportation
    debris, 96
    difficult passage, 95
    Field Guide, 93–96
    finding, 93
    pack trails, 79–82
    road building remains, 94
    wagon roads, 82–84
Rock crushers, 58, 67– 70
Rockers, 27, 29
Rocky Mountain canaries, 80
Rod mills, 69
Rose-root tea, 148
Royal Baking Powder, 231

Sage tea, 148
Saloons, 151, 152, 159 – 160
Salting, 21–22
Samson crusher, 58, 67
Sanguineness, 14, 19
Sanitary Can Company, 206, 207, 228
Schilling's Baking Powder, 231
Schools, 145–146
Screening devices, 74
Seafood cans, 238–239
Sears, Roebuck Catalogue, 10, 36, 218, 220, 247. See also
        Montgomery Wards

Catalogue
Sevres china, 7
Sewing, 144–145
Shadowgees, 3, 6, 7, 181, 216
Sheave wheels, 49–50
Sherman Silver Act, 162
Shikes, Robert H., 151
Shirley, Dame, 136, 152, 186
Side seams on tin cans, 208 – 212
Silicosis, 37
Silver, 21. See also Assay tests, Gold
Silver Jack Mine, 13–14
Silverton, Colorado, 174, 183, 187, 219
Simonin, Louis, 86–87
Single-jacking, 39
Sluicing, 27–29
    long toms, 27, 29
Smelters, 62
Smelting, 123
Smith, Duane, 187
Snubbing posts, 77, 83, 96
Socks, 145
Sound Democrat Mill, 54–55, 57, 59, 60, 61, 62,103
South Dakota, 10, 266
Souvenirs, 8
Splits, 121
Splitters, 121
St. Elmo, Colorado, 174
St. Louis, 240, 242
Stables, 91–92, 97. See also Burros,
        Horses, Mules
    Field Guide, 97
Stagecoaches, 84, 87
    Concord, 85
    drivers, 86
    roads, 93
    robberies, 136, 137
Stamp batteries, 56,57, 58–59, 68
    Field Guide, 68
Stamp mills, 55
Stark, Bill, 3
Stationary assay furnaces, 130
Steam engines, 47
Steam saws, 155
Steele, John, 15, 161–162
Stevens, Hutch, 13
Stores, 157
Stoves, 11, 178,187–188
Strasser, Susan, 142
Stumps, 107
Sunnyside Mine, 150
    boardinghouse cook, 189

coffee, 219
Swandyke, Colorado, 172
Syphilis, 151
Syrup cans, 234–235

Tabor, Augusta, 140–141
Talbot, John, 27–29, 31, 120, 125–126
Taylor, Baylord, 17
Taylor, W. L., 139
Teaching, 145–146
Thayer, William, 17, 38, 85
Thompson, Harold, 38, 51, 52
Tin cans. *See also* Household clues,
    Shadowgees, Trash
    baking powder, 213, 230–231
    and California gold rush, 202–203
    can openers, 229
    canning factories, 204
    changing manufacturing
        characteristics, 206–212
    and Civil War, 203, 205
    and Colorado gold rush, 203
    condensed milk, 205, 232–233
    contents, 203, 205, 212–215
    development of, 202–203
    distinctive shapes, 230–237
    1870s and early 1880s, 208–209, 210
    embossed, 212, 213,
    hole-and-cap, 203–204, 206–207, 210, 214, 226, 227
    invention of canning, 202
    Lard buckets, 240
    Norton's side seam (1887), 208, 209, 210, 212
    open-top, 205–206, 207, 210, 228
    seafood, 238–239
    size of hole as clue to contents, 214–215
    syrup, 234–235
    timeline, 211
    tobacco, 236–237
    Towle's Log Cabin Syrup, 234
Tin Cup, Colorado, 174
Tobacco, 148
    cans, 236–237
Todd, Arthur C., 180
Tomboy Mine boardinghouse, 189
Tombstones, 249
    from Sears, Roebuck, 247

Tommyknockers, 38
Toms, long, 27, 29
Tools, 16, 18, 21
    and blacksmiths, 99–102
Top Hats, 20
Topographical maps, 5
Tours, 255–267
Towle's Log Cabin Syrup, 217, 234
Towns, Field Guide, 163. *See also,*
    Ghost towns, Mining
    camps
Trail guides, 10
Trails, *See* Roads and trails
Tram terminus, 55, 57
Transportation, 79. *See also* Burros,
    Horses, Mules, Roads
    and trails
    aerial trams, 89–90, 155
    Field Guide, 93–97
    freight wagons, 82–83
    railroads, 85
    and stables, 91–92
    stagecoaches, 85–89, 84
Trash, 8, 199-245
    dumps, 8. *See also* Household
        clues
Tread Lightly! program, xiv
Tree stumps, 163
Trollope, Anthony, 218–219
Trommels, 74
Tube mills, 69
Tubular boilers, 53
Turpentine, 148
Tuyeres (tuy irons), 102, 103
Twain, Mark, 14–15, 20, 155, 162, 165

Uncompaghre Peak, 13
Underwear, 144–145
Union-Smuggler Mine boarding-
    house, 189
U.S. Geological Survey
    topographical maps, 5
Utah, 62, 224, 266

Van Westenberg, Ed, 196
Vandalism, 9
Vaseline, 148, 149

Wagon roads, 82–84

Walsh, Thomas, 188
Walters, Henry, 249–250
Wardner, Idaho, 82, 89
Washington,18, 266–267
Washington, California, 161–162
Washington, D.C., 162
Washoe canaries, 80
Wedding Breakfast Coffee, 223
Western Museum of Mining and
    Industry, 121, 122,123,
    124, 125, 260
Wet assay tests, 120
Whiskey, 148
Wilfley tables, 56, 60–61, 71
Wilmington, Delaware, 44
Wire ropes, 49
Witch hazel, 148
Women, 133–134
    and canaries, 140
    and children, 149–150
    cooking, 143–144
    as curiosities, 136
    divorce laws, 135
    and entertainment, 160
    and flowers, 140
    home life, 137–140
    home medicine chests, 148
    and housework supplies, 141
    housework, 140, 141
    laundry, 140–142
    loneliness, 151–152
    midwifery and pregnancy, 149
    and Native Americans, 152
    nursing, 147–149
    prostitutes, 150–151
    relative safety of, 136–137
    and saloons, 159
    sewing, 144–145
    stylishness, 144
    taking in boarders, 142–143
    teaching, 145–146
    Victorian conception of, 135–136
    in the West 134–135
Wood, David, 82, 83, 84
Wooden structures, 8
Workbenches, 110
Writing on walls, 131,170, 179, 194–197
Wyoming, 267

Young, Otis, 116–117, 191

ABOUT THE AUTHORS . . .

Elizabeth M. Sagstetter and William E. Sagstetter are a writer/photographer team living in Denver, Colorado. For three decades their greatest joy has been visiting the ghost towns of the American West.

The Sagstetter byline has appeared on hundreds of magazine articles to date. They have been on the staff of a national magazine and were a correspondent/photographer team for the *Denver Post*. This is their second book.

They produced several documetaries about the West that aired on primetime television. One of their films, "The Mystery of Huajatolla," went on to win a Special Award at the Aspen Arts Film Festival in1978. Beth researched and wrote the scripts for the films. Bill was an honorarium instructor in filmmaking at the University of Colorado/Denver for several years. He has also taught Colorado history for many years.

Bill's name appears on more than twenty patents to date. This patent experience helped to unravel the turn-of-the-century technology while they were working on this book.

Both Beth and Bill are listed in Marquis' *Who's Who in theWest.*

ABOUT THE BOOK . . .

A book is a wonderfully complex object that requires expertise and talent in many different fields in order for it to come into existence. We feel very fortunate to have worked with a talented group of professionals in bringing this book about. Thanks for doing such an outstanding job.

Book Design:	Melanie Smith, Imeo Design
Cover Art:	Rob Bartee, Bartee Photography
Editing:	Dianne Russell, Dianne Russell Editorial Services
Indexing:	Michael Haldeman, Whitehorse Productions
Marketing:	Cassandra Leoncini
Printed by:	Thomson-Shore, Inc.